The
MIDNIGHT
ECONOMIST

Meditations on Truth and Public Policy

WILLIAM R. ALLEN

Introduction by MILTON FRIEDMAN

THE MIDNIGHT ECONOMIST

The Midnight Economist

Meditations on Truth and Public Policy

William R. Allen

Introduction by Milton Friedman

ICS Press

Institute for Contemporary Studies
San Francisco, California

Inquiries, book orders, and catalog requests should be addressed to ICS Press, Institute for Contemporary Studies, 243 Kearny Street, San Francisco, California, 94108.

The analyses, conclusions, and opinions expressed in ICS Press publications are those of the author and not necessarily those of the Institute for Contemporary Studies, or of the Institute's officers, directors, or others associated with, or funding, its work.

Library of Congress Cataloging-in-Publication Data

Allen, William Richard, 1924–
    The midnight economist : meditations on truth and public policy /
William Allen : foreword by Milton Friedman.
        p.   cm.
    ISBN 1-55815-055-2 : $12.95
    1. Economics. 2. Economic policy. I. Title.
HB171.A464 1989
338.9—dc20

                                                    89-11242
                                                    CIP

Contents

General Meditations

Mainly Microeconomics:
Analysis of Relative Prices and Resource Allocation

Mainly Macroeconomics: Income and Monetary Analysis

EMPLOYMENT, OUTPUT, FISCAL POLICY

MONEY, INFLATION, CENTRAL BANKING

GLOBAL THINKING:
TRADE, FINANCE, DEVELOPMENT

Foreword

It is not easy to find an economist who is able to translate the often confusing language of his profession into terms that laymen can grasp and comprehend. Too often, in fact, the economist depends on terms and phrases that needlessly cloud the simple concepts of economics and prevent the non-economist from understanding the basic ideas of this discipline.

Fortunately, there is one man who has devoted himself to educating the average citizen in the lessons of economics. These lessons are extremely important and add a new dimension to any issue. Dr. Allen has been called the Midnight Economist for his late-night, three-minute broadcasts on economics. His second book, *The Midnight Economist: Meditations on Truth and Public Policy,* is a collection of these broadcasts and other essays. He outlines the critical principles of economics and uses relevant examples of social and political problems to illustrate the importance of these principles.

—Robert B. Hawkins, Jr.
President, Institute for
Contemporary Studies

May 1989
San Francisco

Preface

The Midnight Economist has long been providing—on radio and television and in newspapers—purported pithy pearls on various aspects of Truth to a mainly lay audience. He has thereby followed a long and splendid tradition of economists exploring and explaining the nature and workings of the social world.

Some—including giants of the economics fraternity—have been concerned, not only with explication of real phenomena through scholarly lectures, journals, and monographs, but also with reaching wide audiences of nonspecialists. In a world of scarcity, economics is important, and good economic guidance can lighten the costs and burdens of living together civilly and sensibly. The world has suffered more tyranny and poverty than need have been because it has clutched, or had thrust upon it, dumb economics. It behooves competent economists to bestir themselves, to share what they may have learned about what works and what doesn't work, to instill some feel for (and tolerance of) "the economic way of thinking." What economists have learned may be deemed not much, but even a small candle can at least help to make the darkness visible.

The Midnight Economist radio series began in January 1979. Most of the essays have been published as monthly flyers and twice-yearly pamphlets, first by the International Institute for Economic Research and now by the Institute for Contemporary Studies. A book compilation of broadcasts through early 1981 was published by Playboy Press. This second book, presented by ICS Press, draws on more than a thousand scripts prepared from February 1981 through December 1988.

It is not my belief that inscribing these commentaries in stone is either a necessary or sufficient condition for the salvation of Western civilization. Still, there is something of the ephemeral in broadcasting:

the product is consumed—or otherwise disappears—in the moment of its creation. Perhaps for some, preservation of this selection of brief remarks in a form less permanent than stone but less transitory than mere echoes will justify the investment.

These remarks are brief, indeed: each commentary was delivered in less than three minutes. In their preparation, time for presentation was not the only constraint. The audience is diverse in various dimensions, and it includes few specialists in economics; it receives no prior announcement of topics, much less a reading assignment, and it is not to be later tested and graded on how well it has listened; it can only listen—and learning psychology indicates that we comprehend better through the eye than through the ear.

Still, the intent has been to provide laymen capsules of reputable economics, useful applications of well-established, elemental analytics. The analysis itself, the substantive content, was to be dispassionate utilization of those fundamental concepts and techniques which economists have laboriously developed and quite generally adopted. The exposition, however, designed to catch the ear, may at times be rather more vigorous and colloquial than usually provided by an academic.

Despite the commentator's title of "Midnight Economist," these pieces have been broadcast at various hours on numerous stations. By December 1988, the network included: KNUS (Albuquerque, New Mexico); WOI-FM (Ames, Iowa); KIEZ (Beaumont, Texas); KBYG (Big Spring, Texas); KGLT-FM (Bozeman, Montana); WBRD (Bradenton, Florida); WJJY-FM (Brainerd, Minnesota); WHBC (Canton, Ohio); WSCI-FM (Charleston, South Carolina); WCGO/WTAS-FM (Chicago Heights, Illinois); WLTR-FM (Columbia, South Carolina); KETR-FM (Commerce, Texas); KRLD (Dallas, Texas); KNTU-FM (Denton, Texas); KURV (Edinburg, Texas); KXCR-FM (El Paso, Texas); WERG-FM (Erie, Pennsylvania); KRED (Eureka, California); WMMN (Fairmont, West Virginia); WLFC-FM (Findlay/Toledo, Ohio); WQCS (Fort Pierce, Florida); KNYO (Fort Smith, Arkansas); KFAL (Fulton, Missouri); WBCX-FM (Gainesville/Atlanta, Georgia); WCAR (Garden City, Michigan); WHAG (Hagerstown, Maryland); WREB (Holyoke, Massachusetts); KHVH (Honolulu, Hawaii); WJJF (Hope Valley, Rhode Island); KPFT-FM (Houston, Texas); WRPX (Hudson, Wisconsin); KSUT (Ignacio, Colorado); WBCW (Jeanette, Pennsylvania); WWBR (Johnstown, Pennsylvania); KASU-FM (Jonesboro, Arkansas); KLCL (Lake Charles, Louisiana); KDWN (Las Vegas, Nevada); WHLY-FM

(Leesburg/Orlando, Florida); KEES (Longview, Texas); KSNN-FM (Los Banos/Merced, California); WBST-FM (Muncie, Indiana); WCLT (Newark, Ohio); KCSN-FM (Northridge/Los Angeles, California); KRIG (Odessa, Texas); KOCC/KOCC-FM (Oklahoma City, Oklahoma); KNWZ (Palm Desert, California); KXVQ (Pawhuska, Oklahoma); WTAZ (Peoria, Illinois); WPRE (Prairie du Chien, Wisconsin); KKAT-FM (Odgen/Salt Lake City, Utah); KVEC (San Luis Obispo, California); WQSA (Sarasota, Florida); WNTR (Silver Spring, Maryland/Washington, D.C.); WFOG-FM (Suffolk/Norfolk, Virginia); KVTI-FM (Tacoma, Washington); KLAY (Tacoma, Washington); KTXK-FM (Texarkana, Texas); JICR (Tokyo, Japan); WTMB (Tomah, Wisconsin); KTUC (Tucson, Arizona); WNWI (Valparaiso, Indiana); WVSP-FM (Warrenton, North Carolina); WAUK (Waukesha/Milwaukee, Wisconsin); WKRZ (Wilkes Barre, Pennsylvania); KSGL (Wichita, Kansas); KYSC-FM (Yakima, Washington); and KJCO (Yuma, Colorado).

Beginning in summer 1985, a number of newspapers began carrying selected essays as columns. They now include: Charleston Gazette (West Virginia); Decatur Herald & Review (Illinois); Doylestown Daily Intelligencer (Pennsylvania); Knoxville Journal (Tennessee); Los Angeles Daily News (California); Los Angeles UCLA Daily Bruin (California); Madison State Journal (Wisconsin); Montgomery Alabama Journal (Alabama); Pasadena Star-News (California); Paterson News (New Jersey); Pittsburgh Press (Pennsylvania); San Diego Union (California); Santa Ana Orange County Register (California); Shreveport Times (Louisiana); Tucson Daily Star (Arizona); Wilmington News-Journal (Delaware); Woonsocket Call (Rhode Island); and York Dispatch (Pennsylvania).

These analyses and commentaries heavily reflect the work of many people, too many to list here although some noted in the texts. But specific note should be made of the valuable contributions and support of my friend, associate, and co-author, William Dickneider. And while the words of the Midnight (Sound) Economist are (generally) mine, the essentials of substance come entirely from the common heritage.

Introduction

I have always been fascinated by what seems a puzzle about economics. On the one side, the fundamental principles of economics are elementary—simple common sense, seemingly accessible to every intelligent person. On the other side, many very intelligent persons fail to understand them and err egregiously in applying them to specific problems.

Surely, it is the simplest common sense that a low price for any product will encourage buyers and discourage sellers; that a high price will discourage buyers and encourage sellers. Whence then the indignation, the uproar, the charges of fraud and villainy when the legal fixing of a maximum price for rental quarters—that is, an artificially low price—produces more prospective buyers of rental space than prospective sellers? Or when the legal fixing of a minimum price for an hour of unskilled labor—that is, an artificially high price—produces fewer prospective buyers of that labor than prospective sellers?

Economics, it seems, is more than obvious common sense. It is also a way of reasoning, of thinking about problems. Many are the occasions in which I have participated in discussions about policies involving economic issues in which those participating have included economists of all shades of political opinion, together with non-economists of all shades of political opinion. Almost whatever the subject of discussion, the outcome after a brief interval is predictable. The economists will be found aligned on one side of the subject—the free enterprisers along with the central planners, the Republicans along with the Democrats, Libertarians, and generally even the socialists, along with a few allies; the bulk of the group—academics, businessmen, lawyers, you name it—will generally be on the other side. I have been amused to observe the same phenomenon, if in somewhat muted form, emerge even when the subject of discussion has been rather far removed from economics—foreign policy or academic policy, for example.

Some people have a natural instinct for economics and the economic way of reasoning, and some people are completely lacking in such an instinct—just as some people have an aptitude for mathematics or an ear for music and other people do not. And just as a great man may lack an ear for music, so also may he lack a feeling for economics. My favorite example—for economics, not music—is Winston Churchill, surely one of the greatest men of our time or any time. Yet when it came to economics, he came a cropper every time he had occasion to get involved, whether before World War I when he played a leading role in the early development of the welfare state, between the wars when as chancellor of the Exchequer he decided to return the British currency to gold at the pre-war parity, or after World War II when as prime minister he decided to retain a fixed exchange rate for the pound instead of permitting it to float.

A striking example on the opposite side—a non-economist who had a real feel for economics—was Leo Szilard, a famous natural scientist who played a key role in persuading President Franklin Roosevelt to initiate the Manhattan Project to develop the atomic bomb. Leo, a colleague of mine at the University of Chicago, was always coming around, tapping me on the shoulder, and saying, "You know, I've been thinking about . . ." and out would come a sophisticated economic proposition, original with him though generally well known to professional economists. More surprising, it was usually correct—he was almost the only physical scientist, I may say, with whom I have had that experience.

While some people may be tone-deaf to economics and other people born economists, for most people economic reasoning is an acquired skill—and taste. That, at least, is the only way I have been able to justify spending the best years of my life trying to teach elementary common sense—often dressed up, it is true, in fancy mathematical clothes—to successive generations of students.

William Allen is a professional economist with a natural ear for economics. He reasons like an economist, eats, sleeps, and breathes economics, as a good economist should. But he has something else, a quality that is far rarer—the ability to explain his economic reasoning to others, in language they can understand and in language that will intrigue and interest them. He has demonstrated his skill over the years in the classroom. He demonstrates it even more dramatically in the gems of radio and television commentaries reprinted in this book.

Bill's commentaries are not sugarcoated pills to be swallowed by the listener with no questions asked. They seldom tell the listener the answer. That is not Bill's aim. His genius is in bringing into the open the elementary principles involved in an issue so that the listener or reader will be induced to think about the problem on his own and to think about the economic principles in a different way. As the poet has it, "He that complies against his will is of his own opinion still." No one else can persuade us. We must persuade ourselves. But someone else can help us find the right way to think about a problem, to break it down, recognize the familiar ideas in an unfamiliar guise, enable us to make up our own minds.

That is what Bill Allen does over and over again in these commentaries. I marvel at his versatility, the wide range of problems and issues he covers, and even more at his skill at finding a fresh and arresting way to present each item. He is equally skillful at finding arresting turns of phrases precisely applicable to the particular issue he is addressing.

Few people will be able to read—or read widely in—this book without being both educated and entertained, without finding themselves questioning beliefs they have long taken for granted, and forming new beliefs. Best of all, some will even end up reasoning like economists.

—MILTON FRIEDMAN

General Meditations

Introduction

According to a famous definition: "Economics is the science which studies human behavior as a relationship between ends and scarce means which have alternative uses."

Some may gag a bit over reference to economics as a science. And some may sense from the definition a lack of sex appeal, with economics appearing as a deadly dull, dry, and dreary field of arcane doodling and diddling—sort of like accounting and dentistry. In actuality, there is, in good economics, much of feel and flair, of instinct and intuition: economic analysis is not a purely mechanical exercise of grandly grinding out uninteresting answers to artificial problems. And much the same can be said of chemistry and physics. In any discipline of analytic application to important matters, elegant tools and rigorous techniques of thought must be supplemented with accumulated learning and developed wisdom in order to distinguish the profound from the superficial, the appropriate from the inapt and inept, and the feasible from what cannot work well.

The foregoing definition of economics, even if deemed a bit pretentious or portentous, does suggest the core of the broad, versatile field of study and use. It all starts with scarcity: in this world of limitations, we cannot produce all we want. The fact of scarcity has implications of the most fundamental seriousness. Scarcity implies the necessity to pick and choose, for we will never fully satisfy all desires; choice-making implies cost-bearing, for cost is what we must give up or trade-off in order to get the thing preferred. A world of scarcity and choices and costs is a world not only of dealing with stingy nature but of dealing with people; in dealing with other self-centered, aggressive, would-be autonomous people, we sometimes coordinate our efforts to mutual advantage, and we persistently compete in many ways as each tries to get a bigger slice of the finite social pie.

A world of scarcity is inherently a hard world. But with some civility and sense, we can make our lives easier than they otherwise would be. How are we to organize ourselves as a community, what ground rules and institutions can we evolve and adopt, which will enable people, with all their grasping grubbiness, to live together peacefully and productively?

By and large, people and their governmental leaders and masters have not answered that central question well. History is not an impressive story of progressive sophistication in formulating rules and procedures which enable the great bulk of the world's people to live without fear of oppression and want and with reasonable hope of personal fulfillment. But the human spirit is remarkable: people have been denied many options, their initiative has been severely curtailed, they have been abused and oppressed—and yet they have not only stubbornly survived, but commonly have shown much sense in adjusting and making do within the limited alternatives available to them.

People usually have done as well in their personal affairs as they have been permitted to do. How can they be permitted to do better? Much of what we do is "economic" in nature—what we do and how we do it, that is, in allocating "scarce means which have alternative uses." Many sorts of influences impinge upon the human condition, and many sorts of analysts—from the anthropologist to the zoologist—contribute to understanding human potentialities and prospects. But much of our misery has stemmed from dumb economics—inefficient institutions, inappropriate property rights, wasteful processes, debilitating policies.

Dumb economics has included, also, lousy instruction. While people commonly are shrewd in handling their private business, they are not accomplished economists in the broader context, where their expertise and experience are necessarily limited. And they have been taught—by politicians, journalists, academic poets, and even some purported economists—much mythology, including:

- we could have enough of everything if we were fully to exploit our fantastic productive power;

- economic efficiency is a matter only of technology and engineering;

- agricultural and other surpluses stem from productivity outrunning demand;

- capitalism requires a social "harmony on interests";

- capitalism is the source of competitiveness and conflict;

- business people are self-centered and rapacious, while government people are self-sacrificing and altruistic;

- labor unions protect the natural brotherhood and collective well-being of workers against their natural enemies, employers;

- charging a higher price always increases the seller's profits;

- the American economy is heavily and increasingly dominated by monopolists who arbitrarily set prices as high and wages as low as they please;

- the minimum-wage laws raise the income of the poor;

- rent control expands and improves housing;

- there is unemployment because workers outnumber jobs;

- government jobs programs increase employment;

- a government budget deficit reflects failure to tax enough finance needed government services, and increasing tax collections will surely reduce a deficit;

- inflation is caused by greedy domestic monopolists and disruptive international cartels;

- inflation is required for full employment, and full employment must lead inflation;

- fluctuating prices create wasteful uncertainty and rising prices create inflation, so government should make it illegal to change prices;

- tariffs increase domestic employment and wages;

- we cannot compete in a world in which most foreign wages are lower than wages paid domestic workers;

- economic sanctions against our enemies are highly effective, and economic aid is necessary and sufficient for our friends to grow.

Good economics of description, diagnosis, and prescription will not solve all our problems. The best of achievable worlds will still be a world of scarcity—and thus a world of choices, costs, and competition. But good economics will help us to do best, even if not well, in a hard world.

There are some important things economists can explain in part. Most commonly these are things to be explained at quite a formal level—things dealing with production relationships, uniformities of human behavior, the structure and operation of market institutions, the repercussions—not all of which were intended—of government policies. Such conventional investigation and deduction is reflected mainly in the essays of Parts II and III.

Ultimate decisions in our messy world of hopes and fears are not generally made elegantly at a formal level. To be sure, technical analysis can help to set the stage and provide some framework and focus for final choices: theory and its applications help to define options and identify returns and costs. But then, in determining just what to do and how to do it, we lean heavily on habit and predilection, trial and error, mores and preconceptions, the instinct of the race.

Theory is an exercise in logic. But logic without application is only an intellectual game. A given theorist at a given time can legitimately confine himself to pure abstraction: it is important to get the logic straight. But sooner or later, directly or indirectly, there is to be some tangible payoff to the community if the community is reasonably to continue to subsidize the navel contemplators.

All of the essays presented here are oriented toward interpretation of real-world phenomena. But those of Part I go beyond the traditional domain of economics, confined basically to marketplace institutions and activities. As these "general meditations" of Part I illustrate, the modern economist is scarcely confined to sharply delineated boundaries. He has found it useful to follow "the economic way of thinking" into any area of activity which entails the use of means which are scarce and versatile.

Society, Order, and the Quality of People

Great Lights and Social Systems

People appear to be rather an unpromising species—selfish and quarrelsome in a limited world. How to arrange our affairs so as to get along together with reasonable prospects of survival?

A scientist is likely to respond—as does noted biologist Lewis Thomas—in terms of identifying a presumed coherency in the grand scheme of things: ". . . the deepest and oldest of human wishes," he tells us, is "to discover that the world makes sense."

The search for the secret is as frustrating as it is compelling. The universe began as "the Great Light." But we do not see nearly all we want to see. ". . . we feel the need of proofs all around, . . . where there is as yet no clear prospect of proof about anything. Uncertainty, disillusion, and despair are prices to be paid for living in an age of science. Illumination is the product sought, but it comes only in small bits, only from time to time, not ever in broad, bright flashes of public comprehension. . . ." But, Dr. Thomas concludes, through the cumulation of puny endeavors, "we can at least come into possession of a level of information upon which a new kind of wisdom might be based."

But Edmund Fuller, a distinguished reviewer of the essay of the scientist, is skeptical of any "new kind of wisdom" required to save us. The problem is not that we do not know enough—we have "a heritage of much profound wisdom." Rather, we endanger ourselves by failing to use what we already know. Still, Mr. Fuller shares with Dr. Thomas a final pessimism. "There are," the reviewer concludes, "too many of us humans with too many conflicting desires and needs for our wisdom and our means to accommodate. We need a moral equivalent of his Great Light."

For all their sensitivity and erudition—or perhaps because of it—the scientist and the man of letters indulge in misdirected sophistication.

Of course desires outrun means. But no Great Light will change that. Salvation calls, not for metaphysical dissolving of the immutable problem, but for cost-minimizing adaptation to the inescapable condition of scarcity. If a high level of ubiquitous public comprehension is required for such adaptation, we surely are doomed. But there can be ground rules which channel and direct efficient and civil—although selfish—individual efforts to our general advantage. Each atom of the social structure need only look reasonably rationally to his own affairs.

We all can be in favor of scientists being scientific. But the human fortune will depend—as it always has—not so much on "a new kind of wisdom" as on the experiences and perceptions of average people, their mores and aspirations, the institutions which constrict them and provide them opportunities and options. People are not basically to be saved by science or cleansed by scholarship. Attainment of potential will come mainly through coordinated autonomy and mutually beneficial fulfillment of personal interests.

(July 1984)

Hobbes and the Ugliness of Competition

In the game of life, there are various criteria of success—wealth, power, influence, stature, contentment. But by any given criterion in a given setting, those who gain much are a minority.

So sour grapes are pervasive. Having fallen short of early dreams and suffered frustrated ambitions, we are inclined to dismiss success as an aberration and ascribe failure to bad luck or a dastardly plot. And we provide a large audience susceptible to silly talk about "the ugliness of competition."

A newspaper essay tells us that "hostility is a frequent result of competition in the workplace, the classroom, the home, the playing field—any place where my success depends on your failure. This is what competition means: mutually exclusive goal attainment." But, the author assures us, ugly competition can be avoided. Instead of working against one another, we can labor together toward a common end. All we have to do is "devise non-competitive alternatives to our mania for winning."

The newspaper poet ran out of space before he could tell us how unsullied "cooperation" can replace gamey, brutalizing competition.

He should deem the lack of space to be convenient, for a vastly wiser analyst of the human condition has persuasively taught us that, whatever our institutions and mores, competition will always be with us.

Three hundred years ago, Thomas Hobbes, among the giants of political philosophy, explained the nature of man, the condition of scarcity, and the inevitable consequence of competition.

According to Hobbes, man is not naturally sociable, but is selfish, pugnacious, and competitive. He is guided by a plurality of passions. Animated by appetites and aversions, he calls "good" simply that which he desires. But whereas desires are boundless, the means of satisfying them are limited. Reason is a servant of the passions, devising ways and seeking power to secure what one desires. Power is sought because desires of different people collide and conflict. So, says Hobbes, ". . . if any two men desire the same thing, which nevertheless they cannot both enjoy, they become enemies," opposing one another with force and fraud.

Here, then, is the problem of social order. In a world of limited resources, we cannot have all of everything we want, so we somehow contest to see how much of what each of us can get. By definition, we are competitors.

The realistic issue is not cooperation versus competition, for that choice is not available: there *will* be competition. The only operational issue—but it is critical in determining how and how well we live—is *which* forms and modes of competition we will applaud and nurture. There *are* many ways to compete, to adapt to a world of scarcity, to make do in a world of conflict; and it *does* make a difference which way we choose.

(July 1985)

Nature of the Game: Production and Charity

We individually get along either by producing or by mooching. We either earn our way by being useful to others or we rely on charity. When motivated by compassion and directed with sense, charity can be commendable. But it is a costly error—costly both to giver and to receiver—when aid is confused with production.

We live in a *performance* economy. One is rewarded on the basis of *productivity*, being paid for productive services, for contributions to the social product. If one supplies substantial quantities of services which the community values relatively highly—if one is relatively valuable to the community—the rewards are relatively great.

The performance, or productivity, economy is quite impersonal. For the great majority of people, *all* economies are quite impersonal. But the impersonality of the free-market economy is very different from that of the political-command economy. *All* economies are economies of scarcity; therefore, *all* economies are economies of competition. But there is a persuasive case for conducting the competition in the expansive market arena of work and trade rather than in the inhibiting governmental arena of centralized control and decree.

Better to earn personal favor through contributing to the well-being of the community than to gain group advantages from a favor-granting bureaucracy. Better to gain personally by economically helping to create more aggregate wealth than to rely on skewing the distribution of a smaller total of wealth by politically subsidizing low productivity. Better to prosper by effectiveness in market-coordinated wealth production than by effectiveness in government-imposed wealth redistribution.

Indeed, can large numbers of people persistently prosper through any strategy other than being economically productive? Some people can, for a time, gain by pleading that all their difficulties stem from unfair discrimination. They have long been taught that ignoble and debilitating tactic. They have been led astray and crippled by both the knowing cynical and the confused compassionate.

Most of the political tactics promoted for redress of biased treatment not only stultify future, long-term competitiveness, but do more harm than good even immediately. In a performance economy, powers of competition and independence are not fostered by such paternalistic foolishness as minimum wage laws, rent controls, interest rate ceilings, and quotas in hiring and in college admissions.

To the extent that one wishes to prosper—not simply survive—in a stingy world, economic performance is the nature of the competitive game through the efficient apparatus and procedures of an enterprise society. It is a monstrous misfortune for us all to cripple some of our neighbors and divert them from the kinds of investments and strategies which would enable them to play the game to the utmost. Of course, we insist that we cripple them in the name of compassion—

but that simply makes the crippling poignant and perverse rather than deliberately dastardly.

(August 1981)

Bunnie Rabbit and Birthrights

In a cartoon of wry subtlety, two Russian citizens are walking together in Moscow. In simple contentment, one says to the other, "How fortunate we are, comrade, that we do not live in one of those decadent capitalist countries where we would be burdened with the necessity of making choices!"

To many of us capitalists, freedom does not seem an intolerable burden. Indeed, we can find much good in an enormous range of individual choice in how we work and have our being. Shrewd students of social organization and personal adaptation to circumstances are inclined to generalize that more options are better than fewer.

But there are costs and inconveniences of, as well as returns from, freedom. Sometimes, the drawbacks are deemed to predominate. Bunnie Rabbit, my long-eared, nose-twitching friend, seems to find it so. Bunnie has spent most of her life in a hutch. Safe, well-fed, and gently treated, she has comfortably adapted to her circumscribed circumstance. She may dream of freedom—dream perhaps of hopping where she pleases and chasing dogs. But, when occasionally given the run of the yard, she appears tentative and even bewildered. Disappointed and fearful, she finds a secluded corner in which to hide.

All of God's creatures tend to adapt to their familiar conditions. Adaptation is a requisite of survival. But adaptation to confinement can generate inertia. While vaguely dreaming of an imaginary freedom never experienced, the emotional and intellectual capacities essential for competing in a free environment of reality remain stunted. And if the slave or serf suddenly finds himself a free man, faced by both the opportunities and the obligations of freedom, he may resemble the rabbit—tentative, bewildered, disappointed, fearful, seeking the haven of the hutch.

A recent Russian immigrant, who entered this country only after much struggle, finds too much freedom of choice in America. There are too many stores, he says, and too little government regulation. Reality has fallen short of utopian dreams. He had innocently "thought of America as a place where people not only lived in comfort, but managed to satisfy all their hopes and passions as well." His wife adds that "he is really afraid that he is not going to make it, that he is going to be a failure and look like a fool. . . ."

To a degree, we can understand and pity the shy rabbit suddenly in an alien environment. It may not be as easy to comprehend the innocence of those who were born free but dream longingly of being chased by dogs. For newcomers, freedom—with its special requirements and disciplines—may have to be an acquired taste. But how can those who have inherited freedom be so easily seduced into losing their birthright?

(May 1983)

Revolution and "Les Misérables"

Utopians appreciate the power of imagination—and the deadly constriction of trying to spell out mundane details. Thus it was with Karl Marx and the utopia of ultimate "true" communism: just how we will get there, when we will get there, and what we will find when we get there are conveniently left to the imagination.

And thus it is with the impressive popular opera, "Les Misérables." Based on the massive novel by Victor Hugo, it is a story of personal degeneration and final remorse and also of personal nobility and survival, culminating in a setting of revolutionary romanticism. The depicted uprising was a bloody but inconsequential skirmish. The opera stirs the senses with passionate song and sight. Does it help to teach us anything?

Scholars Robert Scalapino and Walter Laquer give us guidance in generalizing on the history of revolution. Revolution can result when society is rapidly changing and institutions are rigid. Societies heavily repressed, in a degrading and deteriorating situation, are not likely to have the cohesion and the hopes which lead to revolutionary expectations and endeavors. There must be some potentiality and anticipation of change. While mass activity (or at least acquiescence) may be required, the inspiration and leadership come from those who are not economically and educationally underprivileged. Revolutions typically have been of middle-class origin, with articulation from alienated intellectuals. Revolutions tend to follow a certain sequence of generations. The initial leadership, ideological and committed to overthrow, is succeeded by administrative types who seek to avoid total breakdown and to build a revised organization; in due course, there is the rise of specialists, with a proliferating bureaucracy, who preside over a new, stodgy status quo.

Revolution provides a vehicle of change, but the first, fervid generation would often be appalled and frustrated by the new situation presided over by the technocratic third generation. Revolution may remove stultifying encrustation of the old order, but it does so at heavy cost, wiping out talent and useful institutions indiscriminately. The more violent the revolution, the more likely that the old despotism will be replaced by a new tyranny. An adaptive evolution of sense and civility can achieve more without the bloodshed and destruction.

"Les Misérables" is a spectacle of emotional power—but it gives no hint of what the grievances were and no suggestion of what to do and how to do it. We are to be content with noble but vague commitment, warm camaraderie, and a romantic vision of "dreaming a dream," of "seeing a world you have not seen"—and we all die gloriously, if futilely, at the barricade.

Cost is borne, but nothing is gained except the exhilaration of the moment—and great cost which yields little return is known as waste.

(December 1988)

Bunnie Rabbit, Winnie, and the Grand Plan

People, with their uncertainties and fears and aspirations, do much fretting and flailing. It is a hard world, to be sure. The best things in life may be free, but the multitude of second-best things are costly. So we work and save and plan—and we compete, struggling with one another as well as with stingy nature. And in our scheming and striving and struggling, the veneer of civilization is worn very thin. The veneer is worn completely through at times and in places, exposing our greed and gaucherie and petty preoccupations.

A vastly more attractive and assuring aspect of being is provided by furry friends. I have been blessed with companionship of my rabbit, Bunnie, and my dog, Winnie. Winnie is still with me; but recently Bunnie had to leave.

Little Bunnie—she of the pretty face and long ears and button tail and velvet coat—like the lilies of the field, neither spun nor sowed. She directly contributed nothing to gross national product. She was a consumer, not a producer, absorbing a bit of the world's scarce resources and returning nothing—nothing but an example of poise and patience and beauty and grace and affection.

The poet assures us that they also serve who only stand and wait. Presumably, we shall never fully comprehend the Grand Plan of the Universe. But much of what we can suspect and infer is to be gained— if we are willing to learn—from the humble likes of Bunnie and Winnie. While people meanly scheme and worriedly strive and struggle, the Bunnies and the Winnies seem instinctively to have found their role and purpose. And they play their part with an innate dignity and beauty of nature which should humble us.

There are many ways in which we can do ourselves in, individually and collectively, and the human race has worked assiduously to discover and utilize them all. Occasionally, a Shakespeare, a Rembrandt, or a Beethoven reminds us of our angelic heritage. And we have very slowly accumulated some successes of medicine and mechanics. And a few of the world's peoples have grudgingly permitted some experimentation in social arrangements of freedom and individualism which can ease the pains and constrictions of our plight of scarcity. But it is not surprising that progress in reclaiming our heritage is, at best, slow and unsure, for it is perversely protested and opposed by most. Unlike the Bunnies and the Winnies—the supposed lesser of God's creatures—people persist in rejecting their role and subverting their purpose.

Certainly, it is a world of scarcity. But the scarcity is not confined to iron ore and arable land. The most constricting scarcities are those of character and of personality. All our cleverness and wit, all our tools and technology, will leave us poor, indeed, a disgrace in the eyes of the Deity, as long as we lack the goodness and grace and gentility of Bunnie Rabbit and Winnie.

(March 1984)

On Sense, Integrity, and Courage

The world operates most fundamentally—not through massive immanent forces of history being made mysteriously manifest and not through activities of impersonal corporate or racial or religious or national conglomerates—but on the basis of decisions by individuals. It is the average person who faces options, reaches conclusions, makes choices, and implements decisions. To comprehend social phenomena, we must account for how decisionmakers perceive the situation confronting them, for their orientation and objectives, for their incentives and the manner in which they calculate returns and costs.

If specific persons are critical in how the world works, then we had better pay attention to qualities and characteristics of those who participate in the formulation and implementation of public policy. Indeed, since public policy can greatly shape the context within which we live our individual lives, why not the very best in critical government positions? Why not the best in government? The question provokes embarrassed titters. Well, then, why not the pretty good? Who would settle for the minimally reputable?

Or perhaps you would prefer the *very* best to be in business or in the religious or education establishment. The problems are not less severe in such centers of power. Corporate board chairman, bishops, and university chancellors can be as dull-witted, venal, and shiv-sticking as bureaucrats and senators.

Still, our reach should exceed our grasp, and we can consider what might be reasonably sought in choosing government personnel. A great economist once mused, in conversation, about the distinguishing features of anyone he would be content to see appointed to the Board of Governors of the Federal Reserve.

First, he said, it would obviously be appropriate for the person to be highly qualified in monetary analysis—although in some know-nothing circles, such sophistication would be deemed a detriment. But, the economist went on, a high level of professional competence in monetary analysis, while desirable, is not as important as some other considerations. It is more critical that the person be teachable, that he be approachable and receptive to sound argumentation and pertinent evidence, that he be attuned to competent thought and dispassionate assessment of thought.

And having been systematically exposed to empirical analysis, and having determined his best policy conclusion, he must have the strength of character to pronounce his position and defend it. Being intelligent and perceptive are not enough. Even being right in the quiet of one's office is not enough. On the battleground of policy debate and administration, one is called upon to exhibit integrity and courage.

All this is not peculiar to the Federal Reserve. In the world at large, to the extent that we are blessed with good decisions and good policies, we generally can impute our fortune, not so much to sheer brilliance as to reasonable judgment, stubborn integrity, and dependable courage.

(January 1982)

Society, Character, and Government

Without the horses—otherwise known as jocks—an athletic coach will win few games. Without students of some sense and seriousness, a teacher will develop few scholars. And without a citizenry of character, constitutions and institutions will not generate a fine society.

Political scientists and economists have not always well appreciated the subtle role of private virtue as they have dealt with issues of public procedure and policy. They are much inclined to put aside the critical but camouflaged consequences of character. Character is commonly classified as a given, perhaps immutable and surely not deliberately malleable. Scholars are generally more technically proficient than insightfully profound. It is relatively easy to manipulate models of possibly measurable variables; it is not to be attempted to incorporate into formal, dispassionate analysis the nuances of proper conduct.

Professor James Q. Wilson laments the lack of attempt to include character in analysis and prescription. Nor is the omission minor or marginal. In a wide array of public concerns and policy issues, he finds character—or the lack or faulty nature of character—to be central.

This is the case in *schooling*, where discipline, commitment, and work habits apparently are more important than buildings, libraries, and student/teacher ratios. This is the case in *welfare*, where some people seem more readily debilitated by adversity and seduced by aid than are others. This is the case in *public finance*, where evident changes in the community's perceptions and predilections have diluted discipline and led to government spending which is out of control. This is the case in *crime*, where self-control and core values of personal accountability, nurtured critically by family influence, can counterbalance such diversions and temptations as growing ethnic diversity of society, urbanization, and industrialization.

Professor Wilson is a bit impatient with economists who neglect "the important subjective consequence of acting in accord with a proper array of incentives." It is tempting simply to take people as they are, and rely on counterbalancing ambitions to generate an acceptable social equilibrium. So he turns to government—national as well as local—to recognize, and then correct, defective human character, "to induce persons to act virtuously." But he adds, "It is easier to acknowledge the necessary involvements of government in character formation than it is to prescribe how this responsibility should be carried out."

Indeed. Government *will* influence the character of people, for government commonly shapes the other institutions, the options, and the incentives of people. But that influence of fallible and clumsy government does not invariably promote virtue. Even genuine intent to do good can harm more than help.

(February 1986)

The Message of Malthus

Thomas Robert Malthus was not the first to discover the question of possible population pressures on resources. For twenty-five hundred years, there have been wonderments and suggestions concerning the potential importance of the size and growth of population on various aspects of personal and social well-being. But Malthus—writing at the end of the eighteenth century and in the early years of the nineteenth—established population as an appropriate and significant topic of economics.

The Malthusian message was not a light and happy one. It was, indeed, a major contribution to the reputation of economics as "the dismal science."

Malthus was interested in explaining real aspects of the real world. And in reality, he inferred, population *tends* to increase at a faster rate than does food. By definition, people *cannot* increase faster than the means of subsistence. But the checks and constraints which keep population growth from outrunning food either involve mischief and tragedy or require uncommon strength of character. If we do not curtail the birth rate through "vices" of abortion and prostitution or bloat the death rate through "miseries" of famine and war, then we must rely on "moral restraint"—a chaste delaying of marriage until children can be adequately provided for.

Malthus was not an elegant formal theorist; his historical and empirical generalizations were too easy and sweeping; his anticipations of technological advance and communal adjustment were inadequate; and his moralistic and sociological entreaties have been too confining for many. Still, he was on sound ground in urging us to face the fact that the world has its limitations and that much depends on the sense with which we make our unavoidable adaptations to scarcity.

In particular, problems of population will be aggravated, not solved, by relieving those who breed too much of the consequences of their actions. If the community takes care of the children of those who cavalierly think only of the pleasures of the moment, the improvident will forever continue to be parasites on the prudent.

More generally, Malthus is telling us, you do not change a condition by subsidizing it; you do not end a difficulty by continuing it; you do not engender responsibility by sympathetically relieving people of responsibility; you do not conduce rationality by compassionately rewarding irrationality. If people are not to bear the costs as well as enjoy the benefits of their own decisions, then all of us—including innocent offspring of the promiscuous—will bear grievous costs which could have been avoided.

In language which seems harsh and callous, this—and not the details of his doodling—is the real and critical message of Malthus. Malthus was not a magnificent analyst. But he was neither an ogre nor a fool. And in his major message of responsibility and accountability, he was not wrong.

(June 1985)

The Inglorius Revolution

A three-car, one swimming pool, forty-three year old adolescent tells us in a newspaper essay that in 1970 he was a law student at Yale.

With presumably heaving bosom, he rhapsodizes that: "To be alive then was bliss, but to be young was very heaven. . . . Because to be young and alive in that day was to believe in the Revolution." In the Revolution, we were "together," but "it's lonely in middle age. Earning a living is lonely work. Responsibility is lonely." Poor baby. It is distressing and discouraging to see a man-child whimper.

The ungracefully aging yuppie acknowledges that the Revolution had its "silly and even embarrassing" aspects, such as "well-to-do white kids masquerading as radicals" and "pretending to be risking something in a completely risk-free environment." He insists—perhaps not wholly dishonestly—that the masquerading radicals really "believed that we would make the future better than the past," relying on "a moral yardstick," "compassion," and "justice."

It would be perfectly splendid to have a world inspired by my conceptions of morality, compassion, and justice. But my conceptions might not be the same as yours. And, in any case, inspirations and ideals alone are not enough. How do we make the standards effective and the ideals operational? What are the institutions, processes, and ground rules which induce, guide, and constrain real people in their activities of gain seeking?

We do have problems, difficulties, and frustrations in this miserable world of poverty and tyranny. And societal frailty and evil are not confined to "free enterprise, dog-eat-dog America." I could have told that to our blubbering hero twenty years ago.

I could have told him about making choices, bearing costs, and paying prices; I could have told him that for most people most of the time, this is more a world of trying simply to minimize losses rather than of maximizing returns; I could have told him that survival of the community relies more on the quite conventional work of unglamorous but sensible and responsible common folk in the chorus than on the precious posturing of pampered prima donnas in the spotlight; I could have told him that men are not angels and are not made angelic by growing beards, wearing sandals, sharing joints, and chanting slogans; I could have told him that we must produce what we consume and the high productivity reflects personal ambition and striving for reward, that one prospers much by competing well, that it is dangerous and degrading to rely on the kindness of strangers; I could have told him that sensitive compassion is a virtue only when directed and applied with sophisticated comprehension, for vast harm has been done by the self-consciously pietistic who are too anxious to do good and thereby do it badly.

It is a great pity that no one in the Yale law school told him such things.

(May 1988)

Capitalism, the Community, and Economists

Capitalism and Gary Cooper

When capitalism does well, it does much good in many dimensions for the entire community. But *is* capitalism doing well? The answer turns heavily on what is meant by both the noun and the adverb: what is capitalism, and what constitutes doing well?

One of the world's most eminent economists suggests that American capitalism is now in a golden age, flourishing in a high noon of anticipated persistence. But we are provided neither definition of concept nor measurement of condition. It seems to be suggested that capitalism is simply what capitalists do, and the degree of contentment of capitalists—or some of them—is, or is an adequate measure of, the state of the health of capitalism.

More particularly, the suggestion goes, business leaders are people of such ambition, intelligence, and political power that the governmental ground rules of commercial activity are, in general, highly agreeable to them. There are regulatory nuisances, to be sure, as well as taxation excesses. But, we are told, "our ocean of regulations could" hardly "have been achieved under high capitalism except by the consent of the capitalists. American business likes what it is getting. . . ."

It may be that "the larger part of the regulations that businessmen are subjected to must be of their own contriving and acceptance." But the success of some business leaders in using government for some purposes may not reflect the typical political prowess of the total business sector. Success in affecting direct regulation may not reflect common ability to control most of the elements which shape the well-being of business. And success in obtaining business advantages through state power may not imply general economic and social health of the entire community. Big business is not the whole of business; government regulation is not the whole of the business context; and business convenience is not the whole of capitalism and its health.

Whatever is reasonably deemed the basic nature of capitalism and its broad implications, huge and growing intrusive government is the enemy of capitalism, whether or not conspicuous business people feel comfortable with the state and its regulatory bureaucracy. And government *is* huge and *is* growing. It has been growing throughout our history. During the last fifty years—in depression, then war, and finally welfare paternalism—the growth of government has become faster and more pervasive. And with that increasing direct and indirect interjection of Big Brother into our activities and our expectations, plans, and aspirations, the performance of our economy and society has degenerated. We have been first hobbled and then corrupted. As efficiency is diminished and freedom is diluted, the crime is rape even if some have learned to relax and enjoy it.

In the famous movie, "high noon" was a time of crisis, not contentment. In that instance, the good guy won. Gary Cooper, where are you now that we need you?

(April 1983)

Capitalism and the Historians

"Liberal history"—which is to say most history—"is reminiscent," it has been said, "of a Peter Paul Rubens woman—mounds of soft pink flesh in all directions." Liberal history over several generations probably has not done a greater disservice than in its treatment of the so-called Industrial Revolution.

We have been taught lurid generalizations of the economic history of England in the late eighteenth and early nineteenth centuries: abruptly, hours of labor were onerous and conditions of work disagreeable as happy peasants were forced from the fields to factories; for the first time, cities became overcrowded and housing deplorable; women and children were massively exploited; real income—along with personal fulfillment—steadily fell; and the economy was wracked with crises and unemployment. Clearly, by modern standards, conditions for many in the early industrialized cities *were* wretched. So were conditions in *non*-industrialized cities; so were conditions well nigh universally in previous centuries.

There is no wholly satisfactory way to compare even material living standards—much less the overall quality of life—over substantial periods of time or between very different communities at a given time. Still, we are justified in concluding that—as measured by selected but pertinent variables—many centuries of virtual economic stagnation for the bulk of the world's people have been followed over the last 200 years by slow, irregular progress. Obviously, that progress was not inevitable, but resulted from the innovation and enterprise which many historians denigrate as the cause of misery and poverty.

It is true that, in these last two centuries, great numbers of workers have owned little personal capital. But in earlier times, as noted by Nobel economist Friedrich Hayek, those with no tools could not survive, and now tools have been provided by investors, which enables non-capitalists not only to exist but to prosper enough to increase their numbers. It is true that patches of poverty are now conspicuous and repugnant—precisely because most of our community is no longer in poverty, and growing wealth engenders both greater sensitivity to grievances and higher aspirations.

With individualistic adaptation to technological advance and fluctuating markets, the enjoyment of gains and burdens of costs have been spread unevenly. But, if it were feasible, surely few would give back the gains in order to avoid the costs. What comprehending people *would* choose is to stop the persistent governmental errors of regulation and taxation and disequilibration which have diluted the gains and exaggerated the costs.

With distressing consistency, historians have been guilty of bad evaluation of source material which is aimed at documenting poverty and pain, of faulty inferences which conclude that all failures and frustrations stem from something called "capitalism," and of naive preconceptions and idealizations of "the good life" and "the natural order" which glorify the primitive farm and hamlet.

Even legions of analysts can scarce hope to prevail against legends of history.

(October 1983)

Economists and the Perversion of Purpose

Why does the community subsidize professors of economics? What is the social payoff of the investment? What is to be the output of economists, and who gains what from its production?

Campus economists are to figure out, explain, and account for certain sorts of real-world phenomena. This enhanced knowledge of the world is justified first as any knowledge enhancement is justified: it is a good thing to know more of what we are and why we do what we do, to satisfy our curiosity about where we have been and how we may best adapt to and even mold our options.

In economics, there can be pragmatic, operational dividends from effective research. Economics deals with interlinked causes and probable effects, with functional relationships of various actions and inputs and consequent results and outputs. To understand *how* parts of the world work makes possible some conditional *predictions*: *if* we satisfy certain conditions and do certain things, *then* we can assign substantial probability to certain subsequent outcomes. Finally, if we can understand and predict, we may be able to exercise a degree of control. Both business managers and government managers have found some economists to be of some aid.

Much lies behind the payoff activity of solving real problems of the real world. There are tools of analysis to be forged, and techniques to be developed in using them; there is much to be learned about social procedures and institutions and individuals adaptations. In this varied effort—building tools and techniques of theory, formulating problems and gathering information in ways which are amenable to analysis, and finally grinding out and communicating solutions—there is division of labor. A few specialize in rarefied meditation; most do less glamorous work of applying theory.

One might suppose that all who participate in a team effort would be appreciative of all other team members. That is not invariably the case. Many of the innovative designers of tools and even some of the imaginative wielders of tools are not motivated primarily by concern to learn and explain.

For all work of all economists, analysis is central; but for much work of economists, the analytics are to be largely invisible to the naked eye, essential but undisplayed scaffolding and girders which give shape and strength to the final structure. The world of scholarship is bastardized by those who pursue esoteric elegance, formalistic rigor, and virtuoso display for their own sake rather than ultimate worldly comprehension and effective conveying of what has been learned.

The community may not be forever tolerant of specialists who are less interested in what they say than in how awesomely precious they are in saying it. A producer flirts with disaster when he loses interest in the substantive product he is to produce and forgets the consumer for whom he is supposed to do the producing.

(December 1985)

Sense and Silly Psychology

I am an economist—you know, an unromantic meditator on scarcity, its manifestations, and its consequences of competition. Does that mean that I favor gaucherie and belligerency? Not at all. In particular, I favor the young being nicer to their elders, students being nicer to teachers, children being nicer to parents, and wives being nicer to husbands.

But while it is nice to be nice, I am no longer surprised when grubby people in a stingy world persist in acting like grubby people in a stingy world. What *is* surprising is when those who should know better are surprised by such behavior.

People are self-interested; they would like to be better off; they prefer to have more rather than less of things they prefer. Preferences differ enormously in detail, but everyone wants more of *some* things: more command over goods in the market; more stature; more friendship; more beauty, grace, and charm; more talent; more time. For everyone, some or all of these and other things are scarce. And economics pertains to scarcity.

Is all this so obvious as to be trite? A psychologist—presumably in pursuit of more applause—has rejected such premises. People are not really self-interested, he tells us. We do not suffer from some innate, biological necessity to act selfishly. Rather, we had to be taught through cultural institutions and pressures.

If so, we have been ready learners. Whether through the instinct or the acculturation of the race, we well comprehend that more resources are better than less, high returns are better than low, and efficiency is better than waste in a world where we cannot obtain and do all we should like. What *is* to be the criterion and the standard of sensible behavior, if not efficiency? It is the manifestation of rationality to seek maximum output per unit of input. *Sophistication* pertains to the *choice* of the ends, but *sense* calls for efficiency in *attaining* the ends which are chosen.

Sense, rationality, efficiency—such guides and criteria are as relevant for the priest and the poet as for the businessman and the bureaucrat. They pertain to living, and are not confined to the marketplace. Nor were they invented two hundred years ago by Adam Smith, who—contrary to the imaginative psychologist—did not create either economics or capitalism.

Sense, rationality, and efficiency became pertinent long before Smith, when, following the fiasco in the Garden of Eden, frail sinners had to adjust and adapt and make do in a world abruptly made harsh and stingy. To be sure, good economists have helped us to learn lessons of how best to survive. In particular, they have told us of the equilibrating and optimizing characteristics of open markets, which are cleared without waste.

We may even have become sufficiently wealthy to survive the silliness of some psychologists.

(July 1986)

What Works: Economics and Conservatism

Does systematic study of economics tend to make people more conservative? A fine journalist, Daniel Seligman, of *Fortune* magazine, believes so. "Liberals go through life worrying about what's fair," he says, "and conservatives go through life worrying about what works. Economics makes you keep thinking about what works."

George Stigler, one of the great economists, agrees that education in economics conduces a conservative orientation. The economics student "is drilled in the problems of *all* economic systems and in the methods by which a price system solves these problems. . . . He cannot believe that a change in the *form* of social organization will eliminate basic economic problems."

If true, the purported connection between economics training and conservative view is not surprising. Dealing systematically with questions pertaining to how we can best use resources which are much less than we want—questions of choices, costs, and prices—tends to sobriety and an acute concern for "what works." Economists look with some suspicion on those who conjure visions of full contentment in an idyllic, post-revolutionary world.

Non-economists, too, profess to know something of the world. We all have perceptions of reality. And it is with, and through, those perceptions that we judge situations and processes as good or bad, interpret the ways of the world, and decide whether and how we can improve our lot.

But perceptions are not received directly and cleanly from the thing observed. The light rays are distorted and diffused as they pass through the many lenses of bias between reality and perception. When people consider the world, they may see quite different things, and then their brains can play different games with what they see.

We are creatures of passion, aspiration, and impatience, as well as thought and rationality. None of us has the commitment and discipline to be an animate logic machine all the time. And that is just as well. The stirrings of the heart and the strivings of the soul are not wholly in vain, for they cast light of their own on beauty and truth, contributing to a context of compassion and civilization. But understanding well matters of economics calls for economic analysis of some system and rigor, and it is mischievous for the poet or the priest to pretend to play scientific analyst.

It can be as bad for the purported economist to slip into the role of poet or priest. The economist surely is not innately more pure than the non-economist. But the most able economists are well aware of what they seem to know and presumably can do with their theory and technique. They believe in their analysis and consistently rely on it—and they use it only for useful elucidation, not pretentious obfuscation.

So cherish good economists—even if their training has made them soberly conservative—for their analytics help us get straight what works.

(February 1987)

Mouse Wisdom: The Measure of Marshall

"I don't know how you and your economist friends can be so two-faced," mouse Karl said pleasantly to his mouse friend, Adam. "You talk about individual well-being and social welfare, but you really are thoroughly grubby. For you, everything of interest has a market and carries a price tag."

"Money and markets *are* important," insisted Adam. "How we earn our living and how good is the living we earn have much to do with how we look at and adapt to the world. But the economic way of thinking can be applied to a wide variety of problems and phenomena involving *choosing, substituting* more of this for some of that; economics is *not* confined to obvious matters of work and business. And the emphasis of economists on use of money does not reflect miserly obsession."

"Pish, posh," sneered Karl. "Alfred Marshall, the famous English economist of a couple of generations ago, was always trying to cluster economic thinking around money payments and receipts. He *was* obsessed with money."

"Marshall," Adam replied patiently, "was a philosopher, a historian, and a mathematician as well as an economist, and he considered being a missionary. His essential concern was the condition of life and how to improve it. For him, economic analysis is not disinterested observation of markets, but rather a practical engine for human betterment. And economic analysis tells us, he generalized, that individualistic, competitive capitalism—an arrangement he called, economic freedom—is our best form of organization. For, in the discipline it demands and the incentive it provides, economic freedom yields not only economic efficiency, but personal cultivation and social coordination."

"Pietistic talk is cheap," grumped Karl. "How can one say, with honesty and sense, that everyone grubbing for money builds character and cohesion?"

"Talk *is* cheap," Adam responded. "That is why we want to measure people's preferences, not by what they *say*, but by what they *pay*. How much does a person want another apple or another minute of someone's labor or another borrowed dollar? He reveals his demand by how much he is willing to pay. This does not measure all we should like to measure. In particular, when two people each offer a dollar for a widget, it does not mean that they attach the same inner, subjective value to the item. But in understanding how people act and the world works, it is significant that each of those people is willing to give up a dollar's worth of any other thing to get a widget."

Karl brightened. "I see the light," he beamed. "The use of money is a reflection of preferences, and seeing how it is used is an indirect way of understanding what people want and what they are willing to supply."

"That was Marshall's *technique*," agreed Adam. "His stated concern was: 'How to get rid of such evils in society as arise from a lack of material wealth?' For a man destitute of material wealth 'cannot be, if we may say so, what God intended him to be.'"

(November 1985)

Economists in Government

The federal government is well infested with economists, genuine and pseudo. *What* is done by the economist in government, under what *circumstances*, for what *audience*, subject to what *constraints*, with what *analytics*, with what evident *impact*?

In speaking with economists who are or have been in government, one obtains a picture which is sobering. The government economist typically is not a highly independent researcher and analyst, free first to pick many of his subjects and then free to broadcast generally the results of his labors.

He is a member of an organization, commonly devoting the bulk of his time to topics specified from on high—the specification often given only days (or, indeed, hours) before the deadline.

He is conscious, also, that the decisionmakers he is more or less directly advising are themselves subject to constraints of worldly realism and political feasibility—along with innocence in economic analysis.

He brings to his task an accumulated intellectual capital which, even if impressive at the outset of his government work, may not thereafter be greatly enlarged or even well maintained. He has available a corpus of theory and an arsenal of techniques which, for all their elegance and academic glamor, are often too time-consuming for purposes of shooting from the hip and too esoteric for the data, the colleagues, and the audience.

And he has little reason to suppose that his work has significant impact in the making of policy, being largely confined to support of programs and procedures determined earlier and by others and for which he may have only modest sympathy.

Perhaps a moral is suggested by this review of the activity and the contribution of the economist in government: social welfare might be enhanced by "minimizing" the number and the scope of governmental endeavors which normally call for discretionary policymaking services of economists. The economist knows so little, relative to the complexities of the world, and is in a position to contribute so marginally, in policymaking practice, that it is unrefreshingly simple to ask him to do more than—if, indeed, as much as—he is now doing in government.

An eminent economist, with extensive experience as a government advisor, concluded that, as economists grow more competent in dealing with policy problems, the questions asked are made broader in scope and more complex. Any community tends to press its government—and the government, in turn, presses its economists—to levels of incompetence. Those in government demand more at any given time than can be delivered.

"One has to distinguish," we are told, "between the attempt to *use* economists and an attempt to *absorb* what economists have to say." It would appear, then, that "the government is always going to be a disheartening game for the honest economist. . . ."

(July 1986)

Marx, Socialism, and Russia

The Misery of Marx

His contemporaries described him as self-centered, arrogant, domineering, and impetuous. Even with members of his family, he was not loving and caring. Yet, many believe that Karl Marx, who had little regard for individuals, was driven by a love of humanity.

The same inconsistency festers in the followers of Marx today. In the name of humanity, Marxists violate individuals' dignity. They intimidate, imprison, and impoverish. They crush free choice, destroy hope, and snuff out lives.

The brutality is excused as a means of ending the so-called capitalist exploitation that Marx claimed stunted human development. He asserted that the value of a nation's output is produced entirely by labor. As a condition of letting workers use their tools, machines, and other investments, however, capitalists keep some of the value as unearned profit. Workers are exploited as a consequence, and they are forced to labor in conditions that alienate them from their work.

The growing misery of workers, said Marx, would cause them to unite in struggle for power and overthrow the economy of private property and markets. Long after the death of Marx, however, workers in sophisticated economies were becoming wealthier, not poorer, and they showed no interest in revolution. Consequently, V.I. Lenin argued that an elite, revolutionary corps would have to seize control and force on the uncomprehending masses the changes the elite decreed to be necessary.

Neither Lenin nor Marx could analytically support the dogmatic assertion that the value of output is produced entirely by workers. Instead of a surplus squeezed from workers, profit is a return to owners of capital and managers for innovating, organizing, taking risks, weeding out inefficiency, and successfully anticipating what consumers value.

These are vital tasks, and history shows how well they are performed by free individuals in an economy of private property and open markets. Such an economy works well because it is a system of losses as well as profits. Profits reward the risk-takers for correctly identifying and efficiently satisfying consumer preferences. Losses punish those who do not efficiently satisfy demands. As Winston Churchill put it: "It is a socialist idea that making profits is a vice. I consider the real vice is making losses."

Coordinated by the prospects of profits and losses in a system of private property and markets, free people in our nation have produced a bountiful harvest of productivity. They have pushed up wage rates and employment, improved working conditions, and shortened the work week.

In contrast, the pursuit of the perverse Marxist dream offers a nightmarish reality where individuals are robbed of both their dignity and their productivity. In this grim, totalitarian reality, individuals inevitably suffer the misery of the humanitarian Marx.

(June 1987)

War, Government, and Socialism

If socialism prevailed in most nations, would war thereby be less likely? Many have believed—if not rigorously thought—so.

From authoritarian and devious communists to genteel and earnest liberals, it has been standard silliness that the special business interests and economic classes of capitalistic societies, in their competitive chase after profits and with their great influence, would often goad governments into conflict. Ever-greedy, ever-scheming Daddy-Warbucks-types would shatter the common interests of the masses of people around the world and seduce the establishments of state into militarily promoting and protecting the economic interests of the monied few.

Jacob Viner, one of the world's great economists of a generation ago, found such devil dogma to be disingenuous.

Nation-states do, indeed, engage in war; and the battlefield quarrels of governments certainly have had purported economic elements which the statesmen sometimes actually took seriously. But Professor Viner suggested that, first, the more society and its activities are controlled by government than by people of commerce the more likely is war; second, government as such—not government of capitalist countries uniquely—is the problem; and third, socialism, far from diluting the potentiality of war, adds to the likelihood.

There are mutual gains from trade, and established means of adjudicating disputes among private parties. But as state control is more and more substituted for private enterprise, an increasing political element is injected into economic transactions; largely competitive activity becomes largely monopolistic; judicial settlements are replaced by ad hoc diplomacy backed by threat of military force; and limited frictions become patriotic causes.

Government quarrels—with confrontations of great accumulations of resources and fired with cohesive community emotions—are inherently more dangerous than the limited and fragmented quarrels of commerce. But governments have been bellicose when their countries have been debtors *or* creditors, when they have had small and slowly growing populations *or* large and rapidly growing populations, when their economies have been flourishing *or* stagnating, and when they have been democratically capitalistic *or* fascistic *or* communistic.

More specifically, socialism exacerbates the problem of government and war. The socialist state, with its centralized administration, is technically well organized for war mobilization; egalitarian ideology could provide a moral basis for aggression against wealthier countries; at home, egalitarianism supposedly guarantees that the spoils of successful war would not go to a small, privileged class; and there would be no "powerful middle class with property interests to protect against risks of all kinds, including the risks of war."

There may be promising paths to peace. But socialism is not one of them.

(April 1987)

Churchill and the Seductions of Socialism

Following the British general election of 1945—shortly after the collapse of Germany and shortly before the surrender of Japan—Prime Minister Winston Churchill was obliged to lay "down the charge which was placed upon me in darker times." Churchill, while magnanimous in manner, was grievously wounded. Why this immediate peacetime rejection of the wartime leader whose strength of character and eloquence had sustained his people through massively perilous times?

One suggestion has been that Churchill conducted an imprudent campaign. An already largely radicalized community did not react well to assertions that "there can be no doubt that Socialism is inseparably interwoven with Totalitarianism. . . ." and to warnings that a socialist government "would have to fall back on some form of Gestapo. . . ." Ironically, the radicalization in part reflected socialistic pamphlets issued during the war by the Army Bureau of Current Affairs. And evidently many in confusion believed that Churchill would continue as prime minister even if his Conservative party lost.

Churchill was more popular than his party. Clement Attlee, the new Labor prime minister, distinguished "between Mr. Churchill the leader of the nation in war and Mr. Churchill the Conservative Party leader. Many people," he claimed, "looked upon the Conservatives as a reactionary party which would not carry out a policy answering to peace requirements."

Ah, yes, peace requirements. In a commentary of Kenneth McDonald, noted was not only the subversion of the leader by an army agency, but the further irony that wartime experience had psychologically prepared much of the public—both military and civilian—for the herdlike protections and processes of socialism.

For armed forces veterans, "it made sense that the same government that had been feeding and paying them for the past six years should go on doing so. . . . Many saw government as provider and protector." And there was the residue of patriotism, magnificently inspired by Churchill himself, which could take the form of "a collective shoulder to the wheel for a Britain that would move forward to a new, secure future rather than back to the insecure past with which Winston and other pre-war politicians were associated."

Perhaps dignity and pride—and also individualism and accountability—are to be defined and assessed in light of the temper of the times. Perspective and standards and criteria are molded by experience and evident options. The proud English, led by a magnificently defiant lion of history, could stand alone against the hoards of Huns threatening invasion. But seductive socialism was not sufficiently widely perceived as a threat at all. After decades of unfulfilling frustration and then years of governmentally coordinated effort, they were susceptible to the seeming shortcuts of socialism, doing directly by decree what can be accomplished only by free men in free markets.

(September 1988)

Russia: System Failure and Reform Futility

Every economy is a market economy, for people must buy and sell productive inputs and produced outputs. Prices are the ratios at which things are exchanged. Market-determined prices make possible rational calculation and economic coordination. But in Russia prices generally are decreed by Big Brother and thus do not reflect values, bearing little relation to either production costs or consumer preferences. Small wonder that the Russian economy works poorly: per capita income is low and is rising slowly, if at all.

At fault is not the innate character and competence of the Russian people. Hormones and hopes do not differ much among God's children. Everyone wants more of what he prefers.

People are similar also in responding and adapting and making do as best they can by their own criteria in light of options open to them. Imposition of socialism does not mysteriously kill concern for personal well-being. All people are characteristically human—shrewd, self-interested, attracted to prospects of improvement and gain. But their circumstances differ enormously, and they can be stymied by the system in which they live.

An efficient economy is a coherent arrangement and procedure of calculation and conduct of transactions, with the returns from activity made comparable to the costs of activity, and with incentives for seeking social returns which are greater than social costs.

In Russia, political ideology and bureaucratic decree have been largely substituted for individual incentive; weakening of incentive has diluted and diverted initiative; perverted initiative has generated endemic inefficiency; inefficiency has yielded massive economic waste; waste has led to frenetic tinkering with centralized controls and shuffling of the controllers.

Economist Allan H. Meltzer, of Carnegie Mellon University, finds that Western observers of the Russian comedic tragedy tend to be mesmerized by ongoing trivial tinkering and shuffling. The system itself—not superficial symptoms of socialistic silliness—must be restructured:

> By rearranging some ministries, firing some . . . bureaucrats, chang-
> ing some prices and exhorting everyone to greater efforts [writes
> Professor Meltzer], . . . [the government] may be able to get some
> increases in output. However, the changes will not be a reform of the
> Soviet economy. . . . The key issue for success or failure of reform is
> whether the Soviets will . . . reverse Lenin's error and permit private
> ownership. . . . The problem in any economy is to introduce the pro-
> per incentives. . . . If the incentives remain unchanged, the system
> remains unchanged. . . . A private property system gives people in-
> centives to use resources . . . efficiently.

But official promotion of such a second Russian revolution is not expected. The Establishment will not depose itself.

(July 1988)

Russian Military Strength and Economic Weakness

Russia is self-consciously a superpower. Her status and stature rest solely on her massive military strength, not on her inept economy. Military might provides quiescence at home and instrumentality for subversion and political power abroad. The governing elite thus has great *demand* for armament.

But what of armament *supply*? The Russian military budget is absolutely greater than that of the United States, although the Russian gross national product is less than half as large. How can such a rickety economy provide such a massive military machine?

Although the Russian economy—muscle-bound with central planning and direction—is largely a mess, in one respect it is not as inefficient as might be initially supposed.

Economic efficiency has to do with effective use of available resources in satisfying preferences. Whose preferences? In our sort of individualistic society, with an economy based on production with and exchange of privately owned assets, the pertinent preferences are those of the members of the community. The Russians do not generally make very effective technological and industrial use of their resources, but at least the boys in charge do not have to be much concerned about whose preferences will dominate. The preferences which count are those of the few who run the show, not those of the bulk of the population.

There are two corollaries of this great unrepresentative and unaccountable concentration of power at the top, corollaries relevant to the development of military might in the face of a bumbling economy.

First, the cost of devoting a very large share of the nation's output to the military is not great. For the cost of anything is the value of alternatives foregone in achieving the chosen end. The Russians do give up civilian goods in order to produce military goods. But, in the eyes of the governmental decisionmakers, those sacrificed civilian goods have little value. When the well-being of the general population counts for little, there is little cost in squeezing the standard of living in order to feed Leviathan.

The second corollary of concentrated power is that the planning and production of armaments is done relatively effectively. Professor Dwight Lee makes this point: "When the task is increasing military power rather than accommodating the diversity of consumer demands, technical engineering considerations become more important, and subjective evaluations and tradeoffs become less important. Also," he adds, "central planners are capable of directing resources in a way so as to overcome well-specified technical problems and to achieve narrowly specified goals."

The belligerently autonomous Russian leaders *want* to be massively armed, partly *because* of the lousy Russian economy; and they *can* be massively armed, *in spite* of the lousy Russian economy.

(January 1987)

Apartheid:
Problems and Potentialities

Divestiture: Defeat by Default

Strident, supercilious voices—mainly on college campuses and in local and state nests of politicians—have a new cause. The current grand—or grandstanding—crusade is to rid the world of South African racial oppression. The means is forced selling by government institutions of stocks of firms doing business in South Africa.

The University of California has a considerable portfolio of stock in a who's who of American firms, many of which have commercial ties with South Africa. Suppose the University were to sell its General Motors stock. What would be the consequences?

First, General Motors would not be directly involved. G.M. issued that stock a year or fifty years ago, and it is not a party to today's transaction when the University sells to another investor. Second, the *price* of the stock may not be affected, depending on how much is sold over how long a period in what procedure. Any price fall will be only modest and momentary, so G.M. will be punished little, if at all. Third, if the price *does* fall, those injured will include the University and the thousands of individuals, insurance companies, banks, and pension funds still holding the stock. Fourth, the University would pay millions of dollars in *brokerage commissions*, first in selling the contaminated stock and then in buying pure replacements. Finally, the revised *portfolio* would be weaker than the original, so again the University is made poorer. Thus do college kids and phony politicians have their fun in playing with wealth which does not belong to them.

Does all this financial mismanagement have a positive payoff? The purposed objective is to help the black people of South Africa. Will they be better off if American firms refuse to sell to and buy from and produce in South Africa?

If United States firms stop *supplying* South African buyers, the South African economy will be injured but will not crumble: it can turn to second-best suppliers. If United States firms stop *buying* from South Africa, we would have much more difficulty in replacing several critical sources of supply than they would have in finding alternative buyers. If United States firms stop *producing* in South Africa, the facilities will be sold to others, in either South Africa or other counties, which is not likely to help the lot of poor workers. By definition, the poor are most vulnerable: in any injury imposed upon the South African economy, the oppressed blacks will be hurt first and worst. Thus do we have our fun in playing with the lives of others.

The divestiture tactic is inherently peculiar if the purpose really is to pressure and persuade the South African establishment to mend its ways. Pressure will be stubbornly resisted, and we can hardly expect to persuade by ending contact. On the scene, participating in work-a-day affairs, we can be—as we have been—some influence for good. But spiteful withdrawal means simply defeat by default.

(June 1985)

Apartheid and Capitalism

Many who loudly condemn odious South African apartheid associate it with and describe it in terms of capitalism. The kindest comment on such commentary is to note its ignorance. Apartheid is *not* a form or reflection of capitalism, and it is *not* a consequence of capitalism. It is, indeed, an *enemy* of capitalism.

The essence of capitalism is, first, minimal limitation of private rights to use of property, including rights to buy and sell assets, including labor services; and, second, clear and consistent containment of government. The first helps assure options and incentives, rationality and coordination—in short, economic and technological efficiency; and the second helps assure the first.

All this ill defines the South African economy. That arrangement provides only limited private property and massive favoritism. With centralized political control concentrating economic privilege on the criterion of race, it has been called "ethnic socialism." And with a small urban economy ruled by whites and dominating a large rural economy filled with blacks, there is much resemblance to feudalism.

Business interests of efficiency and growth more and more coincide with liberalization of the segregated society. And even Karl Marx found dynamic, adaptable capitalism to be a beneficial wind of change in blowing away static, structured feudalism.

Capitalistic industrialization—with the stability and forethought it requires and the sophisticated interdependence it engenders—is a significant instigator of integration. A conspicuous characteristic of a capitalistic economy is large numbers of competent, disciplined workers available at open-market-determined wages. The thrust of apartheid has been just the opposite. By curtailing geographic and occupational mobility of black workers, apartheid *reduces* labor supply in urban industrial centers, *hampers* education and training of black workers, and *raises* wages of white workers.

Apartheid has discriminated in favor of white *labor*—and thereby injured white *employers*. This is hardly a capitalistic strategy.

Still, the muscle of the market is considerable, and some civilizing progress has been made. Largely as a consequence of increasing demand for workers of increasing minimal levels of skill, the economic aspects of apartheid have been increasingly circumvented and diluted. Reduction of that labor demand by weakening of the economy through outside isolation and inside insurrection would reduce the motor force of liberal change.

But our own activists of the left prefer the politics of protest to the economics of wealth; and the South African neanderthals of the right prefer the comfort of hierarchy and privilege to the productive dynamism of the market. Neither are friends of a progressive and prosperous South Africa.

(June 1986)

Dealing With Apartheid: Barriers and Incentives

The world is well filled with problems. The problems come in many shapes. But near the heart of the difficulties of gracefully surviving in a stingy world is the question of how to deal with other people. Most of them are as unlovely—greedy, self-centered, and aggressive—as you. So how do you get others to do what you want? How can you get them to work for you or to sell to you or to join forces with you in joint effort?

Basically, there are two alternative tactics you—and the community generally—can adopt. Either you *conduce* people to do what is desired or you *coerce* them. You *bribe* them or you *bash* them. You *pay* them or you *penalize* them. You *reward* them if they do what you wish or you *ruin* them if they do not.

These are very different sorts of worlds. And most of us find vastly more attractive the kind of social arrangement in which we enjoy *mutual* gains, with people coordinating their activities through making themselves valuable to each other. This is more productive, as well as more genteel, than a world of economic discrimination and physical domination of some people over others.

More and more people are comprehending this message in the context of our domestic economy. They like a social order of occupational and geographic mobility, of rights to use of property they own, of wide options of an open market.

Well, if market coordination—capitalism, if you please—is a good prescription for us, wouldn't it be good for South Africa, too? Yes, it would. But, unhappily, that is not what noisy politicians, silly college kids, and illiterate media and entertainment types are currently promoting.

Against a background of assassinations by burning automobile tires around the neck and talk by Nobel peace prize clergy sorts of holy war and black nannies poisoning white children, there are growing calls for punitive sanctions. Demagogues seek, not solution, but retribution and revolution. We are to coerce and bash and penalize and ruin South Africa.

The South African social-economic arrangement is not satisfactory today. But it was worse yesterday, and there is increasingly acknowledged incentive to make it better tomorrow.

This improvement and this hope surely has little to do with altruism and feelings of brotherhood. Rather, the white establishment of South Africa has been growing in awareness of what is required—including hopeful, committed, and trained workers—for the progress of a modern economy. What is required obviously is *not* apartheid. Apartheid is the enemy of adaptable, progressing capitalism.

Apartheid already is heavily diluted; if opportunity is permitted, it will persistently dissolve. But opportunity will be denied by destroying the South African economy and reducing the community to the tribal tyranny, political ineptitude, and economic idiocy which characterize almost all the rest of the African continent.

(September 1986)

What Comes After Apartheid?

It is easy to oppose odious South African apartheid. But what is to replace it?

Those who loudly demand annihilation of evil instantaneously have made realistic correction and reform more difficult. Simpleminded insistence on sanctions and disinvestment have accomplished little other than stopping of significant progress and solidifying of defiance by South African society. If, as a consequence, further change is to come only through revolution in the name of retribution, then South Africa will be reduced to the tribal tyranny and poverty which characterizes the rest of the miserable continent.

But if South Africa is to be saved without destroying it, what is to be the scheme of salvation? One can be against sin, but what is to be the way of virtue? Can we do better than simply replace whitedominated apartheid with black-dominated apartheid?

Indeed, the question of how the new South African community is to be organized and carry on its affairs is critical to the prior problem of how the ground is to be cleared of the old structure. So long as the white establishment sees only humiliation, destitution, and possible death as the alternative to stubborn resistance, they surely will resist. That resistance likely would be prolonged and effective: few spoils would be left for the victors.

But if it is feasible constructively to reconstitute the South African state and society—discarding the bad, keeping the good, innovating the best—what sort of structure should it be? Hysterical sanctionsmongers do not help. But a few thinkers have indicated a promising model. The fullest statement is by a white married couple of South Africans, Frances Kendall and Leon Louw. Their book—*After Apartheid: The Solution for South Africa*—is a best-seller there and now available here through the Institute for Contemporary Studies. It is endorsed by such strange bedfellows as radical Winnie Mandela, Zulu Chief Buthelezi, and moderate Alan Paton, along with *Time* and the *Wall Street Journal*.

The essence of the Kendall-and-Louw plan is both democracy and protection of minority rights with a confederation of largely autonomous states and severely contained national government, buttressed by a detailed bill of rights, including broad and universal rights to use of property. To maintain major reliance on a powerful, centralized, interventionist government, chosen on the basis of one-man, one-vote, is a recipe for economic and political debacle in a polyglot country of many languages, many races, many tribes, and many religions.

Switzerland has splendidly demonstrated the effectiveness of a confederation, with small cantons dealing with matters of basically local and regional concern and with the national government confined mainly to defense and to maintenance of constitutional rights. Africa—and the entire world—could gracefully tolerate another Switzerland.

(September 1987)

Government and Politics, Administration and Tyranny

Political Voting and Economic Voting

In the political polling-place, we vote with ballots. In the economic market-place, we vote with dollars. The socialists among us sarcastically note that in the political realm, we have one-*man*-one-vote, whereas in the market, it is one-*dollar*-one-vote—and some people have more dollars than other people have.

Socialists find it less convenient to note that the ballot vote is a much clumsier, less satisfying way to register preferences than is the dollar vote. We cast ballots from time to time for a politician. If our candidate loses, we are essentially unrepresented. Even if our candidate wins, we still are not likely to acquire just what we want, for, first, the politician will not always do what we prefer on the myriad issues he faces during his term, and, second, even when he does vote as we would have acted, he may be outvoted by other politicians.

Voting with dollars is infinitely neater and more precise. In the economic market, we pick and reject, choose and decline among innumerable alternatives every day. There is no periodically chosen intermediary, standing between us and the goods and services, as in the political world. We make our own economic decisions, directly and continuously.

Day by day, we buy this instead of that, we buy a little this time, a lot next time, and none the time after that, as our fortunes, our tastes, and our known options evolve. Much better than in the political world, we know what the economic products are, and we have vastly greater choice in what we buy, in what quantities, and in how purchases are financed.

Economic "efficiency" is much more than a matter of engineering. Technological, physical input-output efficiency obviously is important. Less obvious, but even more fundamental, is another aspect of efficiency, namely, production in accordance with preferences of the individuals who make up the community. The market provides a medium for constantly, precisely recording community preferences and a process for effectively directing resources toward the indicated preferences.

But government, in the nature of government—even representational government—*cannot* be so precisely efficient in directing the use of the community's resources in reflection of the community preferences. Government does have command over vast resources, to be sure, but how is it to be determined how to use them? What criteria are to be applied? Whose preferences are to prevail? It would be utterly astonishing to find that the preferences of Big Brother happen to coincide, persistently and exactly, with the shifting, evolving preferences of his serfs. And if Big Brother is simply the personification of the serfs, why have Big Brother at all?

In the economic marketplace, we are voluntary consumers, using our own wealth for our own purposes by our own criteria. In the political realm, we are very largely involuntary subjects, in a position of pay-your-taxes, obey-bureaucratic-directives, and-like-it. When we speak if economic efficiency, found only through the market, we speak also of personal freedom.

(April 1981)

Politics and Economics

For the policy decisionmaker, what is the distinction between caution and cowardice and between boldness and bumptiousness? Unhappily, in the real world of affairs, the delineation between virtue and defect is not always perfectly clear. Indeed, it is often obscure in football, war— and politics.

In early 1968, a widely experienced economist told me that his favorite in the approaching presidential was Richard Nixon. For Mr. Nixon, he assured me, would do whatever was required to correct inflation—even if such policy would be so unpopular as to imply only a one-term presidency.

In early 1971, inflation was at the astronomical altitude of some 4 percent annually, and unemployment was a horrendous 6 percent. The Administration was widely denounced for reveling in the miseries of the downtrodden.

The President was told by his advisors in the summer of 1971 that a steady course of moderate policy, notably including appropriate curtailment of growth of the money supply, would gradually yield a situation of minimal inflation and unemployment. How long would that take? Maybe a year and a half. But the President noted that he could not wait that long, for within that period, there would be an election. So, in August, to great public applause, this free-market President, who allegedly had been prepared genuinely to solve the inflation problem even if that meant losing his bid for reelection, instead imposed wage-and-price controls.

Mr. Nixon told us in his memoirs that he was persuaded at the time—and that he is still convinced—that controls are lousy economic policy. ". . . in the long run," he says, the controls decision "was wrong." Then why did he pursue such a strategy? Well, while it was wrong "in the long run," it was "politically necessary and immensely popular in the short run."

"It is unfortunate," Mr. Nixon philosophizes, "that the *politics* of economics has come to dictate action more than the *economics* of economics." And, he testifies, "even someone with strong economic ideas can be affected by the sting of criticism and the clamor of those who want a different policy."

It is easy, in such a case, to charge—and heroically to condemn—cynicism as well as cowardice. But heroism comes easily for those who do not bear the responsibility of the decision. It is a wise general who knows when to retreat: do we stubbornly face the enemy on this issue now and, as a result, possibly lose the war (or the next election) even if we win the battle?

Even among people of both sense and honor, opinions can differ on the importance of today's battle decision and on the probable relative losses of fighting and of retreating. The net costs of retreat in August 1971 were enormous. But the intellectual error of bad calculation of returns and costs is different from the character weakness of cowardice.

(August 1981)

Truth and Hope

It has been my fortune to participate in an international conference on advances in electronic communications and computerization. The conference was attended by technicians and economists from both sides of the Iron Curtain.

During the bulk of the conference sessions, engineering and administrative considerations predominated. There was much talk of invention and physical application. That was dispassionate ground, stirring few philosophical wonderments. But little attention was given to economic aspects of information costs, investment, and adaptation of both producers and consumers to use of the new knowledge.

When questions of demands and preferences, financing and resource shifting *were* raised, they were supposedly resolved by referring them to government. Should research be pursued and investment made? That is for government to decide. From whence will come required resources? Government will provide. How are resources to be shifted and people to adapt? Government will guide us.

Late in the conference, there was an additional effort to bring economic questions and criteria before the group, with emphasis on utilization of resources in accordance with revealed *community*—not governmental—preferences. It was claimed that personal freedom and economic efficiency walk together in the private-property, open-market society.

But economics discussion was perceived by some as unsafe. A scholar from central Europe offered the hope of quiet accommodation, of acquiescence to dominant power. We do well, he suggested, to confine ourselves to the currently probable, the apparently feasible. Benchmarks of freedom and efficiency set too high, he seemed to say, are more discouraging than productive. Do not criticize or try to guide us. We have lost most of our autonomy, our constraints are severe. We can discuss technology, we can trade, but please do not speak to us of freedom and its efficiency. If you were to be persuasive, we might try to follow, and therein would like disaster. You can be the last, best hope of earth only for those who can afford hope. But we are realists, and in our realism we are without hope.

Many nodded in agreement—not only those who would appreciate a freedom unattainable to them, but those who still have appreciable freedom but do not comprehend it sufficiently well to defend it or fear it or find it an inconvenience in shaping the world to their own designs.

Did the courtly, erudite gentleman speak his actual mind? How far has he professionally accommodated and acquiesced to the brutal stupidity of political masters? It is sobering to have occasion to ask such questions. Distressing as is the occasion, it is also a warning, lest we, too, find ourselves beyond a point of no return, when the alternatives are only to acquiesce or to die.

"Truth crushed to earth shall rise again," we tell ourselves, and "hope springs eternal." But for some, truth is an unaffordable luxury, and hope has died.

(October 1981)

Ideology, Economics, and Survival

Perhaps the elderly become more philosophic. I shall not be able to test that hypothesis with personal experience for another two or three years. But an older friend—a highly successful, retired businessman—recently philosophized at me. He is concerned about how best to delineate and nurture the conditions of survival of the open, individualistic society.

We are confronted, said my friend, by a collectivist, imperialist ideology supported by massive resources. His primary fear is not military subjugation. How shall we more likely be done in? Philosophically. We are in peril of forgetting, misinterpreting, or ignoring our intellectual and inspirational heritage. Without the instructions and guidance of Jefferson and Madison and Lincoln, we will lose our birthright and sink back into the engulfing slime of history.

And, my friend added, in this decisive contest of thought and comprehension of first principles, of dedication and motivation to prevail, economics is only a minor, unglamorous consideration.

Much of this reflects profundity. A free society, by its nature, is bound together and operates through devices and channels of *individual* aspirations and anticipations. It relies not on authoritarian decrees enforced with the thumb screw, but on induced coordination of largely *autonomous* people who, in pursuing their *personal* ends, contribute to the well-being of the community.

But what are these personal ends, what is the nature of these coordinated activities, what is the content of this community well-being? For nearly all of us, ends, activities, and well-being will be predominantly economic.

Ideology, dogma, philosophy have their considerable significance. But they are an adornment built on, and deriving from, how and how well we earn our living. We shall never make many of the community into economic analysts; we shall do even less well in trying to make them into political philosophers; and neither failure need be fatal. There is required little analytic elegance or philosophic subtlety in real people—as contrasted to professors—conducting well their nitty-gritty affairs in the real world.

If we are not physically overrun by barbarians, what *will* destroy us? Not learned quibbles on the nuances of what the Founding Fathers really meant. Rather, we will ruin ourselves with minimum wage and comparable worth laws; with controls on prices of goods, apartments, and loans; with erratic changes in the price level; with governmental domination through the budget, environmental regulation, and antitrust intrusions; with progressive attenuation of property rights; with subsidization of inefficiency and sloth and divisiveness.

Political liberties lack both substance and longevity unless based on an efficient economy. Free men require free markets. If we lose the battle of economic freedom, we lose the entire war.

(August 1985)

Bad-Mannered Government
Is Bad Government

Black shirts and hob-nailed boots may be out of fashion, but stormtrooperism has not been entirely eradicated.

Last year, a Los Angeles restaurant was trampled by officers of the Internal Revenue Service. The firm was delinquent in a modest amount of taxes. But different IRS notices specified different amounts, and the restaurant was unsuccessful in pinning down the exact figure. A required final notice may never have been received; a required meeting of a revenue officer with the taxpayer was not held; and the restaurant was seized and closed prematurely—indeed, the seizure took place in the very afternoon of a scheduled meeting between the business and the government and just before mail delivery of two IRS notices which called for payment *nine days later*.

The seizure itself was conducted with the finesse of a retarded rhinoceros: arriving unannounced during the lunch period, IRS agents ordered customers to leave immediately—without being allowed to take food with them, for the doggie bags were declared government property.

A peccadillo of the federal tax act of 1982 gave the IRS authority to prosecute people filing "frivolous" income tax returns. Under that provision, according to the publication, *Human Events*, more than 5,500 citizens who filed *complete* returns and paid their taxes in *full* have been fined for attaching comments to their tax reports—comments which did *not* interfere with processing the returns but which were critical of the IRS, the government, or the tax system.

Such foolishness is worse than regrettable: it is tragic. And the tragedy extends far beyond the relatively few immediate victims.

The size of government can be variously measured. It is also reflected in the sinews of everyday life. More government spending and taxing mean more government—and more government means more rules and directives, more personal uncertainty and unease, more private concern and efforts of self-protection, more informers and enforcers, more reliance on autocratic bureaucrats and a broader realm of discretion for their unaccountable lackeys.

While there can be much resiliency in a nation, sufficiently massive and prolonged violations of trust, inconsistencies with community mores, and flauntings of administrative authority will transform society and how it conducts its affairs. The transformation corrupts and corrodes, entailing restriction of initiative, suppression of individualism, and withering of confidence.

Ineptitude, unreliability, and nastiness are not confined to the IRS or to government. But such attributes rarely flourish in the private sector. In a competitive market, mistreatment of customers is not the way to prosper. But government relies on coercion rather than persuasion and permits few competitive alternatives to itself.

A community which does not contain its government will be controlled by government. Contempt for and fear of government are not a firm foundation for survival of the Land of the Free and the Home of the Brave.

(August 1984)

The New Deal and Fascism

It has been argued that there were two New Deals in the 1930s. The first centered on "the cartelism of the NRA," and did not last long. The second was a "free-spending and experimental period that saw . . . the injection of the federal government into every aspect of national life."

The dichotomy can be too neatly drawn. The psychological and philosophical orientation toward dominant government initiatives and assumed responsibilities; the reliance on state intervention in and appreciable superseding of the market; the increasing pervasiveness of bureaucratic decree and manipulation—such characteristics provided an underlying consistency for a long episode otherwise marked heavily by analytic incoherency, strategic uncertainty, political inconstancy, and policy improvisation.

In the early 1930s, some articulate people professed to see the workable future in the Russian experience. But communistic state ownership of property was a bit much for all but a few. For many more, fascism approximated the best of all worlds: the trappings of private property and enterprise would be largely retained but in a setting of close alliance among big government, big business, and big labor—with government being the overarching director and final arbiter.

It is not to be suggested that President Roosevelt and his Brain Trusters applauded Mussolini's aberrant political attitudes—the exultation of violence and ruthlessness and irrationality. But the thrust of fascistic *economic* intent and organization looked good to many New Dealers.

The "corporate" economy would eliminate the individualistic competition of the marketplace and the struggle between capital and labor. Such wasteful disruption would be replaced by collectivized economic sectors, with mandatory confederations of union and of industry leaders agreeing on fair wages, fair prices, and fair modes of business behavior, all coordinated and approved by government, and with personal gain subordinated to the community's good.

Basic aspects of the New Deal's NRA and AAA and Wagner labor act have obvious resemblance—explicitly noted by some at the time—to the Italian model. So, too, did some of the New Deal doctrine.

Six weeks after the inauguration in 1933, in a fireside chat, the President characterized the United States' version of economic fascism:

It is wholly wrong to call the measures that we have taken govern-ment control of farming, industry, and transportation. It is rather a partnership between government and farming and industry and transportation, not partnership in profits, for the profits still go to the citizens, but rather a partnership in planning, and a partnership to see that the plans are carried out . . . . Government ought to have the right and will have the right, after surveying and planning for an industry, to prevent . . . unfair practices and to enforce this agreement by the authority of government.

The President is reported to have remarked that he had "never felt surer of anything in . . . [his] life than . . . [he did] of the soundness of this passage."

(September 1982)

The New Deal: Ideology and Performance

Karl, the usually cynical mouse, was uncommonly solicitous. "What is wrong with Professor Allen?" he asked his rodent friend, Adam.

"I am afraid," replied the usually solicitous but now bemused Adam, "that Professor Allen can't decide whether to laugh or to cry. But, of course, he is not permitted to do either: economists are not supposed to laugh, and men are not supposed to cry."

"Hoo, boy," sighed Karl, "it sounds like another attack of his-torianitis."

"That's right," confirmed Adam. "A historian friend has sent the first couple of pages of an article by another historian—a Harvard historian, no less. In the first page, the author has made a magnificent blooper."

"Harvard historians do have a way with words," murmured Karl. "When they have silly things to say, they don't mess around. Just what silliness did he bloop?"

"The historian," Adam replied, "describes his lasting love of Franklin D. Roosevelt's New Deal of the 1930s. The scholar concedes that 'the New Deal was not a "social revolution"'; 'it did not bring full employment'; it 'did not bring significant redistribution of income'; and it did not 'set the country on the path toward economic growth.'"

"Well," asked a confused Karl, "if the New Deal failed in all its efforts, what was so great about it?"

"Why, the glory of the New Deal," said Adam, "is that it was 'a revolution in political *ideas*.' The historian was ghostwriter for two of the 'brain trusters.' In both positions, he says, the 'preoccupation [was] to persuade people to look to Washington for help, to convince them that "government is the solution."' That government failed, that government could not do what the rousing rhetoric called for and claimed, was not very important. The critical thing was for the President and his brain trusters to convince people that there is no beneficial market mechanisms; that the community cannot prosper or even survive through individual initiative and accountability in a stable setting of wide options provided by a severely contained government; that government—with neither market incentives nor market guidance—must be our chief producer (and distributor) of wealth; that government—reeking of purity and wisdom—will save us from the nefarious forces of greed and stupidity."

"But," Karl protested, "the historian agrees that the New Deal did *not* succeed. And he must realize that history has been dominated by dominating government and that that domination has yielded a consistent story of both tyranny and poverty."

"Oh, fascism, communism, and socialism—along with the New Deal—have failed to produce the goods," agreed Adam. "But the historian claims—unhappily, with much reason—that in the 'revolution of ideas,' the New Dealers 'succeeded.' It matters little to these purported descendants of Thomas Jefferson that the people live poorly, so long as they embrace Big Brother. For them, ideology is vastly more important than performance."

(August 1985)

Economics and the Imperial Presidency

In order to manage well the might of government, one's policy orientation had better be philosophically profound and one's policy strategy analytically sound.

In spring 1962, the serenity of Camelot was disturbed by dramatic confrontation between Big Business and Big Government. President Kennedy was worried about inflation and the balance of international payments. And apparently he took seriously the faulty "cost-push" notion of inflation.

Labor union contracts with steel companies had just been renegotiated. This was the second increase in steel-worker wages since steel prices had been raised four years earlier, but the President believed, seemingly with reason, that steel management would hold prices constant.

The President was surprised to be informed in April 1962 that U.S. Steel—whether or not shrewdly by business criteria—would be raising its prices about 4 percent. Several other steel companies quickly made similar announcements. The President was furious, feeling that he had been insulted and claiming that his economic program of non-inflationary growth had been endangered. He said that he was finally convinced that, as his father had told him, business people were not nice.

The President had no authority to order the steel companies to rescind the price increases. But, with a fine jungle instinct for indirect uses of power, he put such pressure on the companies—through public denunciation and threats of government retribution—that the business managers backed off in confusion and fear.

What are we to make of the remarkable episode?

The diagnosis of the economic situation by the President may be deemed peculiar. While inflation can never be finally killed, it was then quiescent, and had been for a decade. The basis of inflation is excessive expansion of the amount of money, and money, like prices, had long been increasing at less than 2 percent annually.

At the same time, the balance of payments, gross national product, and employment were steadily performing well in the difficult postwar period.

But the major cause of wonderment was not faulty economic diagnosis. Rather, it was faulty presumption of the economic role of the President and of government generally. The young President supposed that the great economy of a great nation is properly subject to his personal price controls. His supposition of legitimate bashing of business firms on the basis of idiosyncratic concepts of "the public interest"—implementing autocratic policy by blackjack—was wholly improper by both philosophic and analytic criteria.

It is sobering when a man has to become President of the United States in order to learn that some people can sometimes be naughty. It is frightening when a man who has become President never learns the essence of a society of private rights to use of property, market-determined prices, and severely constrained government.

(November 1986)

Universities: Professionalism, Diversity, and Promise

Majorities, Minorities, and Intellectual Heritage

People, in contrast to dogs, are hardly fit companions. Living together civilly and productively is delicate, at best, and it is complicated by ethnic differences. Minimal good will is necessary, but it is not sufficient: some degree of comprehension of, and agreement on, certain fundamentals also is required.

A writer of Mexican background has written a poignant newspaper essay concerning the plight of racial minorities on university campuses. "For generations," he suggests, "the university accepted scholarship students with the expectation that they would become different from their parents." Indeed, the proper point of educational experience for anyone is to become different from what he would otherwise have been. The individual, even while retaining and cultivating his individuality, is to be introduced to a heritage, and initiated into a community, broader than national demarcations and racial distinctions.

But in the 1960s, much of the university establishment—both administrators and faculty—with belligerent stupidity, denied the academic heritage of the common pursuit of the individual life of the mind, and threw the academic community into confusion. " . . . the university began accepting the minority student," recalls the essayist, "on the assumption that he was somehow still connected with his past. The university," he continues, "expected me to represent my working-class past; my presence would represent disadvantaged Latinos to the academic community. The logic of affirmative action made each minority student a beneficiary of the disadvantaged condition of others outside the campus. Their defeat justified my advantage and advancement."

Now, twenty years later, the fun of fraternizing with romanticized barrio and ghetto delegations has evaporated. It has been replaced, we are told, with "resentment of minority-student privilege." Both then and now, minority students had reason to believe that they were *in* the academy by special dispensation—whether given readily or given grudgingly—but were not accepted as *of* the academy.

People—white, black, brown, yellow, or polka dot—are to be on the campus only because they have legitimate business there. They are blessed with those innate and acquired qualities and characteristics which will enable them to absorb, and then contribute to, the shared intellectual and professional legacy. But the discovery, acceptance, and cultivation of the qualified few cannot be accomplished by the crude process of counting ethnic noses in order to satisfy politically decreed quotas.

Minorities are not to be on the campus neither to amuse the majority or to assuage warm feelings of majority guilt for historical transgressions. And those minorities who are rightly on the campus, having warranted their opportunity, are to be neither romanticized nor resented.

(October 1987)

Quality, Diversity, and the University

When resources and options are limited, we must make choices. In a world of scarcity, we cannot do and have all we want, and different goals and criteria may be mutually inconsistent. Acquiring more of some things means giving up some of other things; doing this means we cannot do that. There are trade-offs to determine, prices to be paid, costs to be borne.

All this applies to the evolving and sustaining of a university. A university is to be an institution through which very able and thoroughly committed people preserve, enhance, and disseminate accumulated knowledge and acquired techniques of thought. All those who are prepared, in aptitude and attitude, to participate effectively in the life of the mind are welcome, for there is sophisticated work to be done. But that work is diverted and resources are wasted by campus politicians among the faculty and the administrators and by students who find brash promotion of Good Causes more fun than laborious study. It is such professional charlatans and intellectual wimps who prattle about university "greatness through diversity."

Great diversity is inherent in a university. The very word—university— suggests a fruitful bringing together of diverse elements and activities. But the latest cause of campus agitators is for still more diversity.

The agitation typically is incoherent at any level above sloganeering, but doubtless the main pressure is on race and gender. Everyone with legitimate business on a university campus agrees that it is totally reprehensible to *deny* faculty employment or student admission on grounds of race and gender—or on grounds of religion, as was done in an earlier day. Should it be more acceptable to *favor* people on such grounds?

Presumably, there are *some* sorts of gross gains from diversity itself. It is surely possible that a campus will be more attractive in *some* respects in being populated by women as well as men; by including pink, black, brown, yellow, and red skins; by having Christians, Jews, Muslims, atheists, and Druids; and perhaps by fat and thin, tall and short people. But *professional excellence* has nothing to do with such extraneous criteria. And it is already shamefully the case that criteria and standards of competence have often been diluted and even discarded, subverting the university in the specious name of diversity.

It is not at all to be expected that we will be blessed with the coincidence that in maximizing diversity we will maximize quality. A choice is required. If we are to be faithful to our trust, we shall seek the professionally *best* faculty and students, not a variously *diverse* group. In the process of obtaining the best, diversity will take care of itself. But if we consciously and insistently seek diversity for its own sake, quality will be a casualty.

(September 1988)

The Campus Children's Crusade

My, these *are* hard days of great concern on the college campus!

One understands the frustrated discontent of would-be revolutionary students over the tepid quality of today's protests. "I'm tired of going to demonstrations where the major goal is to get a large number of people and then not do anything with them," whimpers one young scholar who longs for action and martyrdom. "We go out there knowing no one will get arrested, knowing we'll all just return home safe and sound. It might as well not have happened."

Senior scholars, too, are concerned about the values and vitality of the braves of the tribe. A professor of education detects fascistic subversion in the findings of a poll that over two-thirds of today's freshmen want to be "very well off financially" and that fewer than half put great weight on developing a "meaningful philosophy of life."

We are told that instead of idealistic students shaping society—as in the 1960s—materialistic society is now shaping students. One proffered bit of evidence: sociology enrollments are down, and economics enrollments are up! Alas—the end of the children's crusade!

A survey by professors of psychology and history of high school valedictory addresses reveals limited criticism of society, little social consciousness, and few solutions to world problems. At the same time, these leading high school graduates are friendly, praise achievement, call for individual responsibility, and seek best use of personal resources. They even say that one reason for their going to college is "to learn more about things."

I have learned not to expect profundity in all matters from eighteen-year-olds. It is asking a bit much for people of such years, training, and experience to provide wise counsel and erudite guidance on the great social, economic, and geopolitical issues of the day. But they are more sensible than some professors of education, psychology, and history. It is quite enough that students be civil, ambitious, accountable, and reliant on their own resources.

Nor need such people be bloodless wimps. Although the 1960s babies of Berkeley and kids of Columbia would never comprehend, compassion and gentility and generosity are consistent with interest in one's own productivity and well-being. Cultivated sophistication is compatible with adding value in the marketplace. One can study mathematics and chemistry and law and economics, and still be concerned about the human condition. Ignorance and incompetence are not prerequisites of sensitivity.

The hope of tomorrow does not rest with insufferable infants who will do nothing but invade the administration building and pronounce "non-negotiable" demands. And it certainly does not rest with still more infantile faculty and deans. If we are to be strong and to use our strength well, it will be largely because of those who quietly live laborious lives in the library and the laboratory.

(July 1984)

School Reform:
Quality and Competition

Education and the Community

The quality of our community and its economy is determined largely by the quality of our people. The quality of people—their knowledge, skills, interests, aspirations, and gentility—is determined largely by their basic education. And much of American public education of its youngsters is an inferior product.

A mountain of evidence of various types—both quantitative and impressionistic—is persuasive that the bulk of our high school students (and high school dropouts) know and can do little, compared to students twenty-five years ago, compared to any reasonable absolute standard, and compared to students in other major industrial nations.

The problem goes far beyond a characteristic lack of facility in skills required to be highly productive in a brutally competitive high-tech world. A huge proportion of today's teenagers cannot usefully function at even elemental levels of literacy, logic, calculation, and communication.

Compounding the distressing condition of technical incompetence is an aura and attitude of intellectual coarseness and professional crudeness, a disdain for sophistication, a flaunting of an almost militant ignorance, all of which promise to dilute our society as it weakens our prosperity.

Myron Magnet reports in *Fortune* magazine that educational concern is not confined to the lamentable fact that "many young Americans lack the basic skills needed to build quality cars or even run cash registers. Many new graduates also lack a solid core of the knowledge that makes America work as a country, that common culture that turns a pluralistic hodgepodge into a unified nation without depriving anyone of his distinctive identity. They lack that modicum of political judgment, based on at least a smattering of history, that makes democracy authentic and not a masquerade. Missing too is the historical and literary knowledge that shows the vastness and variety of human aspirations and achievement, strengthening character and values and enlarging one's sense of the possibilities and worth of one's life."

Faced with such failure of schooling, the business community has increasingly assumed enormously expensive burdens of remedial training for new employees. But crash courses for twenty-year-old high school graduates and twenty-five-year-old college graduates in tools and techniques they should have mastered in grade school is only stop-gap strategy. And it is too little and too late for the cultivation of those perspectives and proprieties, those shared values and visions, which must sustain us as a coherent and cultivated community.

If a productive process is to be assessed by the quality of the product produced and the efficiency of its production, then the public school system must be given generally low marks. We had best do much better. We will likely generate the education we deserve. But will we generate the education which survival as a great nation requires?

(February 1988)

Educational Reform and Egalitarian Rhetoric

Evidence is distressingly persuasive that appropriate school reform is critical. But more important than institutional educational correction—for it is a prerequisite of reform—is sophistication of perspective and attitude. The question is not only abstract content of proposed reform, but what is required first to delineate concrete improvements and then make them effective.

Are we sufficiently embarrassed and emboldened to want to correct manifold errors of education? Are we sufficiently insightful and receptive to appreciate the nature, magnitude, and possible resolution of problems? Are we sufficiently courageous and committed to face down inhibiting vested interests and to make the investments required for success?

There is no reason to anticipate that required reforms involving competition will emanate from the long-established public school monopoly. But calls for change are coming from the community, including the corporate component. One vigorous voice is that of David T. Kearns, chairman of Xerox Corporation.

Mr. Kearns proposes a multifaceted "education recovery plan for America." The central *organizational thrust* of his plan is attractive. Public funds are evenhandedly to subsidize students, not schools directly. Highly flexible, largely autonomous schools would compete for students with programs tailored for prospective clientele and with teachers who are accountable and well rewarded for professionalism.

But eyebrows can be raised over some of the *substantive content* of education under the Kearns plan. After all the organizational emphasis on autonomy and initiative and product differentiation, we are told that "we must apply the same high standards to everyone across the board. College prep for the favored few has to go. Every student—without exception—should master a core curriculum equivalent to entrance requirements."

Thus does simple egalitarian rhetoric arise. Education—to some extent even at the high school level and wholly at the college level—is, in its nature, an elitist activity and product. People differ greatly in interests, ambitions, talents, and proclivities—and intellectual competence.

Commentator Daniel Seligman, of *Fortune* magazine, suggests cogently that the educational system, while doubtless infested with many faults, fails in large part because "schools are overwhelmed by kids *incapable* of learning much." In powers of comprehension and analytic prowess, we are *not* born equal. It is *not* the case that *every* student—or even a majority of students—*can* master appropriate college entrance requirements.

Trying badly to do what cannot be done at all generates frustration for those who fail and dilutes the program for those who are inherently capable of doing well. We squander our resources, demean the academically less talented, and fail to nurture our brightest. That is not a recipe for social prosperity and community greatness.

(February 1988)

Common Denominators, Chaos, and School Vouchers

In this Land of the Free, there is a certain seemliness in citizens having much freedom. At the operational heart of freedom is the availability of many alternatives among which one can make choices. Unhappily, in primary and secondary education, the dominance of the public school system allows alternatives which are very few and very costly.

Over two generations, the situation has worsened. In earlier days, numerous, small school districts could closely reflect the aims and values of the largely homogeneous and independent communities which financed them. Now, with school districts much fewer and much larger, with state and federal authority and financing increasingly superseding local, and with unionization of teachers and bureaucratizing of administrators, schools autocratically deal poorly with the diversity of their inmates.

The people who run the quasi-monopolistic school system presumably are not more evil or inept than the rest of us. But the ground rules are stultifying. When the families in the school district disagree sharply on what is be taught and how, when demand preferences greatly differ but supply must be uniform, no one can be satisfied with the resulting bland offering aimed at some minimal common denominator.

There are occasional rebellions. Members of a Tennessee community have successfully challenged teaching and assigned reading which offends their religious beliefs. They can hardly be faulted for having beliefs and wishing to make their preferences effective. But the court decision merely excuses the children from certain classes; it does not provide alternative schools or alternative textbooks.

One can feel also for the beleaguered school board, which must try to hold the lid on the pot while being unable to satisfy all citizens, if any. A commentator fears that "educators may face chaos as they try to accommodate everyone. The danger is that the schoolhouse will become a giant restaurant where parents, and presumably students, have great freedom to pick what they will study."

But the notion of "smorgasbord" certainly is not inherently repellent. Not *every* school reasonably should or realistically could cater to every interest and preference. But much greater educational *variety* can be provided through *competition* among schools. And, as Milton

Friedman and others have long urged, the variety of competition can be made feasible at no increase in total costs through use of *school vouchers*. By providing parents with dollar vouchers, they can effectively bid in the education market, choosing among schools. And the schools will have economic incentive to respond to preferences thus revealed.

What does a market do? It provides information about options, and it provides means to make effective preferences among options. Through an education market, we can escape the present lowest common denominator and also the looming chaos.

(December 1986)

Media Cowardice and Incompetence

Economic Thinking and Pursuing Trivia

Economic institutions and economic policies bulk large in determining what we do and how well we do it in our economic activity. It might seem that substantial public knowledge of economic procedures, institutions, and policies is a good thing. But evidently it is not essential for a viable society of considerable wealth.

The Hearst Corporation has sponsored a survey of "the public's knowledge of business and the economy." The report of the survey reaches two conclusions which are deemed "distressing."

The first conclusion is that "a large segment of the American public is sadly deficient in its knowledge of basic business and economic facts of life." On some matters of relatively immediate personal interest—the level of the minimum wage, current mortgage rates, and eligibility for Social Security—people *are* well informed. But they typically are innocent about such random matters as the number of non-agricultural jobs, the proportion of the federal budget spent on defense, the size of the balance of payments deficit, and after-tax corporate profits as a percentage of sales.

The second conclusion of the survey is that "the media, which people say are the primary source of their business and economic information, do not appear to be making any significant impact on [the public's] ignorance."

How distressing—and how surprising—is this failure of the media? One need not applaud ignorance in order to acknowledge the limited significance of miscellaneous erudition. The essence of the open, individualistic community and its economy is that no one and no institution is "in charge." There is no central plan, no central control. The interaction of market activity—accountable individuals taking care of their own limited affairs—will meld self-interested people into an efficient economy and provide the basis of a free society.

But here we are talking about *economics*, not *business minutiae*. People are not likely to absorb isolated, unconnected factual details of seemingly remote pertinence to their own situation. The Hearst Report notes that, at best, the media "have been informing, not educating," and contends that television, newspapers, and radio must "interest and explain, . . . educate as well as inform." But you cannot teach what you do not know—and few reporters, editorial writers, and anchor-types know much economics. The failure of the media to instill facts is disappointing but hardly distressing, and it certainly is not surprising.

The real cause of distress is that the media so rarely try to teach economics—and even more rarely call on economists to help them teach economics. Indeed, media people commonly have little notion of what economics is and what economists do. There *is* an "economic way of thinking." But the economic way of thinking is a process of using analytic principles to elucidate the world, not a way of memoriz-ing facts and pursuing trivia.

(March 1985)

Professional Courage and Business Sense in Media Economics

In our sophistication, we have become a community largely of watchers and listeners instead of readers. This is the case with respect to transmitting news and commentary on the news. As an economist has put the point—in a written essay—this is the age, not of Thomas Paine, but of Walter Cronkite.

How well done are the analyses of our condition and of proposals to improve it? The head of a conservative foundation is generous, finding the media to be looking for ideas. "They like to talk about people, personalities, and events," he acknowledges; "but," he reas-sures us, "basically ideas are their raw material."

Maybe so, but a Los Angeles producer of television documentaries concedes that the small core of reality is distorted, if not lost, behind the fun facade. Television news, he says, is hardly journalism. It is "headline," "tip-of-the-iceberg business." "It is a kind of amateur show business," and only a "minority of those who work in TV news qualify

as journeymen journalists." The television "advisors and counselors
. . . are grounded in advertising and market-research techniques, not
journalism," and they say that "people don't want to think seriously or
for very long." The producer concludes: "We are guilty of giving you
too little because we are desperately afraid that you don't really want
any more."

Desperately afraid, indeed. Boldness in radio and television news
and commentary programming is as rare as analytic respectability. If
one is to err in targeting the audience, it would be refreshing to a
non-trivial proportion of listeners—and, partly because of its rarity,
perhaps even better business—to err on the high side.

The editorial page editor of a major newspaper warns—in writing,
to be sure—that "it can be tempting, even perversely satisfying, for an
editorial writer to confuse an absence of knowledge in some of his
readers with an inability to absorb it." But he adds that famous
newspapers have financially failed by underestimating the intelligence
of their readers, while "the most successful papers have spent great
sums to deliver hard news of the kind that's hardest to get, along with
commentary that's rich in data and reasonable in argument."

Of course, topics of an "economics" sort are much referred to by
broadcast reporters and commentators—matters of inflation and taxes
and shortages—but the references typically, almost invariably, are
analytically adrift, with no attempt to illustrate deduction of an
answer or to summarize testing of a hypothesis. There is no suggestion
of rigorous logic, and little hint of evidence other than anecdotal.
There is no foundation except bias and no technique except cutesy or
purple prose. One may be either comforted or outraged by the
reflected perspective—generally socialistic—but one cannot be formally persuaded.

Typical media commentaries, especially in the electronic media,
are not pabulum, for pabulum is nutritious, even if soft and bland; the
product is merely puree of sophomoric garbage.

(September 1982)

Television News:
Consciousness and Comprehension

A producer for a television network news program laments journalistic restrictions imposed by the government of South Africa. He refers to forming and raising of the nation's "consciousness" through "constant television images." But does television news raise *comprehension*? Outrage and revulsion alone cannot adequately substitute for research and rationality.

Contrary to the television show-biz image types, the eyeball is not the only important part of the head. Righteous indignation and wrathful denunciation not only are far from enough, they can get in the way, absorbing energy and misdirecting effort required to generate and make effective optimal resolutions. Simply damning a problem does not magically yield a best answer. Sanctimoniously giving us a steady diet of gut-wrenching pictures does little to generate thought and action which will do net good. Indeed, such a diet can lead through confusion and desperation to tactics of retreat and strategies of destruction.

One cannot expect the television audience to get much of educational value from television news when very little of educational value goes into producing the programs. In no other area is the deficiency of television news more egregious and dangerous than economics. On topic after topic, television news gives old wives' tales and populist prejudice and crocodile tears instead of even the semblance of hard-nosed, systematic review and analysis.

Showing teachers on strike tells us nothing about proper management of school budgets; showing housewives picketing grocery stores tells us nothing about the cause and cure of inflation; showing showboat activists invading private property at a nuclear plant tells us nothing of the efficiency and the safety of alternative sources of energy; showing unemployment lines tells us nothing of productivity, wages, resource mobility, and the money supply. When the pictures do show something, incorrect interpretation hides the real message and substitutes more mythology—showing long gasoline lines in 1979 did not demonstrate conspiracy of greedy oil companies or irresponsibility of greedy consumers.

And in such misinterpretation, the bias is clear: the pretty heads speaking in dulcet tones with clipped enunciation overwhelmingly prefer government manipulation over open markets, regulations and restrictions over prices and profits, paternalistic collectivism over private calculation.

One cannot expect much other than mush from those who traffic in "consciousness" rather than comprehension. We cannot know if they can provide economic analysis, for they have never tried. But there is little reason to presume that the anchor-types and those who write their scripts could pass the final exam in my elementary economics class. It is not a foregone conclusion that they could do so even after taking the course.

(October 1987)

*Mainly Microeconomics:
Analysis of Relative Prices
and Resource Allocation*

Introduction

In a world of scarcity, choices among available alternatives must be made.

So priorities must be established, production must be organized, and bearing of costs is unavoidable. How are consumption, saving, and production plans to be made and implemented? Who makes and implements, through what processes, and on the basis of what objectives and criteria?

Some of the many considerations involved in the administration of scarce resources can be illustrated with a diagram. The figure below presents a "production-possibilities" curve, measuring output of guns horizontally and butter vertically. Given current technologies and resources, the economy's maximum production of guns alone is OA units; if nothing but butter is produced, OB is the maximum output; if some of both are produced, maximum combined outputs—such as at points C and D—are production possibilities. The line from A to B,

FIGURE 1

Production-Possibilities:
Feasible and Infeasible, Efficient and Inefficient

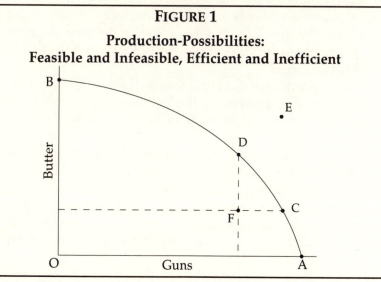

here bulging out a bit from the origin, is the *boundary* of production possibilities: we do not have the resources to go beyond the boundary to some such point as E. That there *is* a boundary of production possibilities reflects the existence of scarcity.

Since the production-possibilities curve shows the alternative *maximum* combinations of guns and butter, it is a curve of *technological efficiency*. Of course, we may produce *less* than the maximum, locating ourselves inside the boundary, as at point F. F is a combination of *technological inefficiency*: we could continue to produce the amount of guns measured by the horizontal distance to F while increasing output of butter vertically to D (or continue to produce butter in amount up to F, while increasing guns horizontally to C).

We are productively efficient when, with a given output of one good, we cannot produce more of the other. To produce more of the other we would have to reduce output of the one: in moving from point C to D, we increase butter, but with the *cost* of decreasing guns. And as we move further up the curve, there is an *increasing* horizontal amount of guns foregone to release resources to produce a given increase in butter.

Which of the infinite possible combinations of production is "best"? This is a matter of choice. *Whose* choice? And *how* is the preference manifested? In a predominantly "open," "private property" community, the controlling preference is that of the members of the community, and they register their choices (and provide guidance and incentive to producers) by voting with dollars in the market. In such a society, *economic* efficiency subsumes technological efficiency and involves also the stipulation that we produce at the particular point on the production possibilities curve which the people in the market deem to be preferred.

Every society, from dictatorial to democratic, values technological efficiency: produce a given output with minimum cost, and maximize output with a given cost, with full use of resources. We want to be on the production possibilities curve; more broadly, we want *economic* efficiency by being at the most preferred point on the curve.

We now are necessarily talking about more than just mundane "producing" and consuming," more than dreary details of market procedure and "business administration." To think broadly and fundamentally about the economy is to think of the entire society and its members. Adam Smith and Karl Marx agreed that how individuals look at the world and form their attitudes and aspirations are determined very largely by how they earn their daily bread.

More than considerations of psychology are involved. The essence of the processes of the economy is critically intertwined with the structure of the society. The ground rules of the one must be compatible with the orientation of the other. The classic problem of "order" has been how to establish or nurture institutions and practices and attitudes which will enable self-centered, acquisitive, and would-be autonomous individuals to live civilly and productively as a community.

Many have thought that order must be achieved at the expense of liberty. Some person or small group must be in charge, to whip the boys into line: we must impose a prison or a zoo in order to avoid anarchy. We have been told that individual liberty must be severely curtailed to achieve national honor—and to have the trains run on time.

A few thinkers have provided a different approach to the problem of order. Among others, Adam Smith took men as they are but envisioned a set of fundamental rules and general procedures—private rights to use of property—which would not only indicate options and constraints, but would permit and encourage personally inspired activity to serve (without intent) the general community interest. We can hardly expect to extinguish self-interest, but we can establish rules of the game which will channel strivings for personal gain to the common good.

This is a *market* mechanism. In an individualistic community, individuals can bid and offer, save and invest and produce, as they please, in the use of their own resources for their ends but to mutual advantage. They pay one another to obtain what they want and sell their own products and services to gain income. One prospers much when what he offers for sale is highly valued by others. The community in general prospers when people are useful to each other. Producers typically make themselves useful in anticipation of reward, uninspired by self-sacrificing altruism. Seeking reward may be grubby, but it is a stronger, more reliable reed on which to lean than relying on the kindness of strangers.

Market activity not only generates prices—prices both of commodities and of productive services—but it tends strongly to generate *equilibrium* prices. Equilibrium prices "clear the market," equating amounts demanded with quantities offered for sale. The diagram is a simple format combining a downward-sloping demand curve with an upward-sloping supply curve for a commodity. At price OP, buyers want to buy and sellers also want to sell OM units: there are no frustrations of sellers wanting to sell more than buyers want to buy, as when the price is too high at OP^I, nor is there buyer frustration from quantity demanded being greater than quantity supplied with the price too low at OP^{II}.

FIGURE 2

Demand and Supply:
Equilibrium, Surplus, Shortage

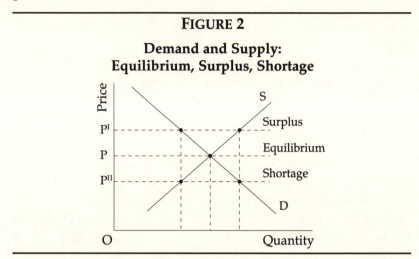

If price is above or below the equilibrium level, free market activity would move it toward equilibrium: frustrated would-be sellers would bid the price down from OP^I, and disappointed buyers would bid it up from OP^{II}. But markets are not always free and open. Government pegs many prices at non-clearing levels. Price floors thus generate "surpluses" of agricultural goods and of labor (minimum wages); price ceilings generate "shortages" of apartments (rent control) and of gasoline and of foreign exchange in international money markets.

Can we have efficiency with freedom? To organize an individualistic society's economic activity, we require more than technological, engineering knowledge. We must have, in addition, economic values. Those values are manifested as prices stemming from activity in the market by all the members of the community. Efficiency requires, and freedom yields, market-determined and market-clearing prices. We cannot have efficiency without freedom. Because for us, economic efficiency is defined in terms of well serving personal preferences, and a productive *result* is attained through rewarding personal performances.

Exchange:
Free and Restricted Trade

Truth and Free Trade

"You may think me a bit slow," said mouse Karl slowly, "but when I do see the truth, I firmly clutch it to my bosom."

Talk of bosom-clutching tends to make mouse Adam a bit nervous. "So long as you adhere only to genuine truth," he said, "I applaud."

"You should agree this time that it is truth," Karl said reassuringly, "for you taught it to me. I refer to trade. Trade is a very good thing. It must be, for everyone does it. And no mouse would participate in exchange if he did not gain from it. No one will trade unless he himself puts a greater value on what he *receives* than on what he *gives up*. Since each participant in the swap deems himself to be better off, then it is unambiguous that trade is terrific. And an activity which benefits everyone involved ought not to be curtailed."

"We may reasonably say," Adam said cautiously, "that the burden of proof is on those who propose to prevent freely consenting mice from trading. But not everyone agrees that it is unequivocally desirable to permit the buying and selling of everything."

"Then they are demented mice," cried Karl caustically. "If some gain and none lose from an activity, it is crazy to forbid it."

"Still, the community *does* forbid or restrict selected trading," Adam pointed out. "It can be claimed that some traders do *not* well know their own preferences; and some supposedly know their preferences *now* but will be disappointed *later* by their actions today; and some *do* know what they want, but *should* not have those preferences; and some trades which are beneficial to the traders will have bad side effects on *third* parties. I doubt that anyone is a full-fledged free-trader, unwilling to accept any restrictions on any possible trade."

"All you are saying," said Karl, "is that the woods are full of blue-nose and dictatorial types who are eager to impose their arbitrary standards and preferences on the rest of us."

"One mouse's idealist is another's ideologue," observed Adam. "Is trade in naughty pictures and sinful activities and mind-blowing drugs a good thing? Many quite rational and reasonable mice fear that such transactions harm not only the immediate traders but also others in the community. How about required licensing of professions? Probably most believe that untrained people, equipped with only an ice pick and a fingernail file, should not be permitted to do brain surgery—even if the patient is willing. College students—all of whom are ever so liberated—will riot over a university contract for research in national defense."

"Sigh," sighed Karl. "I do understand the explanation of trading activity. But to *account* for trade is not in itself to *condone* trade. The theory of trade tells us much about *why* and *how* trade takes place; it does not pass final *judgment* on the ultimate *desirability* of trade. And it is well to understand what theory explains—and what it does not explain."

(November 1987)

Diseased Kidneys, Pure Hearts, and Dialysis for the Brain

I am quite attached to my kidneys. So far as I know, they feel the same toward me. But I have two of them, and the National Kidney Foundation assures us that one good kidney is enough. Some people do not have one good kidney. At some finite price, I would be willing to sell one of my kidneys; it is easy to imagine a person in grave kidney difficulty being willing to meet my supply price. I would sell my kidney for his money; he would sell his money for my kidney; in our respective assessments, each of us would be better off.

A person with bad kidneys has available only limited strategies of survival. Possibly he has access to expensive, cumbersome, and confining dialysis treatment; possibly a kidney is available from a deceased donor; possibly someone will simply give a kidney. Obviously, the patient's situation would be improved by adding to his possibilities the alternative of *buying* a kidney. But according to the National Kidney Foundation, such "cash payment" is "immoral and unethical." And there is strong support for a Congressional bill which would prohibit the purchase and sale of human organs.

Surely, economics is not to be the ultimate arbiter of morality and ethics. Indeed, economics is amoral, being simply a technique of thought to help explain—dispassionately, even (if we may say) cold-bloodedly—certain cause-and-effect relationships. In uncoerced exchange, both parties gain, and, if no one else is hurt, it might seem pretty clear that the transaction should be permitted. But maybe the National Kidney Foundation and congressmen are attuned to a higher, more subtle Truth. Perhaps it is better for the kidney patient to die—morally and ethically, to be sure—than to participate in utterly contaminating market exchange. Some will suspect that a more likely explanation of the anti-market position is sophomoric sophistry.

The registering of demand preferences, the inducing of supply responses, the freedom to exchange privately owned assets—all this is not a trivial or doubtful luxury, tolerable only in halcyon and unstrained circumstances. The market produces sinews of adaptability to and survival in an unfriendly world.

The contribution to our well-being of market processes of trade are never more apparent than in rolling with the kidney punches of fate. A house burns down, a car is stolen, disease strikes. We are confronted by grave misfortune, and tears, wit, and government cannot undo the initial injury. But there are ways and ways of dealing with the problem. We can *minimize* the costs. We achieve our *best* possible situation by pursuing the best of the available options. Those options commonly involve other people, and through market procedures—procedures of bidding, offering, and contracting—we improve our condition.

All this strikes reasonable people as reasonable. It is reasonable, not only with respect to houses and cars, but also kidneys. The unreasonableness of some is a pity—especially since there is no dialysis for the brain.

(April 1984)

Mouse Wisdom:
Advertising and the Demand for Mouse Wash

I have spoken before of Adam and Karl the two mice who live in my office. Their conversations often profoundly analyze important economic issues which affect us as well as mice. The other day they argued the merits of advertising. Adam had returned from shopping and surprised Karl, who was nibbling on a piece of honey wheat berry bread, his favorite food.

"Look at what I bought," said Adam excitedly as he reached into a bag of mouseries and pulled out a red bottle of mysterious fluid.

"What nonsense is it this time?" questioned Karl in a patronizing tone.

"It's a bottle of mouse wash," answered Adam. "It's that new product advertised on television. A capful in the morning bath will eliminate offensive mouse odors all day."

"Superfluous junk," railed Karl, who was visibly upset. "Another victim of advertising. You've confirmed my belief that advertising should be banned in the public interest."

"That's ridiculous," responded Adam, who was beginning to assume his more reflective nature. "Advertising gives me a lot of information: it tells me about new products, their prices, and where they can be bought."

"That's just it," said Karl angrily. "Advertising makes you want things you would never have wanted on your own. Producers don't make what consumers want; advertising makes consumers want what producers make."

"Nobody *forced* me to buy the mouse wash," retorted Adam. "It was *my* money; it was *my* choice; and now it is *my* mouse wash."

"But don't you see," persisted Karl, "that your desire for mouse wash is a *contrived* want—a want which would never have existed without the persuasion of advertising. It's a shame that so few of your wants originated with you and not with advertising."

"Poppycock," snapped Adam. "Is your preference for honey wheat berry bread wholly an 'original' want? Mice do not live by bread alone. Just about everything we want is learned to some extent. We were not born with our present preferences for the kinds of food we eat, the clothes we wear, the music we listen to, or the literature we read. All these wants, and many more, were learned—and continuously relearned as our tastes have been molded through our lives. There are all kinds of persuasive elements in society—parents, teachers, clergymen, politicians, girl friends—telling us to do this and not to do that, to admire some things and shun others. Advertising is but one of those many elements."

"Preposterous!" fumed Karl. "Look at all the unimportant, nonessential goods mice now buy but would not buy without advertising. They are silly, contrived wants."

"That's the point," Adam said calmly. "You can say that all wants have been contrived in the sense that we learned them. But that does not make them imaginary or any less important. Just because *you* don't agree that mouse wash is a useful good doesn't mean that it is unreal or unimportant to *me*. Because you can't understand why other mice could possibly want things you do not, you suppose they must be dupes of advertising. Wouldn't you say you are being a belligerent elitist?" asked Adam.

Karl, busy chewing his money wheat berry bread, did not reply.

(March 1981)

Mouse Wisdom: A Multitude of Gratitude

Adam, the scholarly mouse of my office, had just opened a jar of peanut butter. "Everyone loves this stuff," he said to his friend, Karl, "It's filling, and it tastes great."

Karl wiggled his nose in agreement.

"We ought to thank peanut butter producers," said Adam teasingly.

"What do you mean?" asked Karl, taking the bait.

"We mice should appreciate the producers who give us this scrumptious food," said Adam. "Although we take peanut butter from producers, we never give them any back. To show that we value producers, we should return some of what we take from them."

"That's ridiculous," chortled Karl. "They provide us peanut butter, and we pay them money. It's not a matter of *gifts*; rather it's an example of the *mutually beneficial exchange* you and that fellow Allen are always extolling. We mice obtain peanut butter which we value more than the money we pay; and producers obtain money which they value more than the peanut butter they produce. The exchange makes every mouse better off because everyone receives more value than he sacrifices."

Feigning ignorance, Adam continued, "You mean that each mouse 'thanks' the other by offering something in exchange?"

"If you want to put it that way," retorted Karl. "Mice consumers 'thank' peanut butter producers by handing over money. And once consumers have paid for the produce, the transaction is completed, and no further 'thanks' are required."

"Then we don't have to return any peanut butter to thank producers," concluded Adam.

"You've got it," affirmed Karl.

"Then why do you support the boycott of Big Cheese Corporation?" asked Adam.

"The purpose of the boycott," answered Karl, "is to get the Big Cheese Corporation to put back some of the money it takes out of the mouse community. We want the company to appreciate the community that spends money on its product."

"But you are contradicting what you just said about our thanking peanut butter producers," admonished Adam.

"I don't see how," snapped a befuddled Karl.

"Well," said Adam patiently, "you said that the community thanked peanut butter producers by providing money in exchange. Producers would rather have the money than the peanut butter. In order to show my appreciation, I don't have to give back any of the peanut butter I bought from producers."

"Right!" agreed Karl.

"The same principle holds for Big Cheese Corporation," continued Adam. "Big Cheese supplies the community a product that mice value more than the money they spend. So Big Cheese shows its appreciation for the money it receives by supplying cheese in return. It is two-way trade which makes both parties better off. The trade need not be supplemented with gifts. Mice don't have to give back peanut butter to show they appreciate producers; nor does Big Cheese have to give back money to show it appreciates the community. The company 'thanks' the community by giving cheese, and the community 'thanks' the company by giving money. That's mutually beneficial exchange— something for which we should all be thankful," said Adam.

(June 1984)

Competition, Costs, and Accommodation

Competition and Efficiency, Innovation and Monopoly

One of my wise friends warned me of the worth and the limitations of mathematical doodling in economics. "The blackboard can be a very useful device," he said, "but do not confuse it with the real world."

Economic theory—and the curve bending and equation solving in which it is often exposited—*is* highly useful when used well. It helps to identify key variables and their functional interrelations in the problem at hand. It helps to turn general wonderment into coherent thought, to convert unstructured conjecture into consistent deduction, to provide systematic speculation amenable to real-world examination.

But not all possibly pregnant wonderment, conjecture, and speculation can be readily reduced to neat, self-contained models. Not everything worth concern and consideration can be measured to the fourth decimal place. One need not denigrate formal rigor and manipulative elegance to note the need for imagination, erudition, and wisdom. Esoteric technique cannot well substitute for sophisticated sense.

A model which serves well in its own proper province may require considerable adaptation for other proper questions and purposes. The economic theory of "perfect competition" is a case in point. It typifies much of economic thought of the past century. Many modern economists have worried much about how to make the most efficient use of resources now available to the community.

The theory of perfect competition tells us the conditions—conditions of costs and production, price and purchase—which must be satisfied in a market of many sellers and many buyers if efficiency is to be attained. But it is a theory of a particular kind of market in a context that is largely static, pertaining to the moment, not to process and evolution over substantial time.

A major economist of the twentieth century, Joseph Schumpeter, tried to push out the boundaries of our concern. The real world is one of change, and the life of the market is one of flux and adjustment stemming, in part, from *innovations*. Innovations may involve a new product, a new method of production, a new market, a new source of supplies, a new organization.

Being *first*—first in lowering cost, first in merchandising—establishes a degree of monopoly. Monopoly power tends to be quickly diluted. Still, progress calls for innovation, and the innovating entrepreneur is trying to get a monopolistic edge which generates profit. Some degree of seeming short-term inefficiency may be a necessary but tolerable cost of greater long-term productivity—although it is not convenient to incorporate such insightfulness into mechanical models.

Does this mean that Professor Schumpeter favored monopoly for its own sake? Does his picture of market activity wholly vitiate the competitive model? No. But short-term, static efficiency is not everything. The competitive model, while answering some important questions, does not well explain the actual world dynamics of innovation.

Let the model fit the world.

(December 1986)

Mouse Wisdom:
On Monopoly and Competition

Mouse Karl was customarily belligerent but uncharacteristically somber. He turned to the characteristically composed mouse Adam.

"If you really are concerned with the efficiency of the economy," said Karl, "you would try to do something about monopolies. The game Daddy Warbucks tries to play is monopolization, and he is pretty good at it. The community in general is at the mercy of big businesses, who decide by whim what and how much to produce and what prices to charge."

"Curious," mused a composed Adam. "Nearly everywhere you look, you see autonomous, impervious monopolists. Nearly everywhere I look, I see dependent, adaptable competitors."

Now Karl was more excited than somber. "Businesses are dependent and adaptable?" he shrieked. "Don't make me laugh," he laughed.

"Businesses which survive, much less prosper," Adam elaborated, "recognize that they function in a highly interrelated world, usually buying inputs from many suppliers, organizing those various inputs in production, and selling output to many buyers. There are many options, so there must be many decisions. Managers of even big businesses must satisfy customers while containing costs. And those decisions are not made once-and-for-all, because the input and output markets and production technology are incessantly changing. A firm has wealth today because of wise decisions and good work yesterday, but it will be wealthy tomorrow only if it operates well today."

"Pure theory," sniffed Karl, "otherwise known as mythology."

"On the contrary," replied Adam quite sternly. "I am speaking of the uncertain real world of blood, sweat, and tears. In a single recent issue of the *Wall Street Journal*, there were at least half a dozen stories of various sorts of enterprises—sizable and small, sophisticated and simple—fighting for their lives in hard, changing markets.

"One story," Adam went on, "dealt with the gambles and experiments of magazines who are suffering from a long slump in advertising income. Another recounts the difficulties and possible strategies and tactics of a struggling metropolitan newspaper. There are the various retailers who are obliged to modify merchandizing techniques in the face of shifting shopping mannerisms and characteristics of the community. More than a dozen fast-food restaurants are challenging the increasingly elaborate giants by going back to the sort of simple hamburger shops of the 1950s. Financial advisers are struggling with the new specifications of optimum portfolios in light of new tax provisions. And in hard-hit 'rust belt' states, there is a surge of garage-shop, blue-collar entrepreneurs who, after losing their jobs with big manufacturers, are staking all they have in small outfits of their own."

"I infer," said a somber but no longer belligerent Karl, "that not every business person is an unassailable, fat cat Daddy Warbucks."

(October 1986)

Losses, Profits, and Use of Resources

"I try to be tolerant," said mouse Karl quite intolerantly, "of the open, competitive market. But one thing wrong with it is that it doesn't work very well. If widget output is greatly increased, widget prices crash, and profits turn into losses. In a world of scarcity, it is a ridiculous economy in which great output means disaster for producers."

Mouse Adam tried to tolerate the intolerance. "Losses for widget producers," he said gently, "are evidence of bad use of the community's resources and incentive to shift some of those resources to better uses."

Karl was offended. "Look," he snarled, "we want more goods, producers produce goods, so producers should not be penalized when they produce more."

"Losses certainly are misfortunes for producers," Adam agreed. "But we should recognize what they reflect and what they imply from the standpoint of the economy."

"A loss," snapped Karl, "means simply that some unlucky character is losing his shirt because his costs are greater than his receipts."

"But what do the costs and the receipts measure?" asked Adam. "Business receipts are a measure of the worth of the product in the eyes of the buyers. Anyone paying two dollars for a widget is saying that he prefers the widget to two dollars worth of any other good."

"Obviously," said Karl, "people pay two dollars for widgets only because they consider the widget to be worth the money. But what do costs reflect?"

"Costs," replied Adam, "reflect the value of *other* goods which *could* have been produced by the resources embodied in the widgets. To produce widgets, labor and other inputs must be bid away from other uses. Inputs derive their value from the value of the outputs they produce. The price which must be paid for inputs is a measure of the most valuable alternative good which is *not* produced when we make widgets."

Karl's beady little eyes sparkled with comprehension. "So," he said, "if business receipts indicate the value of our product and business costs indicate the value of the best alternative product, and if receipts are smaller than costs, then the community prefers that the resources we are using here be used elsewhere. They consider some other good to be worth more than widgets at the margin, so widget production should be cut and the output of the other good increased."

"You are a pretty smart mouse," commended Adam. "A loss is a sign that the resources of the community are misallocated. We would be better off by shifting inputs from widgets to something of greater value. And, in an adaptable market, that will happen. Widget producers, with their losses, will not find it feasible to compete for the previous amount of inputs against profit-making competitive producers. And owners of inputs will have incentive to sell their services to the highest bidder. So—with no five-year plan decreed by an economic czar—resources will shift to where the community values them most."

"I conclude," said a now wiser Karl, "that the market works."

(December 1986)

Mouse Wisdom:
The Gains and Pains of Closing Plants

Karl, the radical rodent of my office, had learned that the cheese factory which employs him was closing down in order to relocate in another region where production costs will be lower.

"Outrageous!" he screamed. "All they think about are profits. They have no sense of social responsibility. They don't care for the mouse community. There should be a law against plant closures."

"Such a law would harm the mouse community," mused Adam, the relaxed mouse. "The plant's relocation will provide more benefits than costs to the community,"

"Nonsense!" roared Karl. "Don't give me that cold logic of economics."

"But only by thinking clearly about issues—like plant closings—can we make the best decisions for all mice," replied Adam. "Moving the factory will reduce employment in our village, but new jobs will be created elsewhere. Since production costs will be lower at the new location, more cheese can be made and sold at lower prices. Cheese consumers will be better off, and the community will be wealthier."

"All you talk about is consumers," snapped Karl. "What about workers? Costs and benefits, indeed, but you fail to consider employees' security, self-esteem, and job attitudes."

Adam responded thoughtfully. "You are implying that the maintenance of particular jobs is an end in itself, regardless of what the workers do and on what terms. But jobs are the price we pay to get things we want. We want more than we can ever have, so it is important that the jobs we work at be the most productive ones.

"By relocating," Adam went on, "the factory will provide more cheese at lower prices. To the community, the *cost* of the relocation is the value of the output no longer produced at the *old* plant. The *benefit* is the value of the cheese gained at the *new* plant. Since more cheese is gained than lost, the benefit to the community outweighs the cost."

"Well," said a befuddled Karl, "the only reason the factory is moving is because labor costs are lower in the other village. We should have the right to prevent other workers from underbidding us. We can't maintain our decent living standards if we have to compete with low-wage workers."

"The problem is not wages elsewhere which reflect economic realities," corrected Adam. "The problem is your unrealistically high wages, which are unsupported by the amount of cheese you produce per hour. If your higher wages were matched by correspondingly higher productivity, then the cost of producing cheese would be no higher here. But your productivity is not high enough to offset your greater wage rates."

"Are you saying we should work for lower wages?" asked Karl with astonishment.

"*I'm* not," replied Adam, "but *consumers* are. And producers dare not ignore consumers. The real purpose of the law you propose is to compel consumers to underwrite our village's high cheese-producing wages, which are not generated by our productivity. This exploitation of consumers through stifling the market adaptability of producers— this forceable subsidization of community waste for your personal benefit—is no more a reflection of sensitivity than it is a manifestation of efficiency."

Karl sighed and tucked his tail.

(February 1983)

Productivity, Costs, and Efficiency

Technological Efficiency, Economic Efficiency, and Government

In a certain sort of journalistic economics, the editorial writer can quickly characterize an involved problem and provide a seemingly commonsensical solution with no complications of analysis and leaving no doubts of wisdom. And editorial advocacy tends toward commands and impositions by governmental authority.

When people can choose widely, they may not choose wisely. So government is to limit alternatives, leaving only choices which are autocratically deemed to be good. Thus, Congress is setting very high "efficiency" standards for electrial appliances.

Government, at both federal and state levels, has a very long record of very bad management of energy production and use. Massive misconception and confusion, heavy-handed intervention and enormously wasteful manipulation, culminated in the ridiculous responses to OPEC in the 1970s. And now Senator Snort and his propagandists of the press are energetically messing around with energy again.

Supposedly, no one pure of heart could disagree with these statements in a recent editorial:

> One easy way for Americans to stretch their supplies of energy is to buy a better toaster or air conditioner or refrigerator. They will be assured of that opportunity if Congress approves the National Appliance Energy Efficiency Act. . . . The administration [has] argued that the free market should be permitted to work its will and that mandatory minimum efficiency standards would force up the price of appliances. This is saying in effect that if Americans want to buy shoddy, energy-wasting appliances, that is their right.

Well, my heart is pure, and I say that the editorial is disgraceful.

First, the *market* has no "will." The market is a means through which *people* work their will, expressing their preferences, using their own resources as they think best.

Second, in a free society, there is more to *economic* efficiency than *technological* efficiency. Physical input/output engineering efficiency is obviously important. But, in a world of scarcity, it is not invariably shrewd to choose state-of-the-art technology, for it can be too expensive. The very best gadget is not always worth the cost, especially to those with low incomes or who make little use of the gadget or those of advanced age. The very notion of economic efficiency is based on satisfying consumer preferences.

Third, we require no constricting law to provide greater consumer opportunities. A substantial proportion of appliances already on the market meet the proposed standards.

Finally, the proposed bullying of consumers is not expected even by the bullies to reduce energy consumption much—less than 2 percent. And consumption could go *up* as consumers are induced to make fuller use of appliances which are technologically more effective.

Pull the plug on silly energy regulations.

(May 1987)

Mouse Wisdom:
Efficiency, Productivity, and Wage Rates

"I find it painful," said mouse Karl in a voice filled with pain, "that I have discerned a massive, fundamental error in economic analysis."

"I am not amused," mused his mouse associate, Adam, "by massive, fundamental errors."

Karl hastened to explain. "You and your economist friends," he explained, "often speak of *efficiency* in production. And efficiency, as I understand it, calls for each person to specialize in doing what he does best."

"Well," murmured Adam hesitantly, "efficiency *does* have to do with exploiting differences in productivities."

"That's what I said," said Karl a bit sharply. "But the theory cannot work in the real world. There are millions of mice, but there are not millions of different kinds of jobs. It cannot be the case that each job is done by the mouse who does it better than can any other mouse. To put it differently, you know that not every mouse is the very best mouse in the whole world in doing some job. So efficiency would mean that most workers could have no job, for most workers are not the world's best in doing anything. And having most workers unused can't be very efficient."

"True," agreed Adam, "most of us would find no place in production if the only ones to work are those who are absolutely the best in their respective occupations, if 'absolutely the best' means turning out the most widgets per hour. But there is work to be done—and done efficiently—even by those who do not have a physical input-output advantage in producing anything, if they will work where their *disadvantage* is *least*. Most of us are not the best in anything, but we are *relatively* less bad in some jobs than in others. Each of us should work where we are least bad. Compared to me, you are slow in making widgets, but you are still slower in making gadgets, so the community gives up very little when you make widgets instead of gadgets."

"But," carped Karl, "how could I compete with you in the market if I am slower than you in producing everything? Being simply less slow in one kind of job than in another is not good enough. The economy sacrifices relatively few gadgets when I make widgets, but no widget producer will hire me instead of you."

"But he will," assured Adam, "provided that your money wage compensates for your physical inferiority. Comparatively speaking, you do best in producing widgets. You turn out only half as many widgets per day as I do, but you do even worse compared to me in any other job. And you can undersell me in the widget labor market if you accept a wage rate less than half of mine. Your *low money wage* more than offsets your *physical disadvantage*, and the wage-expense per widget would be less when employing you instead of me."

"So," exclaimed a relieved Karl, "people of relatively low physical productivity can compete by receiving still lower money wages."

"And," added Adam, "high wages are high because they reflect high output."

(August 1986)

Doctors and Economists, Returns and Costs

In the best of Renaissance tradition, I am steeped in medicine as well as economics. My credentials in health care are impeccable: one of my grandfathers was a doctor, my sister is a nurse, and I used to watch Dr. Kildare on the telly.

So it pains me when my physician colleagues say hurtful things about economists. And it puzzles me when physicians take note of the basic good sense of economists but then stubbornly reject the implications of that sense when applied to medical matters.

There are questions, not only in the science of medicine, but in the delivery of medical care. To concede the existence of an issue is not magically to provide a satisfying resolution of the issue. For most problems, there are no resolutions which are wholly satisfying by all criteria. But we can be confident that the dilemma of medical care will not be well disposed of by doctors claiming that economists are crazy for holding that *costs* should be considered along with *returns*.

The claim has been made, with more vigor than rigor, by a conspicuous physician in a newspaper essay. The doctor finds it quaint that economists believe that people choose among their options, that they have some sensitivity to prices in determining what and how much to buy from whom, and that they will buy more of something at lower prices than at higher prices. Oh, it "may be true," the doctor grudgingly concedes, that such rationality will be found in "commercial" activity, but it is "simplistic" to suppose that either patient or doctor would calculate any economic calculations in concern with medical concerns.

The doctor is bemused and disgusted. "Do the economists really expect a person faced with life-threatening illness," he asks, "to shop around for the least expensive doctor? Do the economists really believe that a majority of physicians will offer patients a choice between first-rate and cut-rate treatment?" And the doctor concludes: "In reaching health care decisions, the public and the medical profession value . . . factors, such as quality and accessibility of care, [which] are just as meaningful as costs."

When less agitated, the doctor doubtless would agree that normally very little of medical care is directed to life-threatening illness, that there is much reason to be sobered by the huge proportion of medical expense concentrated in ministering to the final few months of life, that people do *not* commonly do all they can—bearing any cost necessary—to maximize their safety and well-being, and that consumers will overconsume goods and services which they are subsidized to waste.

In the eyes of non-doctors, medical care is *not* a highly unique commodity—except that it is sold more monopolistically than are most goods. It is hard to imagine any consumer (even an economist) of any good—even medicine—failing to take into account *both* the quality of merchandise and its price.

Economists really do note returns along with costs: that, indeed, is the essence of their business. It would be helpful, in trying to make the best of a stingy world, if doctors would note costs along with returns: *that* should be part of *their* business.

(June 1984)

The Moving Forces Behind Market Prices

Some economic fallacies don't die easily. Take the belief that the only determinant of a market price is the cost of producing the particular good. When a price rises or falls, it is commonly assumed that the item's cost of production must have gone up or down. And there is a tendency to condemn price increases which are not apparently due to higher production costs.

But market prices are not mere reflectors of production costs. To see the real driving force behind market prices, consider rental rates on trucks between Houston and Detroit. The *Wall Street Journal* reports that last year the Detroit-to-Houston charge for a twenty-four-foot U-Haul van was about $1,800 plus gasoline. U-Haul's *costs* for the reverse trip from Houston to Detroit were not different, yet the *fee* for the same van northbound was only $300 plus fuel. The truck rental fee varied six-fold, depending simply on which way one was traveling.

That difference seems unjustified to one who clings to the old wives' tale that only production costs determine prices. What does determine truck rental fees and all other markets is *competition* among consumers for the available supply. An increased demand would cause the price to be bid up. A smaller available quantity would further intensify consumers' bidding. Conversely, a diminished demand or an increased supply would weaken consumers' competition and cause the price to fall.

There are thus two factors which determine a market price: consumers' demand and the available supply. Either or both can change without any change in the cost of production. Last year's decline in the auto industry induced more people to migrate from Detroit to other areas, such as Houston. The demand for rental trucks in Detroit jumped. Inventories dropped. Rental rates soared in order to apportion existing truck supplies among competing renters. Someone who wanted to move from Detroit to Houston, therefore, had to pay a higher rental fee because increased consumer demand and consequent dwindling inventories made rental trucks more scarce in Detroit. Meanwhile, in Houston, competition for trucks was much smaller, and the available supply of trucks increased as people arrived from depressed areas, such as Detroit. Both factors—a smaller demand and a larger supply—kept rental rates in Houston much lower.

The lesson is clear. Prices move up or down in order to ration the existing supply among those who demand it. And market-clearing prices can be very different for the same good at different times or in different locations—even though production costs are identical. So long-distance calls are cheaper at night; matinees are cheaper than evening performances; early-bird restaurant specials are less expensive; and U-Haul trucks from Detroit to Houston were much higher priced than the same trucks from Houston to Detroit.

Production costs do influence market prices, but only to the extent that these costs affect the available supply. It is that supply and consumers' demand which are the real moving forces behind market prices.

(December 1982)

Mouse Wisdom: Alternatives and Costs

Karl, one of the two mice who inhabit my office, was fuming again. "Outrageous," he muttered to Adam, the other member of the rodent odd couple. "That economist fellow, Allen, has gone too far. He can be very irritating."

Adam thought about pots and kettles, and did not want to encourage Karl by replying. Karl continued without encouragement. "Economists are such a dour bunch," he said. "Maybe that is because they deal with alleged scarcity and the purported necessity to economize and bear costs. What a dismal subject!"

"This *is* a world of scarcity," responded Adam gently, "and we *do* have to make economizing choices, so costs *must* be borne. Economists did not construct the world; they simply try to understand it and thereby help us to cope with it."

"They may try," snapped Karl, "but they sometimes mislead us. They seem to have no heart, no poetry of the soul. They are cold calculating machines, and we sensitive types know that there is more to life than economic calculations."

"Oh, Allen seems not to be a bad type," soothed Adam. "Winnie, his noble dog, loves him."

"I bet *fish* don't like him," said Karl. "Look here. Allen has a collection of his broadcast essays published as a book. I can choke down some of his stuff, but not this piece on pollution. He talks about a chemical plant disposing of wastes in a stream. Now, any civilized creature—even a person—would be against that. But does Allen come out four-square against polluting the stream? No, he has to equivocate—to muddy the waters, so to speak. Listen to him straddle the fence:

> The polluted water kills fish for miles. The firm has imposed costs on fishermen. *But* if the firm is then prohibited from using the stream, it is forced either to stop producing or to find more costly ways to dispose of wastes—fishermen have imposed costs on the firm and its customers. There are costs in *either* case. It is not more "wrong" for consumers of the firm's product to put costs on fisherman than for fishermen to impose costs on the consumers.

It was Adam's turn to be irritated. "What is outrageous about pointing out the real-world alternatives? You surely do not deny that there *are* alternatives and that there are costs no matter which alternative is chosen."

"No," conceded Karl, "we have to give up possible options when we make a choice. But the *proper* choice is obvious: unpolluted nature is a good thing."

"Allen doubtless agrees—and so do I—that happy fish in clean water is good," replied Adam. "But when you acknowledge that there is a choice to be made, you have conceded Allen's point. We can debate *who* should best bear *how much* of what *kinds* of costs in achieving *which* goal. But don't foolishly talk as if there are no costs. And since there are costs, obviously it is conceivable that some may deem the costs to be too high."

(November 1981)

Oil Prices and Gasoline Prices

The gradual decontrol of domestic crude oil prices is scheduled to be completed by October 1981. Energy advisors of President-elect Reagan have been debating the ending of controls still earlier. Some fear that elimination of crude oil price controls, whether early or late this year, will result inevitably in much higher prices for refined oil products, such as gasoline.

It seems obvious: price controls hold down prices, and removing controls permits prices to rise. But real world relations are a bit more subtle than that, and failure to get the economic analysis straight leads to, or perpetuates, lousy economic policy.

Decontrol of domestic crude oil prices will not appreciably and permanently raise the price of gasoline and other oil products. The price of a good is not determined simply by its production cost: it is determined by consumers' demand for the product and the amount of it available.

To be sure, in a free market, the cost of an item's production helps to determine the quantity of it made available. Other things the same, a larger quantity will be supplied when production costs are lower—and that larger quantity will reduce the product's price. But when markets are not free, when prices are controlled by decree, the link between production costs and prices are broken. Legislation may lower the cost of manufacturing a good by suppressing the prices of production inputs, but it will not reduce the final sale price of the good.

Suppose a law is passed which reduces the price of cattle, thereby decreasing the cost of producing meat. Although meat would cost less to produce, fewer cattle would be supplied by cattle growers at the suppressed price. With fewer cattle, the amount of meat available would fall. With a diminished supply of meat, consumers would bid up meat prices, even though the cost of producing meat—the price of cattle—had been artificially lowered by the government.

Should the price control on cattle be eliminated, meat prices would actually fall as more cattle and therefore more meat became available—a greater availability because, not in spite, of the higher price of cattle.

So it is with oil. Prices of oil products were not decreased by price controls on crude oil because those controls did not make more domestic oil available. Instead, less domestic oil was produced at the lower, controlled price—and more foreign oil was correspondingly imported. The supplies of refined oil products remained about unchanged and their prices largely unaffected.

Consequently, when crude oil price controls are eradicated, prices of gasoline and other refined products will not rise. It is true that higher domestic oil prices will mean higher cost of products refined from that oil, but higher crude oil prices serve to make more domestic oil available. More domestically produced oil will be substituted for imported oil, and our dependence on OPEC will diminish.

Price controls on crude oil were enacted in the early 1979s in a naive attempt to keep down prices of oil prices. Of course, they did not succeed. But they did increase oil imports. Not for the first time, bad economics led to bad policy.

(January 1981)

Decisions, Choices, and Costs: The Future Lies Ahead

Decisions demand choices—and vice versa. To have more of one thing, some of something else must be sacrificed. We give in order to get, and what we give is the *cost* of what we get.

We judge the sense of a decision by comparing the judged value of what we *choose* relative to the judged value of what we *could* have had. This is a notion of some subtlety, and we are sometimes urged by unfriendly types to ignore it.

In his opposition to President Reagan's so-called Star Wars defense system, the Soviet Foreign Minister garbled the notion of cost. The United States may spend twenty-six billion dollars to research the feasibility of a space-based defense against missile attacks. In response, the Russian complains, "Will there not be people . . . who will then say:

'Sorry, we have spent so many billion dollars on research, why waste all this money? Isn't it better to go on to testing and deployment?'"

But once the twenty-six billion dollars has been spent on research, it cannot be recouped. At that time, the twenty-six billion dollars would not be an additional sacrifice requiring a *current* choice, so it would not be relevant to decisions about continuing the project. Only additional outlays to deploy the system would be a cost to be weighed at that time to judge the wisdom or folly of making the anti-missile defense operational. Because the research money would already have been spent, it would not be wasteful if a decision were then made to *terminate* the system's development. The decision to pursue or to end further work would depend on *future* sacrifices, not *bygone* costs which, like spilt milk, cannot now be undone.

That no-longer-avoidable costs have no importance for present decisions can be seen in all choice-making circumstances. If a farmer spends ten thousand dollars drilling for water but ends up with a dry well, he would not be wasting that ten thousand dollars by deciding against further drilling. The mistake is history, and the money is irretrievable. Nor, like a gambler on a losing streak, should the farmer stubbornly conclude that he has already "lost too much to stop." Whether or not another well should be drilled depends on expected costs and returns of drilling, not on past costs already borne.

Similarly, a marathon runner happily suffering halfway through a race wonders whether or not to continue. The first thirteen miles have already been run, and their cost cannot now be avoided. The decision to continue depends on the expected costs and fun of running thirteen more miles.

Whether it is running a marathon, drilling a well, or developing an anti-missile system, past costs are not relevant in present decision making. As Shakespeare put it, "Things without remedy should be without regard. What's done is done." Do not look to bygones to appraise the cost of today's decision. The past is prologue, to be sure, and experience can teach—but it cannot be changed. Today's decision must be based on expectations of tomorrow. It is the future which lies ahead.

(February 1985)

Price Rationing and Political Rationing

Mouse Wisdom:
Unhappiness and Uncleared Markets

If Karl had been a chicken instead of a mouse, he would have been in a fowl mood. "I'm sick of hearing you economist types talk about market equilibrium," he snarled at his fellow mouse, Adam. "You seem to want equilibrium at any price and suppose that that will solve all our problems."

"I'm sorry to learn of your sickness," soothed Adam. "But you may be sick for wrong reasons. We don't want equilibrium at any price; rather we want a price at which there is equilibrium. And we want an equilibrium price, not because that will solve all problems, but because it generally avoids making a hard life still harder."

"It certainly is a hard life," snapped Karl, "and we mice of sensitivity and compassion want government to make things better. One way is to stipulate fair prices."

"I suppose everyone prefers prices which are fair instead of unfair," murmured Adam. "But your notion, or the government's notion, of fairness may not be the same as mine. Everyone would like to sell at higher prices at least as much as he now sells, and everyone would like to buy at lower prices at least as much as he now buys. But we can't both raise and lower a price at the same time; if a seller charges more, a buyer cannot pay less. And if government starts to diddle with prices, the market will not be cleared."

"Oh," groaned Karl, "you are making my head hurt. Of course, we can't move a price up and down simultaneously. But we should move it to where it ought to be. Who cares if the market is cleared — whatever that means."

"A price which is market-clearing is at an equilibrium level," Adam explained. "At that unique price, the amount of the good

103

demanders are willing to buy is just equal to the amount suppliers are willing to sell, and the price stays where it is. No one is frustrated because he cannot buy or sell more at that price. Avoiding that particular frustration is not everything, to be sure. Whatever is the market mechanism or the bureaucratic procedure of determining prices, it will still be a world of scarcity."

"But can't we ease the pains of scarcity by having compassionate and wise officials decrease prices?" whimpered Karl.

"Unhappily, no," said Adam firmly. "The market, if permitted to do so, will give us equilibrium prices. There is no point in decreeing what we normally would have, anyway. The whole idea in Big Brother specifying prices is to enforce *disequilibrium* prices, which will leave markets uncleared—and mice frustrated. If the imposed price is higher than the normal market level, sellers will want to sell more than buyers will want to buy, and there will be a *surplus*—as with some farm goods and menial labor services. If the price is pegged too low, the amount demanded will outstrip the amount supplied, and there will be a shortage—as with rent-controlled apartments and gasoline in 1979."

Karl had now regained his equilibrium. "It isn't nice," he concluded with cleared mind, "to try to fool the market."

(November 1985)

Education, Sex, and Character

We do not live in a gentle and genteel age. Typically, behavior is neither decorous nor disciplined. Conduct evinces general lack of pride and common rejection of erstwhile conventional proprieties. And irresponsibility has its costs.

Jacqueline R. Kasun, professor of economics at Humboldt State University, has investigated the elemental economics—the logic and the evidence—of sex education. Her analysis has sobering and perhaps generally unwelcome implications for public policy.

Studies conducted by Dr. Kasun indicate two consequences of sex education. On the one hand, such instruction seems to increase the probability of *premarital sexual activity* by 14-, 15-, and 16-year-olds. On the other hand, it appears to increase the use of *contraceptives*. With regard to *pregnancy*, it is likely that the first effect predominates. The pregnancy data are not conclusive, but evidently the number of abortions has been seriously understated, so the probable net result of more sexual activity along with more contraception has been more pregnancy. This likelihood is consistent with the fact that states which have spent most in providing contraceptives and abortions have had the highest rates of premarital teenage pregnancy.

Sexual activity is not a function of sex education alone. Such activity is reduced by family stability, represented by both parents being in the home. It is reduced even more by frequent church attendance.

But probably the most important determinant of premarital sexual activity is *price*, that is, the terms on which the activity is available. The price includes the readiness of access to contraceptives and abortions. And the lower the price, the greater the amount demanded.

As a no-nonsense economist, Dr. Kasun observes: "A youngster who is given free contraceptives by her high school birth control clinic without her parents' knowledge and with the promise of a free and confidential abortion in case of pregnancy, faces a low price for premarital sex activity. She can be expected to consume more of it than a girl with less easy access to contraceptives and abortion. . . .The notion that teenagers can be deterred from becoming pregnant by more and easier access to contraceptives and abortions is like expecting people who are given free gasoline to reduce their driving."

Economics can contribute critically to analysis of teenage promiscuity and pregnancy and to policy implications. Still, the problem is ultimately one of character and cultivation and commitment. When social opprobrium of loutish behavior is severely diluted, when the community has largely succumbed to coarseness, there can be no very satisfying and effective answers. The best we can do in our degenerate condition is to fight a losing rearguard action in trying simply to minimize losses and delay final disaster.

(August 1988)

Economic Analysis and Moral Superiority

A perfectly splendid collection of these radio-television commentaries has been published as a book. One reviewer of the book finds the essays to be "snappy little capsules." But half of the review is devoted to the reviewer's indigestion over one of the 154 pieces which comprise the volume.

The piece is a straightforward application of basic analytics. It deals with the pricing of museum tickets for a King Tut exhibition. It recounts the consequences and implications of selling the tickets at a price below the market-clearing level. Of course, there were long lines of buyers and a shortage of tickets: more people wanted to buy tickets at the suppressed price than could be accommodated. There was "scalping" of tickets, and ticket brokers charged prices well above the initial price, to the outrage of sensitive editorial writers and state legislators.

Evidently, the book reviewer, too, would have prefered a prohibition on exchange which would salvage some rationality from the initial haphazard ticket distribution. Those who succeeded in acquiring a low-priced ticket would not be permitted to resell it at a higher price; those who were willing to bid a higher price would not be permitted to spend their money. Big Brother—and the book reviewer—know what is best for the unwashed masses, and, in the name of doing good, they are eager to prohibit trade.

It was not feasible for the exhibit to be seen by all who wanted to attend at a zero price. At higher and higher prices, the number of people wanting to attend would be smaller and smaller. Somehow attendance had to be rationed. Prices are an efficient rationing device.

But some have more purchasing power than others have. By definition, to be relatively wealthy is to be able to buy relatively much. Perhaps the major interest of the reviewer is not that a virtually random sample of people see the exhibit; rather, heartburn is induced by the fact that some are richer—as well as prettier, smarter, more energetic, ambitious, and luckier—than others.

But even if we arbitrarily divided the social output evenly (despite uneven individual input), we still would do well to let personal preferences determine just how those equal incomes are used. Our preferences are not magically made uniform simply by imposing equal incomes. There would continue to be choices to be made, so there would continue to be a critical role for market prices. And prices arbitrarily pegged below market-clearing levels would still result in shortages and waste. So unequal incomes are not the issue, after all: we want an efficient pricing mechanism in an open market irrespective of initial income distribution.

It is a pity that such analysis is too subtle for those whose ready-made opinions are set in concrete. No line of thought and no kind or amount of evidence will change their opinions, for, along with being intellectual virgins, they are pure in heart and are blessed with social sensitivity and moral superiority.

(September 1981)

Surpluses and Excessive Productivity

Being a confessed professor, let me try a true-or-false question on you: "The United States has long produced agricultural surpluses because of the extraordinary productivity of American farmers." True—right? After all, a "surplus" of something must reflect the fact that we have produced more than we can use—doesn't it? If we were sufficiently less productive, there would be no excess of output over desired consumption. So the remedy for embarrassing and inconvenient surpluses is for producers to be less efficient!

Somehow, that doesn't sound quite right. Are we really to solve economic problems by becoming more wasteful? Are extraordinarily productive farmers a problem in a world with millions of hungry people?

If you still insist that surpluses reflect excessive productivity, consider the plight of India. While Indian agriculture has made appreciable progress over the past twenty years, it is hardly the epitome of efficiency. The rate of growth of Indian agriculture is only a little greater than the rate of growth of Indian population, and some 40 percent of its 750 million people are chronically malnourished. And yet, despite its low and modestly growing productivity in agriculture, India is now plagued with grain surpluses, which the Indian government is trying to export.

How can that be? How can "surplus" mean producing more than we want to consume, and yet India produces surpluses while hundreds of millions of Indians are hungry?

Reconsider the notion and the cause of surpluses. A surplus has no connection with "excessive productivity," whatever that can mean. As the experiences of U.S. and Indian agriculture illustrate, there can be surpluses both in wealthy and efficient economies and in poor and inefficient economies.

So-called surplus is not a *productivity* phenomenon; instead, it is a price phenomenon. And people react to the incentives and disincentives of prices in the same way in all economies.

If government somehow establishes an artificial price above the normal, market-clearing price, then producers will find it in their own interests to provide more than consumers are willing to buy at that high price—and government maintains the high price by buying the excess of the amount supplied over the amount bought by consumers. So too many farmers produce more grain than is demanded by consumers at the bloated price; consumers consume less than they would have consumed at the lower equilibrium price; and the government then has on its hands massive amounts of grain which it tries to sell or permits to rot.

Is this the way to run an economy? Pegging prices means misdirecting resources. Government thereby subsidizes waste. And subsidizing waste in a world of scarcity is unamusingly ludicrous either in relatively prosperous America or poverty-ridden India.

(January 1986)

How Do We Ration a Pie Too Small?

We have a rationing problem. We have had a rationing problem ever since a disgusted Deity sent Adam and Eve packing. All of the currently produced pie of aggregate output is divided among the members of the community, but everyone would like a bigger slice.

If the markets for the many goods are cleared, everyone can buy as much as he is willing to buy at going prices. But we all still want more. So how about forcing down prices? However, if we decree lower prices, we induce greater quantities demanded of the various goods and smaller quantities supplied of most of them. Inflicting shortages through price controls will not magically return us to the Garden of Eden.

Under the best of circumstances, we are confronted with scarcity. We must— somehow, through some procedures, by some criteria—ration most of what we consume. Since we do not have enough of most things to make everyone fully content, inevitably we compete. In an open market, we compete through offering money, bidding up prices to levels where those still in the bidding will wish to buy no more than is available.

In a purported spirit of "fairness" and a striving for "equity," we sometimes stipulate maximum prices, making it illegal to buy or sell an item above the ceiling price. Such stipulation does not eliminate scarcity, and thus it does not eliminate competition. Rather, it simply curtails one form of competition, so alternative forms must now be used. If people cannot buy as much as they want at market prices, how else can they compete? In what other ways can the necessary rationing be done?

One perfectly splendid way is to wait in line: first-come-first-served—with those at the end of the line not served at all. So the relatively small money expenditure must be supplemented with time and aggravation. Happy were the gasoline lines of 1979.

Or the artificially suppressed price may be administered with ration coupons, as with meat and gasoline during World War II. The essence of that scheme is that everyone gets to buy the same amount of the good despite their different demands.

Or there can be tie-in deals. You get the apartment in competition with ten others because you are willing to pay heavily for the pile of sticks which the landlord calls a Steinway piano.

Or you may pay under the table, with no pretense of buying a piano. Irrational, inefficient laws tempt us to cope through cheating and lying.

Or a government bureaucracy may allocate the good on various inspired grounds: age, occupation, geographical location, political loyalty, old-boy connections.

Perhaps the most pernicious basis of rationing is personality and appearance. If not everyone can get the apartment or the loan or the meat, those left out will be those with the wrong skin color, the wrong gender, the wrong age, the wrong religion, or who talk funny.

There is much to be said for the impersonality of the open market. Money is simply money, and mine is no better than yours. If market competition is to be conducted in terms of beauty, grace, and charm, a few of us will do alright. But most of you will be in big trouble.

(July 1983)

Political and Business People and Their Markets

It really is true—cross my ruby heart—that economists know some things of importance and can do some things of significance. Politicians tend to know less of analytics and to be able practically to do more. But we should not wish either group—economists or politicians—to have definitive control of our lives, to be the first mate of our fate.

The community has had some defenses. Responding to the in-grained survival instinct of the race, it has largely ignored economists. And it has often followed the political precept: "Throw the rascals out."

But people are inherently pretty rascally, so we may accomplish little in elections other than replace one set of self-centered, competing, corruptible rascals with another. Even the brightest and best are not psychologically unique. We all—professors, politicians, priests, and poets—are characterized by self-interest, including interest in molding society in our own conceptions of truth and beauty.

It is not, then that the politician acts without principle—but the principle pertains to securing survival and seeking stature. And it is not that the personal survival and stature are inherently reprehen-sible—if the politician loses, the unlovely characters in the opposition party will take power, and he may genuinely believe that that would be a calamity for the community.

All this suggests that there is little distinction between political and commercial activities and the people who participate in them. Indeed, it is true that people are people, individuals who are not al-ways without honor but who quite systematically and sensibly seek to prosper and to prevail.

Such distinction as there may appear to be between the person in politics and the person in business is that the former can be more glamorous and thus more seductive. For the seeker of political power can emotionally appeal to us on larger issues and by nobler criteria. The politician, after all, is not a huckster of such mundane products as washing detergents and potato peelers: he comes to us as a statesman who offers salvation on grand issues of peace and prosperity.

But both are hucksters. Each is selling something—himself or his product or both. And neither is doing it either for sheer love of the activity or from sheer dedication to high principle.

The difference which most matters is not in the nature of the people, but in the nature of the markets in which the people do their selling. The people are much the same. But, as some economists understand, the political and economic markets differ enormously. And the political market does not compare well in the variety of options provided to buyers, in the institutional procedures and the tactics of sellers, in the responsiveness of sellers to buyers, and in the recourse of buyers when stuck with faulty merchandise.

(January 1987)

Time, Conservation, and Investment

Why Invest in a Redwood Tree?

Our majestic redwoods are surely more than lumber—they are a living link to the past, an affirmation of life, a source of spiritual renewal. But economists are said to be coldhearted creatures of calculus who ignore intangible values. Moreover, planting a young redwood to produce a giant tree in the distant future is alleged to be foolish according to economics. A noted ecologist tells us, "Encapsulated in the prejudices of the market place, the economist must advise us not to plant a forest of redwoods." Not so. Advice they *do* offer is that ecologists learn elementary economics.

Economic goods represent anything people value and would like to have in greater quantities. Economics does not say that the intangible spiritual services produced by a redwood are less important than the lumber it would yield. Rather, the economic problem is in choosing which competing uses will be satisfied.

If choice is not to be whimsical or arbitrary—if it is to be in accordance with the community's preferences—then it must be made in light of people's valuations of alternatives. The worth to them of lumber is revealed in the market by the amount of other goods they are willing to pay to obtain it. So, too, is the value of intangible services.

Still, those with more sensitivity than sense complain that no profit-seeker would want to make the long-term investment necessary to produce a redwood, for the investor will become nutrient for the tree long before the tree's old age is reached. By that argument, the maximum time horizon for any investment—to be made by new-born babes—would approximate three score and ten years.

Even ecologists can recognize, if they try, that *current* prices of long-lived assets embody expected *future* values. The rationality of man and the mechanisms of the market link the years and generations. We make decisions today, of course, and we make them on the basis of today's valuations, but today's valuations reflect and incorporate reasonable anticipation of tomorrow. People bid today to obtain rights to the asset's future benefits, and this bidding assures us that today's prices will represent those distant benefits.

But a dollar to be received for an asset in the future is worth less than a dollar received now, for one must delay the spending of that future dollar. As the passing of time shortens this delay, people bid more for the asset and cause its market value to rise. One can thus earn a return by planting a redwood and selling it at any time. As Nobel economist Paul Samuelson put it, "Even if my doctor assures me that I will die the year after next, I can confidently plant a long-lived . . . tree, knowing that I can sell at a competitive profit the one-year-old sapling."

If investment in a redwood is not worthwhile, it is not because the market ignores intangible values or is blind to the distant future. It is simply because the uncoerced community does not sufficiently value those future services.

(April 1983)

Does Resource Conservation Pay?

So-called conservation of resources has been debated—often emotionally and rarely analytically—since the turn of the century. It is commonly argued that the extraction of mineral resources has been at a pace which is too rapid, with the current generation wastefully exploiting the heritage of future generations. And it is equally commonly recommended that greater governmental controls should be used to conserve the allegedly fixed amount of resources.

Economists Gerhard Anders, Philip Gramm (now a member of Congress), and Charles Maurice have approached the issue of conservation as a comparative compound interest problem.

Consider a resource which, for illustration, yields no flow of services to its holder and which can be brought to market without extraction or other costs. The owner has two alternatives: either he can *hold* the asset or he can *sell* it. If sale of a resource is delayed, the price of the resource may rise during the period it is held. Alternatively, the resource could be sold at the beginning of the period, and the proceeds of that sale could be invested over the period. If the rate of *price ap-*

preciation is greater than the rate of *investment return*, then conservation is economically rational.

The authors calculated "break-even" prices for fourteen mineral resources, including coal, petroleum, and iron ore. Break-even prices are those which, over given time periods, would just equate the appreciating value of a conserved resource with the appreciating value of the invested proceeds of the sold resource. The historical record over three-quarters of a century reveals that actual market resource prices have fallen short—generally far short—of those break-even prices which would have been required in order to make conservation economically sensible. In historical fact, further conservation has not paid.

Conservation has been too costly, not only over long periods, but typically over short periods as well. And to identify early enough those exceptional short-term cases in which withholding resource use is efficient would require prescience which would be extraordinary in the market and well-nigh inconceivable in government bureaucracies.

The conclusion that "enforced long-term conservation" in this century "would have been a poor economic decision" is not overturned by doomsday warnings that finite resources are nearing exhaustion. For what constitutes a "resource" changes over time as market values and technology change.

Specific resources can be depleted, of course, even if never physically exhausted. New resources come into use as old ones lose value. When not hamstrung by government, the community adjusts to changing circumstances reflected in the market, and the aggregate of available resources increases. "The only . . . non-substitutable resource," conclude the economists, "is the set of institutions, known as market order, which eliminates crises with respect to physical resources."

(February 1983)

Coherency and Capitalization: Capitalism Versus Communism

For all of us, in different measures, the body is frail and the mind is befogged. Few expect much of the academic bod, but scholars—even academic administrators—do disconcert with flauntings of foolishness.

The president of a technological university is quoted as damning the so-called neutron bomb by calling it "the perfect capitalist weapon: it kills people but leaves property standing." One bit of foolishness pertains to the purpose of using weapons. Since it is not to be anticipated that we shall demolish property without killing people, evidently the university head prefers to destroy property as well as to kill. It is not apparent to us non-scientists how the more completely devastating effects would make the world better.

More subtle foolishness pertains to distinguishing between "capitalism" and "non-capitalism," the latter labeled "communism." *Both* kinds of economy have physical assets, or capital, of course; capitalism is not distinguished by uniquely having capital goods. As UCLA economist Armen Alchian suggests, the crucial economic distinction between capitalism and communism turns on *who* makes decisions on resource use, through what analytic *processes* and institutional *mechanisms*, and by what *criteria*.

No one—capitalist or communist—can know all that tomorrow will bring. But to *some* degree, we can anticipate and plan; to *some* extent, we can enhance net returns by coherent calculation. Whether we do so to the greatest degree and the furthest extent intellectually possible is determined by the ground rules under which we operate.

Rational current calculations involve considerations of future flows and values. Current calculations are made on the basis of *present* market values of those *future* variables, that is, the discounted impact of the anticipated future on the present prices of assets. For such calculations to be made, then, there must be, first, *saleable assets owned by the calculators*, who, being owners, are concerned with use of assets which is rational by criteria of personal wealth-gain and, second, *appropriate capitalization rates*, which, to be appropriate, must reflect both time preferences of consumption and perceived productivity of saving-and-investing in altering income flows and resource allocations over time.

The communist economy, like the capitalist, has managers who make decisions, including decisions of saving-and-investing. But the rewards of those managers will be only weakly and indirectly linked with efficient use of resources, including use with temporal repercussions and implications, if efficiency is conceived of in terms reflecting *community* preferences. The imposed responsibilities and personal opportunities of the communistic bureaucrat—who does not own the assets he manages and has little guidance in any attempt to deduce capitalized values—preclude economic efficiency, so conceived, and ensure a less attractive kind of focus and incentive.

(February 1983)

The Corporation and the Structure of the Economy

Mouse Wisdom: Corporations and Economic Planning

Adam and Karl, my two mice friends, recently discussed corporations and economic planning.

"Our economy needs economic planning," exclaimed Karl. "Too much output is produced by giant corporations which are not controlled by the community. Planning would give the mouse masses control of these institutions and promote economic democracy."

"I agree," said Adam, "that all economies must plan. All societies must determine *somehow* what they are going to do with their scarce resources. They must decide *what* goods to produce and in what *quantities*; they must choose *how* to produce those goods and *who* will get to consume them. These decisions are economic planning.

"But," continued Adam, "it is not necessary for the *government* to make these decisions, because the *marketplace* provides a better method of planning. The marketplace effectively collects information and induces rational decisions in directing scarce resources to the production of those goods which mice value most highly. Only the most efficient production methods will survive, and the goods provided will be apportioned to those who most value them. That's what *I* call economic democracy."

"Ridiculous," ridiculed Karl. "Big corporations don't represent the community. Even the views of stockholders are ignored by corporate managers, because control of corporations is separated from their ownership. Corporate managers represent only themselves."

"That's incorrect," corrected Adam. "Few stockholders have the desire or the knowledge to manage complex corporations. Instead, they invest in specialized skills of managers by buying stock. If corporate managers disregard stockholders' wishes, then stockholders sell their stocks, thereby depressing stock values and punishing managers. Managers want to act profitably for stockholders," continued Adam, "so that their services become more valuable to all potential employers. The better job managers do, the more valuable are their services, and the higher are the salaries they can obtain—and the higher priced is the stock they themselves own. Managers have big incentive to behave as stockholders wish."

"Maybe that's the problem," snapped Karl. "Profits, profits, profits—that's all they think about. Big corporations have so much economic power that they ignore the preferences of the general community."

"What economic power?" asked Adam.

"You know," whimpered Karl. "They're big, and I'm small."

"I can see that," replied Adam, "but what economic power are you talking about? Corporations can't *force* us to buy what they produce. Like mice in general, they try to *persuade* us to do what they want. They present various goods to us, but it is we mouse consumers who accept or reject their offers. We decide how to spend our own money. Even the biggest of corporations can survive and prosper only if they satisfy the community's preferences. Replacing private marketplace planning with government planning would substitute preferences of government commissars for those of the whole community. Surely, you do not want that."

Karl acknowledged agreement through humble silence.

(December 1981)

Societal Subversion and the Corporation

For whatever reason—maybe the Devil makes you do it—suppose you want to subvert an individualistic society and its open economy. How would you carry out the destruction?

There are very direct, ham-handed techniques, of course, including imposition of a dictatorship by a Man on a White Horse and his hooligan followers—although revolution is a messy game, requiring resources and entailing risk. Or, a bit more subtly, rights to use of private property could be abruptly abolished. Even if some trappings of civilization are nominally retained, we would be effectively made serfs and slaves of the state.

But if we are done in, it need not be with a sudden, catastrophic bang. Indeed, it seems more likely that we will whimper our way to disaster.

One whimpering process is widespread, prolonged price controls. No blood need flow, no storm-troopers—other than government bureaucrats—are required, and few tactics are more effective in creating community chaos and contention. And few are more perversely appealing, for price controls can be sold to many in the name of equity and administered efficiency.

Still another way to stick the shiv into freedom and efficiency—a way entirely compatible with price controls—is to stick the shiv into the corporate form of business organization. Just about everyone already questions the purity of Daddy Warbucks types and their massive corporations, which always make obscene profits through all sorts of dirty tricks and have come to dominate not only the economy but society generally. The Ralphs and John Kenneths and Toms and Janes among us play this theme with great effect. There are various sub-themes:

- The corporation, we are told, owes its existence and identifying characteristics to special—and overgenerous—dispensation of government.

- In corporate organization, management control purportedly dominates shareholder ownership.

- Again, the corporation as such has "social responsibilities," and shareholders, who are to be protected from managers, should be required to share their assets with the community.

- Finally, through excessive permissiveness of some states, corporations have become veritable governments, and the community can be protected only through "industrial democracy" or federal chartering or other gimmicks.

In all these propositions, history has been bastardized, and analysis has been garbled. The unrelenting attack on the enormously useful corporation—to constrain it, to exploit it, ultimately to destroy it—is distressing enough. But it is part of a larger campaign. The encompassing assault, Armen Alchian discerns, is "on the institution of private property, the right to make private contractual agreements, and on privately determined, fluctuating prices as a mechanism of economic and social control . . . ," with "voluntary . . . exchange . . . being replaced by political force." But this is a weirdly one-sided Armageddon. The belligerency of subversion is confronted by little other than "the seemingly confused apathy, if not death wish, of the free society."

(December 1981)

Ownership, Management, and Costs

In a simple scheme of society, business firms do nothing but produce goods which are consumed by households. Preferences of people in households are reflected in market demands which guide production. Managers of firms respond to these preferences in order to prosper. And, in their own interests, they respond by producing with minimum costs. So people who consume in households obtain greatest possible well-being with their income, and people who manage firms obtain the largest profits from their production.

Critics of corporate capitalism commonly concede that, in principle, a production arrangement of firms which are managed by the self-interested owners is highly efficient. The owners of the resources have obvious incentive to use those resources profitably, and profits are greatest when customers are pleased most. But, it is complained, the large corporation is *not* managed by the owner. Ownership may be scattered among thousands of stockholders, who hire managers to run the firm. And the hired managers may have goals in addition to making profit for the firm. Separation of *ownership* of the firm from *management* of the firm thus tends to dilute *efficiency* of the firm.

Eminent economist Harold Demsetz, of UCLA, explains that such concern over separation of ownership and management is mainly misdirected.

First, we should acknowledge that consumption is *not* confined to households: the owner-manager may consume partly on the job. He consumes by hiring pretty but dumb secretaries, buying extraordinarily thick carpets, and surrounding himself with people of certain religious and ethnic backgrounds even though they may not be the most productive.

But consuming on the job does not preclude maximization of profit. Market competition requires that the owner-manager, not the firm, *pay* for this on-the-job consumption with reduced take-home pay in order to contain costs. Indeed, if he *chooses* to take some of his compensation in the form of more expensive but less productive secretaries, that means that he is willing to give up *more* dollars in wages than it costs the firm to supply his office consumption. On balance, it can be *cheaper* to the firm to supply office consumption than to pay for home consumption.

Now, suppose that the owner of the firm retires and hires a manager to run the firm—ownership is now separated from management. The owner can no longer consume at the office, and he receives compensating take-home income. But the desire for profit then leads to the selection of a new manager who either consumes less on the job than the owner used to consume or is willing to receive sufficiently little salary to pay for consumption on the job. So the separation of ownership from management can mean thinner carpets and more productive people in the office.

Outside owners do not gain from office amenities. And if hired managers are effectively monitored in their duties by the owners, separating ownership from management can mean a leaner, less-nonsense firm.

(November 1988)

Mouse Wisdom: Corporate Ownership, Control, and Social Responsibility

"Disgusting!" roared Karl, the mouse who is too anxious to do good.

"What is the problem this time?" asked Adam, his rodent friend.

"I have been reading about the evils of the corporate form of business," explained a fuming Karl. "With corporations, the exploited owners, who have invested in the stock, do not run the show. The business is directed by hired managers."

"I suspect," said Adam, "that the investors knew what they were doing in buying the stock. They have their own activities. They did not buy stock in various companies in order to run them."

"So they weren't surprised," replied Karl. "The fact remains that *owners* of a business should exercise *control*. Not only is that aesthetic, it would help efficiency to have decisions made by those who own the resources."

"Oh, people do have to be monitored," agreed Adam. "Managers must keep an eye on workers, and owners have to watch managers. And there *are* ways, even though imperfect and not costless, to hold people accountable for their obligations. We *must* have ways to delegate responsibility and coordinate diverse efforts," added Adam. "Investors efficiently bear risk by pooling resources in an enterprise and then hiring a specialized manager to direct it. That is sensible division of labor."

"Sure," sneered Karl, "sensible for the fat cat investors. You can bet those greedy characters will direct the manager to operate the firm for the good of the investors—and thereby for his own good."

"Yes," Adam said, "people do tend to be interested in their own well-being. And in the business world, one improves his own lot by being useful to others, supplying attractive goods at attractive prices."

"Well," sniffed Karl, "I don't want to rely wholly on bribing people to do good things. Corporations should assume social responsibility and give away much of their profit."

"I should suppose," said a discouraged Adam, "that in this world of scarcity, where wealth is so hard to produce, you would be content with competitive efficiency—and that you would see that hard work, shrewd planning, effective organizing, and assuming of calculated risk is encouraged by minimal constraints and forced sharing. Trying to do good by arbitrarily dividing the pie, with large slices sequestered for some who have not contributed to its production, tends strongly to make the total pie smaller."

Karl did not seem chastened, so Adam made one more observation.

"At least," he said, "recognize the inconsistency in your two points. First you lament the so-called separation of corporate ownership from corporate control; then you want to take from the corporation and its owners some of their wealth for you to use for your own purposes. It is a bit awkward to defend corporate owners and urge greater efficiency for their organization while siphoning off their wealth. And since you are obliged to choose between conflicting objectives, I suggest that what you really are after is to get your paws on the assets of investors in order to remake the world according to your socialistic designs."

The greedy gleam in Karl's beady eyes let the cat out of the bag.

(May 1983)

Golden Parachutes and Stockholder Protection

During the 1980s, there has been a flurry of takeover activity involving major firms. Acquisition of one corporation by another may be a more or less friendly *merger*, approved by the directors and the shareholders of the take-over firm. Or the acquisition may be through an untender *offer tendered to the stockholders* of the target firm, to buy a controlling number of shares at a specified premium price. Or stockholder votes can be solicited in a proxy contest for control of the board of directors.

The owners of a firm taken over commonly gain from an appreciable increase in the price of their stock, particularly in cases of tender offers. But not all takeover attempts are advantageous to the target shareholder, and some terms of possible takeover are more attractive than others. Shareholders want managers to be shrewd—by shareholders' criteria—in determining if a takeover attempt should be welcomed or opposed and in determining optimal tactics in either defense or generating the terms of the acquisition.

By and large, in running the firm, managers have much incentive to please shareholders. Managers will have larger incomes, greater job security, and better options when they run the business well. But when confronted by a takeover attempt, target firm managers may have criteria of shrewdness which are incompatible with those of the shareholders.

The previous managers of a firm taken over are not invariably dismissed, and their personal holdings of the firm's stock may appreciate during the takeover maneuvering. Still, the takeover will seem in many eyes—including the eyes of the managers of the target firm— to be a defeat for those managers. They will have reasons—protection of their own power, stature, and income—to resist even those takeovers which would benefit shareholders.

One device—found in perhaps 30 percent of major corporations— to minimize management-stockholder conflict is the "golden parachute." The parachutes differ from case to case. But the essence of the arrangement is to provide compensation for a limited time—perhaps full salary for two or three years—to the top managers of a taken-over firm. Provisions of such compensation—which generally is quantitatively insignificant in the total context of a take-over—is increasingly important in the competitive hiring of superior managers in the first place. And such protection from the slings and arrows of the corporate control market is to enhance the clarity of mind and promote the corporate orientation of managers when confronted by possible takeover.

Such clarity enhancement and orientation promotion—like any other good thing—can be overpriced. If the parachute is too golden, the managerial agent of the stockholders may be over-eager to give up the company in order to bail out. But Professor Michael Jensen, of the University of Rochester, finds "the principle behind the desirability of the Golden Parachute to . . . [be] airtight." The parachute is not a purposeless consolation prize to a defeated manager. Instead, it is a device to protect the interests of stockholders by making defense of those interests less costly to managers.

(March 1984)

The Profits of Gloom

Here is a recipe for a spicy news story. List the largest corporations which paid little or no income tax last year. Add some somber statistics which reveal a recent drop in the rate at which corporations are taxed, and then mix together with pithy philosophical profundities about tax loopholes and tax cuts. The media dish will appeal to the popular passion which views corporations as greedy tyrants who take most of the nation's income as swollen profits and then abscond without paying their share of taxes.

There are, indeed, tax loopholes for corporations, as there are loopholes for individuals, not all of which go to the wealthy. Perhaps we can justify few of these loopholes through which government types use the tax code to promote their particular goals. We would be better off if we junked all these credits and exemptions and then instituted a much lower, flat-rate tax for everyone.

We might even want to scrap the corporate income tax. The tax on corporate profits provides a small and persistently shrinking *portion of the federal government's tax revenues*. Although the corporate income tax provided well over 20 percent of federal tax receipts in the early and mid-1960s, it now provides only 10 percent. This reduction is not due to increased evasion of taxes, but rather to reduced *size of corporate profits relative to national income*. In 1965, fourteen cents of every dollar of income earned in the nation went to corporate profits—before the tax collector skimmed off two-fifths of those profits. Today, pre-tax profits represent only eight cents of every dollar of national income, a reduction of over 40 percent. Despite the decline in the share of national income earned as profit—averaging over 12 percent in the 1960s, less than 10 percent in the 1970s, and just over 8 percent thus far in the 1980s—the *percentage of corporate profits paid in taxes* did not diminish during this period: it has fluctuated between 40 and 50 percent.

In all this, we should not suppose that the corporation itself bears the burden of the so-called corporate income tax. *Individuals*—customers, employees, and stockholders—bear this burden. Because of the corporate income tax, customers pay higher prices, employees receive lower wages, and stockholders obtain smaller earnings. Obviously, it is politically appealing to speak of shifting the tax burden to corporations, but it is real-life people who pay that tax.

Beware catchy news stories whose distortions and old wives' tales feed the public's paranoia about corporations. Some businesses have, indeed, used tax provisions, such as the investment tax credit, to reduce or even to avoid income taxes in specific years. But these exceptions do not change the general picture. Not only is the relative size of corporate profits in the total economy much smaller than most imagine, but that size has disconcertingly declined. And corporations continue to pay close to half their earnings to Big Brother.

(October 1982)

Small Firms, Opportunity, and Growth

"In numbers, there is strength," and "the more, the better," it is often said. Well, perhaps not always—as with wives and children. But many and much can be promising in some categories and circumstances.

This may be the case in the context of "market structure." Producing and transporting and selling are done mainly through business firms. Business firms are born and organized and directed through the coordinated efforts of innovators and investors and managers. Resources are committed to such endeavors, at considerable risk, in the hope of adequate returns. Those firms will prosper most who best employ productive inputs in responding to preferences of consumers. And consumers, in turn, delight in market options, in many suppliers vying with energy and imagination and boldness to please buyers.

The existence of many firms contributes to much consumer-pleasing competition. And the increasing number of firms is a response to high and expanding consumer demand. The rapid forming of firms both reflects and contributes to the robustness of the economy.

A flourishing economy is one of eager exploitation of expanding economic opportunity. By that critical criterion, the American economy is flourishing. Such is the conclusion of Dale Jahr, a Senior Economist with the Joint Economic Committee of Congress.

It generally takes much time and always takes much success for a firm to grow to great size. Most firms are born small. The vitality of the economy is reflected largely in the rate of birth and of growth of small firms. And Mr. Jahr finds that "small companies are proliferating as never before."

From 1970 to 1983, corporations overall expanded impressively in number, receipts, and assets. In number and receipts, at least, the picture is dominated by firms with assets no more than one million dollars. Such firms doubled in *number* over the thirteen-year period, accounting for more than 99 percent of the increase in all corporations; in 1983, they were over 91 percent of the total. And in *sales*, the proportion of corporations with less than one million dollars increased from three out of four to five out of six.

Large corporations are *not* disappearing dinosaurs. Indeed, the share of all corporate assets held by those firms with more than $250 million in assets increased somewhat from 1970 to 1983. But the wave of the future may not be characterized so conspicuously by "bigness." Liquidity and mobility of resources may be more important than economies of scale in manufacturing.

We cannot *know* the future. We best *shape* the future, not with concrete five-year plans of centralized direction, but by general fostering of economic opportunity. One manifestation of economic health is the vigorous formation of small firms.

(April 1987)

Media Myths About Manufacturing

Many seem to suppose that the industrial sector is collapsing as an employer of American labor. They fear we are becoming a nation of low-paid workers who will only serve hamburgers and sweep up around Japanese computers.

Fluctuations in the economy have caused manufacturing employment to swing up and down, but these swings have been around an upward trend. Between 1950 and 1980, the average yearly growth of manufacturing employment was more than 1 percent. And while employment in United States manufacturing was rising during a recent ten-year period, it actually fell in Japan, France, West Germany, and Britain.

Although our manufacturing employment has increased over the years, it has not increased as fast as employment in the rest of the economy. The result has been a smaller percentage of the labor force working in manufacturing. Averaging about 33 percent in the 1950s, the proportion of all workers employed by manufacturing fell to an average of about 29 percent in the 1960s and to around 25 percent in the 1970s.

The relative decline of manufacturing employment is a healthy change with identifiable causes. One cause is the relatively rapid growth of manufacturing's labor *productivity*, a growth that has enabled businesses to produce our rising output of manufactured goods with proportionately fewer workers.

The relative size of employment in manufacturing has diminished also because the *composition* of the labor force has changed. Waves of new women workers caused the female percentage of the work force to rise from under 30 percent in 1950 to more than 40 percent today. Since women usually have sought jobs outside the manufacturing sector, employment rose faster there than in manufacturing. Thus, the proportion of the labor force employed by manufacturing declined. But manufacturing employment as a percentage of adult male workers has remained at about 40 percent since World War II.

Manufacturing is not collapsing as a source of jobs for American workers. But news stories that emphasize troubled industries or regions obscure this fact. In particular, the steel and auto industries were devastated by the recent recession, and, with misplaced concreteness, that devastation was abundantly and ominously documented by the media.

News stories also have featured particular regions that have lost manufacturing jobs as employment has shifted over time from one geographical area to another. Between 1950 and 1980, the average yearly growth in manufacturing employment was more than 5 percent in the West and close to 3 percent in the South. But in the Northeast, manufacturing employment dropped more than 1 percent per year.

Focusing on defeats and reductions while ignoring successes and increases paints a false picture of manufacturing employment and market adaptation to changing circumstances. One wonders why reporters often report so badly and with such bias.

(May 1984)

Antitrust Policies: Theory, Purposes, and Consequences

Antitrust Policy and the Competitive Model

We have long experimented with outlawing trusts and monopolies in order to preserve (or re-establish) consumer-protecting competition, supposedly too anemic otherwise to persist. If there must be grubby economic activity, at least see that it is not dominated by Daddy Warbucks and other Robber Barons.

So we have generally applauded efforts of lawyers and economists to delineate a coherent antitrust stance and make it prevail in the marketplace.

Much of antitrust policy rests on a conventional model of competition. The market of this model is open, with firms of insignificant size selling a homogenous product; if the competitive market is perfect as well as pure, both buyers and sellers have full information, so it is always in equilibrium, with price equal to average cost.

Whatever its analytic and pedagogic purposes, obviously, such a conception does not describe much reality. It defines a type of equilibrium, but it does not explain or describe the processes of reaching equilibrium. In its essence, it has no place for many of the characteristics and activities of most real marketplaces—different prices and brands for basically the same product; advertising, packaging differences, and other sales devices; firms of appreciable size relative to the market and rates of return of appreciable variation among firms of an industry.

Many have supposed that the competitive model provides analytic criteria and benchmarks against which real, operating markets can be measured and assessed. But there are fatal difficulties in using abstract conceptualization of a never-never world of atomistic, equilibrated uniformity as a guide in grading and possibly circumventing and constraining the ever-evolving, adjusting real world—a world of risk and uncertainty, experimentation and research, disequilibrium and change, sweat and strain.

In such a world, it is naive to suppose that we have available a simple, neat measuring rod of market behavior and influence, enabling us readily to identify the bad and the beautiful, distinguishing monopolists from competitors. It is doubly naive to suppose that, having put the finger on trusts, we can use the power of the state to bust them into competitive fragments which will better serve the community.

Indeed, typically, firms which have been victimized by antitrust enforcements were guilty simply of doing better than most in what the community wants—lowering prices, increasing supplies, broadening consumption options, improving product quality. But if a firm does well enough in thus pleasing customers, it will prosper and grow bigger both absolutely and relative to others who are competing for community favor, thereby perversely making itself suspect in antitrust eyes.

It is entirely sensible to look at market performance rather than market structure, to assess real results of real market behavior rather than market organization on the basis of static and bloodless criteria.

(May 1982)

Antitrust: Mythology and Methodology

A radio news announcer was reporting a story of economic analysis. With sonorous, pear-shaped tones, he twice referred inadvertently to "economic mythology" instead of "economic methodology." Alas, many reporters and politicians actually do confuse mythology with methodology.

Few areas of economics are more distorted by myths than questions of antitrust law and policy. There are myths about alleged innate proclivities of businesses to monopolize; there are myths about the purported necessity of antitrust laws to maintain effective competition; and there are myths about the supposed historical effectiveness of such laws in satisfying their antitrust purposes.

The purpose itself is largely hidden in clouds of mythology. Several economists have peeked into the real record of the late nineteenth century agitation for monopoly legislation, culminating in the Sherman Antitrust Act of 1890. Professor Thomas DiLorenzo, of George Mason University, has reported on the peeking.

Antitrust legislation, one is tempted to suppose, is intended to avoid or correct market conditions of monopoly and to maintain or re-establish competition. And surely what counts in taking the measure of a market is industry *performance* of production and price, not industry *description* of dimension.

The economic history of the latter part of the nineteenth century was highly impressive. It was a period of great innovation and investment. Some industries and firms prospered and expanded; others were losers. While some conspicuous fortunes were made, total national income rose, and there was no "dangerous concentration of wealth": the proportional division of national income between laborers and property owners did not change between 1840 and 1900.

Nor was there "a rising tide of monopoly power." Presumably, such dangerous degeneration would be manifested in curtailed production and bloated prices. The antitrust crusaders of the 1880s professed to be protecting consumers from deprivation and gouging. But the actual record does not support the demagogic ridicule of alleged monopolies. *Output* of the notorious industries—including coal, lead, petroleum, steel, sugar, and zinc—was *increasing* much more rapidly than the economy generally, and their prices were *falling* more rapidly than the overall price index.

Not only were the antitrusters tilting at phantom windmills, hoping to protect relatively inefficient firms from domestic competition, they were simultaneously and cynically raising tariffs to protect all domestic firms from foreign competition. These crusading politicians, we now realize, were not lovers of consumers.

One reason why it is not always easy to determine if legislation well serves its purpose is that it is not always easy to determine the purpose of the legislators.

(October 1987)

Mouse Wisdom: Outlawing Competition

Karl, a gung-ho, red-blooded mouse, was disgusted with the number of penalties called in last night's basketball game. "Let them play," he roared. "Let the game be won by dribbling, passing, shooting, and rebounding—not by free-throwing."

Mouse Adam was sympathetic. "A game can be largely ruined by too many or badly enforced rules. Lots of picky penalties inhibit initiative and hurt the quality of play by interrupting activity. The same sort of complaint," he added thoughtfully, "can be directed toward antitrust laws and their interpretations by the courts."

"Don't be silly," Karl admonished. "Free-wheeling basketball is great sport. But business is different: it must be closely contained and directed. Otherwise, some firms will get too big, and they will then make too much money selling shoddy merchandise at high prices. Competition has to be defined and enforced by government. That's the idea behind antitrust laws."

It was Adam's turn to admonish. "First," he said quite sternly, "the antitrust laws, passed in the late nineteenth and early twentieth centuries, are hardly clear and consistent legislation produced by dedicated devotees of competition. Second, sometimes antitrust prosecution has denounced the very essence of competition and proscribed the happy results of competitive activity."

"I can't believe," protested Karl, "that a judge, in the name of antitrust, would penalize effective competition which benefits consumers."

"You better believe it," said Adam sadly. "In a critical case in 1945, the Aluminum Company of America was accused of 'monopolizing.' The judge said that 'monopolizing' does *not* include instances of virtually automatic or inevitable monopoly. Indeed, he elaborated, 'a single producer may be the survivor out of a group of active competitors, merely by virtue of his superior skill, foresight, and industry. . . . The successful competitor, having been urged to compete, must not be turned upon when he wins.'"

"So the company won," chirped Karl.

"No," Adam replied. "The judge went on to proclaim:

It was *not* inevitable that . . . [Alcoa] should always anticipate increases in . . . demand . . . and be prepared to supply. . . . Nothing *compelled* it to keep doubling and redoubling its capacity before others entered the field. It insists that it never excluded competitors; but we can think of no more effective exclusion than progressively to embrace each new opportunity as it opened, and to face every newcomer with new capacity already geared into a great organization, having the advantage of experience, trade connections and the elite of personnel.

Karl blanched. "It is weird when a firm is deemed guilty of illegally 'monopolizing' because it efficiently serves it customers—expanding supply, restraining price, and improving service—by competing through 'superior skill, foresight, and industry' and 'embracing each new opportunity.'"

(May 1986)

Dollars and Scholars, Cartels and Competition

Especially in "higher" activities—including medicine, religion, and education—some majestically eschew the sordid and castigate the contemptible. And they are pleased to pronounce standards of refinement and punish transgressors. Sometimes they manage to believe their haughty foolishness.

Consider, with economists Armen Alchian of UCLA and William Meckling of the University of Rochester, intercollegiate athletics and their supervision by the National Collegiate Athletic Association. And find comfort in young scholars occasionally bounding about the playing fields and gyms of our colleges, with some "student athletes" representing Alma Mater in friendly strife with equally well-scrubbed sophisticates from other centers of study.

But this wholesome competition of the gladiators camouflages collusion of the schools, with the N.C.A.A. being the enforcement agency of organized exploitation of the athletic employees. The athletes *are* paid, of course. So are students who work in the library, the bookstore, the dormitories, the labs. But maximum payments to athletes are specified by the national collegiate cartel. Why the discrimination against athletes?

Successful athletic programs can generate enormous revenues, so the players are very valuable. And those revenues directly and indirectly aid the financing of the entire school, not just the athletic department. There is, then, the incentive to curtail wages of the athletes in order to maximize net income to the school.

But a given school could not long compete—and generate that massive income—if it *uniquely* paid below-market wages to its athletes. Any school not meeting the labor market competition would have inferior teams and small gate receipts. But employee exploitation which is not practicable for an *individual* school *is* feasible when done by *all* schools under enforced agreement.

The cartel agreement does have to be enforced. For there is temptation to cheat by surreptitiously paying players something closer to their free-market worth. Correspondingly, there is incentive for schools to squeal on each other when they see rules being broken by competing institutions. Finally, authority of the endorsing agent—the N.C.A.A.—is great, for flagrant cheaters would lose academic accreditation, which would cost the school more in lost government and philanthropic subsidies than even the potential athletic profits.

One might justify prohibition of intercollegiate athletics, now packaged and promoted by colleges for sale to the community, for such activities could be construed as diluting the purposes and diverting the activities of higher education. And one might justify non-cartelized, non-exploitative athletics, with each school determining how and to what extent it will participate in open competition of the market.

But it is surely unseemly to play the game (pardon the expression) of cartel monopolization and exploitation in the name of genteel cooperation and protection of purity, of subterfuge and inconsistency in the name of academic honor and intellectual sophistication.

(January 1982)

The Gaucheries of Government: Intervention and Regulation

Commissars of Kitchens and Commodes

We must act now, or yesterday's shortages of gasoline will pale in comparison with future shortages of water. This is the message of doomsayers who argue that supplies of fresh water are running out. Drought, population growth, industrial expansion, pollution, increasingly thirsty appliances—all are said to be gulping down our limited fresh water.

A newly published book makes this claim, and then describes ways to conserve water in the kitchen, the bathroom, the laundry, the garden, the swimming pool. Unless we adopt these water-saving methods now, disaster will occur. "There will be worldwide chaos," say the authors, "if people do not start using water correctly."

What is meant by correct use of water? It is made clear that "correct uses" are those which the authors, not individual consumers, think important. To ignore the book's water-saving recommendations is, by definition, to waste water. And how is the behavior of water users to be changed to fit the preferences of the authors? You guessed it: mandatory controls by government.

The book concludes by listing some of these controls, such as prohibiting ornamental and golf course use of water, unrequested serving of water in restaurants, and use of water for cleaning driveways and automobiles. Made to believe that doom is otherwise imminent, we are thus to surrender to government officials the right to choose acceptable uses.

Freedom of individual choice is compatible with—and, indeed, required for—socially efficient use of a scarce resource, with people paying *market-clearing prices*. If water becomes more scarce, its market-clearing price will rise. Doubtless, individuals would then use less water by adopting some of the conservation practices outlined in the book. But people would decide for themselves the extent to which water uses are not worth the higher price, and the quantity of water demanded would fall to the smaller supply available.

The problem of sensible water use is more economic than technological, but the authors omit economics from both diagnosis and prescription. Water shortages occur when government keeps the price of water *below* its market-clearing level. The lower, controlled price understates the scarcity of water, increases the quantity demanded beyond the available supply, and causes waste. A "shortage" of anything occurs only because people demand more than is available at the existing price. Any shortage disappears when the price rises to its market-clearing level, where the quantities demanded and supplied are equal.

Despite the critical function of water prices, they are nowhere mentioned in this book about water shortages. Since artificially lower prices are not cited as the cause of shortages, equilibrating higher prices are not prescribed as their cure. But if individuals want to choose for themselves the important uses of water that can be satisfied, they must pay market-clearing prices that reflect the reality of scarcity. The alternative is to have government officials make those choices for us—to have commissars of kitchens and commodes.

(November 1983)

Learning From an Industrial Policy Experiment

It is painful to recall silly episodes of elaborate government economic planning and the visionary exhortations associated with the experiments.

But the dirty work should be done. Chemists and botanists can often rely on laboratory experiments to test theories. Economists must find their evidence in the complex welter of many people conducting varied affairs in a non-antiseptic world. And so Dean George Daly, of the University of Iowa, directs our attention to a real-life episode of centralized economic planning in the 1970s.

The United States, with much of the rest of the world, was confronted by an oil crisis precipitated by antics of OPEC. And, unfortunately, government is government. Both the Republican administrations of Nixon and Ford and the Democratic Carter administration, starting with similar preconceptions and predilections, reacted in similar fashion and achieved similar results.

The politicians presumed that resolution of the oil problem was primarily a responsibility of government. This was a responsibility of discretionary, ad hoc direction and decree, for it was presumed that citizens could not sufficiently well understand their options to behave efficiently in a free market. It was presumed that these governmental directions and decrees—these imposed substitutes for the market—could be derived from expert projections and predictions of supplies, prices, and consumption.

Each of the administrations commissioned an elaborate study of the expected consequences of the energy problem and energy policies. One report appeared in late 1974, the other in early 1977. One was quite optimistic, the other highly pessimistic; both were wildly inaccurate in their forecasts and thus misled both the public and the policymakers.

Indeed, the policymakers soon misled themselves. Their handicaps went beyond lack of analytic sophistication and bad projections and predictions. They were handicapped also by the very nature of the political game. There is a widespread "notion that the making of government policy" is "a coherent, consistent process characterized by single-minded, informed pursuit of the public interest." In reality, there are "contending forces or interest groups, each pursuing its own goals," and "policies inevitably reflect the conflicts and compromises, the rhetoric and posturing, attendant to the process through which they are made." With analytic coherency a fatality in the melee, there were "price controls . . . advocated by people who also urged conservation" and "major taxes . . . imposed on an industry we wished to expand."

In this unamusingly ludicrous experience, Dean Daly finds lessons—lessons concerning our ability to forecast and to plan on a grand scale. But lessons must be learned to be useful. And our current "industrial policy" cheer leaders are very slow and reluctant students.

(March 1985)

On Curbing Parking

Manna from heaven is very limited. Since we must produce most of what we consume, production would seem to be a good thing. And good things, one might suppose, are to be encouraged. But we find many exceptions.

Sometimes, even the most humble of producers are harried and hassled—especially when production is not recognized as production. Production includes more than the molding of materials and the performance of services. Production includes *exchange* of assets. We make ourselves better off in a stingy world by appropriate *trading*, with each trader preferring what he gets to what he gives.

Even Mortimer Snerd can suspect that buying and selling would not be taking place unless both buyers and sellers considered themselves benefited by the voluntary activity. But commonsense is occasionally too subtle for Big Brother—or for Little Brother at the local level of government.

The Los Angeles Coliseum is a place where glamorous gladiators cavort for the amusement of affluent audiences. But there is little glamor and affluence in the neighborhood of the Coliseum. One of the few assets of the people living there is a bit of space in driveways and front yards. On days of Coliseum events, that space becomes more valuable. It is coveted by the intruding beautiful people who want to park their cars.

Unsurprisingly, the people looking for space get together with those who have space, and transactions are made. The car owners pay money to the space owners to rent parking space for several hours. Both parties gain from the deal.

But the Los Angeles City Council has declared such productive activity to be illegal. Why? Surely not because of safety considerations: a car in the driveway or on a lawn by agreement and with payment for the privilege is not likely to be in greater peril than a car left at the curb. And "price gouging"—whatever that means—is not the alleged evil of private parking, for these market prices are not out of line with prices charged in commercial lots. The publicly offered explanation for the ordnance is that front yard parking is a "nuisance" and a "blight."

Well, the automobiles may be aesthetically less attractive than the small, old houses they partially hide from view. But that would seem to be a judgment best made by members of the community. And the residents—not Council members who would not allow cars on their *own* lawns—might best decide if it is worth five dollars to despoil the beauty of their estates on a weekend afternoon.

There may be a compromise between the Council and the community. It is proposed that the poor people of the Coliseum neighborhood travel to City Hall and pay for a permit to sell temporary use of their space. No price controls are in the proposal, and the parked cars will not be made more attractive. But some of the grubby productive activity would be curtailed—and the government would get a slice of the remaining action.

Thus are we protected by our protectors.

(August 1984)

For Whom the Bus Tolls

A jitney is not an affliction of the patella. It is a privately owned van or small bus which once was, and could be again, an important means of urban transportation. Unlike the taxi, the jitney picks up passengers until it is full; and compared to the bus, its schedule and route can be flexible.

Decades ago, there were many jitneys operating in Los Angeles, but city officials banned them, because they competed with government-sanctioned transit monopolies. Now, members of the Public Utilities Commission think the jitney should be permitted to operate again in order to alleviate rush-hour congestion on buses. Bus operators oppose the idea, arguing that jitneys would decrease their revenues.

This argument should make us wonder whom the Rapid Transit District is intended to serve—the consumer or the producer of transportation services?

In a free market, the interests of producer and consumer are made coincident. Only by providing a good which consumers sufficiently value can a producer survive, much less prosper. If a producer offers a good which consumers do not value highly enough, consumers will buy alternative goods from other suppliers. In order to pass this incessant, grueling test of the market, producers must satisfy consumers' preferences, and they must control their costs. Producers benefit because consumers benefit.

But city buses do not now operate in a free market. Entry of new competitors is rigidly controlled by government, so consumers are denied the choice of buying alternatives, such as jitney services. Moreover, bus revenues do not depend solely on the satisfying of consumers, for tax dollars are used to subsidize the transit system. Consequently, there is less incentive to keep costs down and to please consumers, for all taxpayers can be compelled to pay for transportation services which some consumers would not otherwise buy.

A bus system faces a peak-load problem. Having enough buses to handle rush hour demand means much excess capacity during the rest of the day; but reducing the number of buses generally standing idle means overcrowding and bypassed customers in periods of peak demand. Better service at lower cost would be possible by minimizing the number of buses and then supplementing buses with jitneys during the hours of largest demand for transportation.

But jitney supplementation of busing capacity smacks of competition to the employers and administrators of the bus system. And they argue for continuation of government protection from competition.

Should the utility commission acquiesce to their argument, we will know for whom the bus tolls are subsidized. Producers of bus services will continue to be protected by, and operations of the transportation network will continue to suffer from, absence of a free market. And both taxpayers and bus riders will continue to pay the toll of this inefficiency.

(July 1982)

Mouse Wisdom:
On Being Railroaded into Subways

Karl, the rather mean mouse who lives in my office, was in a point-scoring mood. "Thank goodness and commonsense," he smugly said, "the economic planners of government are making progress on at least one front."

"Oh," said Adam, his clear-headed compatriot, "what is Big Brother going to do for us—or to us—this time?"

"Big Brother and Little Brother together," Karl said mockingly, "are going to give Los Angeles a nineteen-mile subway. And providing more fixed-rail urban transit will marvelously reduce street congestion, purify the air, provide transportation for the poor, reduce the use of energy, and improve the spatial use of the community's land."

"It would be marvelous, indeed, to accomplish all—or any—of that," Adam agreed. "But transportation economist Peter Gordon of the University of Southern California tells us that *none* of those results have been achieved by past subway monument building, including the recently constructed BART in San Francisco and METRO in Washington, D.C."

"Well," replied Karl cautiously, "surely some subways have done some good."

"Of course, they have done some good for some people," said Adam a bit impatiently. "But the good they have done has been concentrated on posturing politicians and self-serving subway builders. For the community generally, the amount of benefit has been modest and swamped by the associated costs. Subways, for all their enormous expenses of construction and operation, have not siphoned many riders off the streets and thus have done little to reduce surface congestion or air pollution; their massively subsidized use has been mainly by middle-class people, not the poor; they have not reduced energy use in operation enough to offset the energy use in construction. And," concluded Adam, "there is little basis either to predict or to hope that a new subway will reduce urban sprawl. The voters of Houston were uncommonly shrewd in recently refusing to accept the burdens of a subway."

Karl did not surrender easily: "Maybe a subway is inappropriate for Houston, but Los Angeles has a population density twice that of Houston's."

"The only situation in which mass transit can come even close to paying for itself is one of high population density," acknowledged Adam. "But," he added, "that condition is *not* satisfied in Los Angeles. There are more people per square mile in Los Angeles than in Houston, but the population density of Los Angeles is only one-tenth that of Manhattan! Places of employment in Los Angeles also are dispersed on a magnificent scale. But the builders of subway monuments claim—with a straight face and no contradiction by investigative journalists—that the Los Angeles subway will carry more passengers per mile of track than any other subway in the country, including New York's!"

"Well," muttered a chastened Karl, "it does appear that the subway supporters may have been a bit too exuberant. Urban transportation will continue to be a very big problem, and there is not likely to be any very happy resolution. But that is no excuse to let ourselves be railroaded into subways."

(November 1983)

Mouse Wisdom:
Fair and Unfair Housing Discrimination

Adam and Karl recently debated legal prohibitions against renting housing exclusively to adults.

"It's unfair," exclaimed Karl, "that mouse children should be discriminated against in rentals."

"Children do squeak more than adult mice," mused Adam, "and they often are more destructive of property."

"Not *all* mouse children," protested Karl. "Why should all children be discriminated against because of how some behave?"

"Information is valuable," answered Adam. "When you buy cheese, you take a familiar brand. Some other brands might be as tasty, but information is scarce and costly, so you buy the brand you know. As brand names provide information about characteristics of cheese, so does age provide information about characteristics of tenants. Adult tenants are generally more quiet and less destructive."

"Mice and cheese are entirely different," snapped Karl. "Landlords shouldn't be able to exclude mice from rental housing just because they are younger."

"Don't blame it all on *landlords*," said Adam, "for adults-only housing reflects preferences of *other tenants*. When landlords offer adults-only housing, they have reduced the number of demanders for their product. But many of the remaining rental market are willing to pay a sufficiently high price—maybe because they are sedate people who like peace and quiet or because they are swingers who like privacy and freedom—to induce landlords to fragment their market."

"Right," said Karl. "And as a result of having some of the market closed to them, mouse parents have fewer places to bid for. They face a housing shortage."

"No," responded Adam, "there will be no shortage for anyone—unless the community is so silly as to impose rent controls on itself. With or without adults-only apartment buildings, market-determined rents will adjust to market-clearing levels. Each landlord will deter-mine—in light of estimated demands and anticipated costs and incon-veniences of conducting his business—whether or not to adopt an adults-only policy and then what rent would just keep his units filled."

"You are strangely concerned with landlord well-being," Karl sneered. "Why aren't you concerned instead with housing being allo-cated fairly?"

"Don't talk like a ridiculous rodent," Adam said sternly. "What can you mean by 'fair'? We are dealing not only with mouse parents and their kids, but also with mouse landlords and mouse tenants who want to live only with other adults. How can we be 'fair' to some by granting them wider options without being 'unfair' to others by restricting their options? How can it be 'fair' to prohibit childless mice from freely bidding for child-free apartments and to prohibit property owners from responding to such bidding? And by restricting the op-tions of property owners, the value of their property falls, and invest-ment in new housing will be curtailed. How is that 'fair' to any of us? Conflicts which inevitably emanate from scarcity are best resolved by people freely bidding their own resources in open markets—not by legislative and judicial decrees.

"Regulating the housing market," Adam concluded wisely, "is not child's play."

(March 1982)

Cigarette Policies: Actions and Reactions

In economics, there is a law which is not (but should be) known as The Law of Uncertain and Indirect Effects and Delayed and Perverse Con-sequences. The general thrust of the law is: we commonly know little of what we really do when we mess around with the market, and the surprises can be quite the opposite of intended results.

A striking case has been provided by limitations on cigarette adver-tising and mandated health warnings on cigarette packages. The sur-prising tale is told by university economists and newspaper columnists.

The Surgeon General's warning of a causal relation between smok-ing and major health problems may have contributed to the declining per capita cigarette consumption in the United States. But, with fine entrepreneurial flair, the industry has responded well. Indeed, governmental health warnings seem to have helped inspire wise adjustment while protecting the industry, and the advertising restrictions have solidified the standing of existing firms during the adaptations of the industry.

First, if domestic consumption may be gradually curtailed, partly as a consequence of health warnings, then consider foreign markets. Consumption in Japan and in developing countries has been increasing faster than it has been falling in the United States and Europe.

Not only can the tobacco industry adjust geographically, building up a large export market, it can diversify its product domestically. The biggest cigarette firms were warned by the government's health warnings that it would be shrewd to expand quickly and heavily into food products, which, like cigarettes, are sold in supermarkets.

Second, the 1970 prohibition of radio and television ads saved the firms a big bundle in advertising budgets while doing little to curtail the public's consumption. For one thing, eliminating broadcast ads for smoking reduced *anti*-smoking messages, as well. Further, cigarette advertising evidently does not increase total demand for cigarettes; rather, it is a tactic in interbrand competition. That includes competition from new brands. Curtailed advertising not only solidified established firms, it solidified also established brands—so it was made more difficult to introduce new kinds of cigarettes which would be less harmful to health.

Finally, recent court decisions have held that the required government health notices on cigarette packages provide adequate warnings, protecting the firms from product liability claims of estates of possibly prematurely lost customers.

"Quite a record," records one commentator. "The Surgeon General helps the industry avoid complacency, a ban on advertising saves it money, and now government-required warnings save it from bankruptcy." And quite a reminder that reactions from our actions are often uncertain, indirect, delayed, and even perverse.

(October 1987)

Mouse Wisdom:
Licensing and Consumer Protection

"Nonsense!" exclaimed the no-nonsense mouse, Karl. "This foolish magazine article wants to abolish state licensing of plumbers. But most mice know little of plumbing, so they are unable to distinguish good and bad plumbers. Government licensing is necessary to weed out incompetent plumbers and thereby assure consumers of high quality services."

"Licensing may increase the level of quality," agreed the gentle mouse Adam, "if the licensing requirements are professionally sensible. Even then, it does not necessarily mean that consumers benefit."

"Ridiculous," snapped Karl. "How could a higher quality of plumbing services not benefit consumers?"

"Didn't you buy a pair of jogging shoes last week?" asked Adam.

"Yes," said Karl, "but feet and shoes have nothing to do with faucets and sewers."

Adam persevered: "Did you buy the best pair you could find?"

"No," responded Karl. "I'm poor, and they cost too much."

"So you chose not to buy the highest quality running shoe because, in *your* estimation, it wasn't worth the higher price," Adam went on. "You sensibly weighed quality against price, comparing benefit and cost. You did not select the top-of-the-line model because it is too expensive. Instead, you *preferred* to trade some quality in shoes for other goods by buying a less expensive pair of shoes and using the savings for other purchases."

"So I was better off because market *alternatives* allowed me to pick a lower quality shoe that sold at a lower price?"

"Precisely," affirmed Adam. "And the same holds true for consumers of plumbing services. By licensing plumbers, the government may increase the average quality of their services through restricting entry into the business. But by curtailing the supply of plumbers, licensing also increases the price of plumbing services. Consumers are less able to trade some quality for a lower price, as you did with shoes. Competition is reduced, and consumer options are fewer. Consequently, consumers either pay the higher price or attempt repairs themselves or avoid repairs altogether. In any case, the possible protection against poor service is likely to be costly."

"I can see how consumers could be harmed," said Karl, "but I still doubt that they have enough information on their own to avoid being taken by incompetent plumbers."

"Perhaps," said Adam. "But the best answer may be voluntary certification, not mandatory licensing. Voluntary certification—proclaiming satisfaction of certain standards of training and testing—would allow anyone to be a plumber, so it would not reduce the supply and raise the price. Consumers who wanted some assurance of greater quality could then hire certified plumbers and pay a higher price. Others could choose to take their chances with uncertified plumbers and pay a lower price, just as you do with running shoes—and with numerous other commodities. It is a dubious tactic to try to help consumers by restricting their options."

"I guess I was plumb wrong about licensing," concluded Karl.

(February 1987)

Government and Solving Misconceived Problems

We have lots of problems and lots of government. Government can go some way to resolve some problems. But making a sad situation better requires getting straight what the essential nature of the problem is. The adopted remedy must achieve gains greater than the associated costs. And an optimal policy must attain a given good end with minimum costs. Meeting these conditions is not easy even when decision-makers are rewarded for efficiency. And that is not often the case in government.

Heavy exposure to lead is a significant health hazard. But how big a hazard to whom? How is the exposure experienced? What might we do about the problem?

According to the Environmental Protection Agency, lead is a widespread problem, airborne lead from the burning of gasoline in automobiles is a major source of the contamination, and banning lead in gas "will greatly reduce the threat, especially for pregnant women and young children."

It is true, says the American Council on Science and Health, that the bulk of airborne lead comes from use of leaded gas. But it is true, also, that airborne lead is a relatively minor problem. Up to 90 percent of the blood lead level for adults, and over 90 percent for children, comes through food and water, not through the air. Young children, up to age of four, have the highest levels of lead in the blood. Lead poisoning in the very young—concentrated in poor urban areas—appears to stem almost entirely from repeated eating of old leaded house paint and inhaling lead-tainted household dust from peeling old paint. There is virtually no correlation between blood lead levels in children and living close to heavy automobile traffic.

There have been concerns that lead in the blood below levels associated with symptoms of lead poisoning may affect the intelligence and behavior of children. An expert committee of the EPA concluded in 1983 that no relation between low-level lead exposure and children's "neuropsychologic deficits" has been established. But the government agency has found it convenient to ignore the analysis of its own researchers.

The American Council observes that, evidently, "the EPA was determined to reduce lead in gas, even in the absence of scientific evidence of any health benefit to be derived from the reduction." Tinkering with gas will do little good, it diverts attention and resources from efforts which could be useful, and it imposes very substantial costs on gasoline consumers and refiners.

So who gains what from this misleading and expensive bureaucratic foolishness? Government busybodies find glamor from the exercise of power and vindication for an agency which has been accused of laxness and inactivity. Commonly, for Big Brother, the criterion in assessing his activity is not efficiency, and his product is not community wealth. And his rewards are losses for the rest of us.

(August 1985)

Judges, Socialism, and Golden Eggs

The owner of an apartment building wished to tear down his building. A city ordinance required government approval of such action, and the public bureaucrats denied the owner's petition to demolish the structure.

The state supreme court upheld the authority of the city to forbid the owner of the property to destroy the building. The basis of the court's decision was simply that, while the ordinance did infringe on the property owner's rights to use his property, the state has an over-riding concern to maintain the amount of available housing, even when the housing has not been built by the government and does not stand on government land.

Obviously, in a world of interrelated activity, rights to use property must be delimited. But—for those who cherish an individualistic society—the constrictions should be minimal, clear, consistent, and stable, with discretionary government well contained. However, some do *not* prefer a society of individual competitive opportunity and accountability. And even some who do profess philosophic purity are so fearful of markets that they are effective totalitarians. They can always find reasons for imposing consequences different from those which would be generated by free markets—and there is no need for governmental impositions which the community would generate through markets.

But even on its own repugnant grounds—that wise government must supersede the stupid public in directing the use of the community's resources—the court's decision is appalling in its myopia. As is typical with central planners, the court focuses solely on immediate consequences in the short run of the individual case, failing totally to appreciate the indirect effects and ultimate consequences on the general well-being. Whether or not naively, the judges find it convenient to look only at selected aspects of the initial impacts of isolated decrees.

Do the judges actually suppose that production—great in amount, done with efficiency, and directed to the community's preferences—will automatically and persistently occur without incentives and information? Is output simply an inevitable given, decreed by the deity (or by judges) and unaffected by the ambitions and options of the producers? Is the production of wealth—what and how much is produced—unconnected from distribution of the resulting income?

Judges say that it is a good thing to have lots of multiple-unit housing. But the same judges uphold rent controls, restrictions on conversion of apartments into condominiums, prohibitions on adults-only rental, and, now, limitations on leaving the housing business. Investors may not be as compassionate and angelic as judges, but they are not dumb. So with alternative investments available, they will not continue to put scarce resources into an industry severely curtailed by socialism.

Perhaps judges should direct some of their meditations to the source of golden eggs and the physiology of geese.

(February 1985)

Rent Control

Economic Democracy: Refuge for Rogues

Patriotism having fallen into general disfavor, compassion has become the new haven of scoundrels. This is evident in efforts to promote "economic democracy." Greater representation of individual preferences is promised if we permit government officials to control more of our economic activities. But, of course, we get less, not more, representation when decrees of centralized authority replace inducements of the open market.

Rent controls offer a striking example. A common marketing strategy of political candidates is to create an image of compassion— in this case, a fondness for apartment renters, who are much more numerous than apartment owners. In the political market, candidates present themselves as protectors of helpless tenants victimized by cruel landlords. "Vote for me," each implores, "and I'll democratize the marketplace by standing up to these heartless lords of the manor."

The advertising is false: rent controls are based on narrowing, not broadening, the representation of preferences—including the preferences of renters—in the apartment industry. The falsehood can be seen when we acknowledge why rents would otherwise rise in an uncontrolled market. It is not unique greed of landlords that makes rents rise, although they—like the rest of us—prefer a higher price for what they sell. Indeed, the apartment industry is intensely competitive, and landlords know that, if they charge rents above going rates, they will lose wealth from excessive apartment vacancies. Landlords are able to charge higher rents only because going rates for apartments have risen.

Going rates for apartments increase when consumers compete more vigorously with one another for the limited number of apartments in a geographical area. Imagine a city noted for its beauty, temperate climate, sea coast, and proximity to major areas of employment. Many not now living in this city will want to move there, and they will register that preference by offering to pay higher rents. As consumers bid up rents, some tenants will grudgingly leave the city, others will happily move in, and the total number of tenants will increase as apartment builders are persuaded to expand their investments.

But local political candidates sense the payoff from catering to existing tenants whose rents are being bid up. Only existing residents can vote for local officials, so candidates can safely ignore the preferences of prospective tenants who now live elsewhere. Thus do rent controls yield political power in the short run. But in the long run, those controls are perverse and pernicious. Apartment shortages become chronic and mobility of tenants is reduced; further, condominium conversions, reduced maintenance, and less apartment construction erode the city's stock of apartments.

In an uncontrolled market, rents would rise to reflect consumers' real value of apartments, and those higher rents would induce construction of the additional dwellings demanded. But rent controls block many apartment consumers from expressing their preferences. These economically disfranchised consumers are not represented. Only a scoundrel would call that economic democracy!

(December 1983)

Homelessness and Rent Control

It requires little genius to *describe* manifestations of problems in this difficult world. It is much trickier analytically to *diagnose* disease. And if we poorly *account* for woes, we are not likely to *prescribe* appropriate remedies. Indeed, to react inappropriately can make a bad situation worse.

Thus it is with the national blight of homelessness. Measurement of the problem varies enormously, from fewer than 250,000 homeless population in the nation to as many as three million. Still, there *is* a homeless problem. But why? What caused it?

The seemingly obvious reasons are growing unemployment and poverty and cutbacks in federal public housing. But the obvious becomes obscure in light of five years of *declining* unemployment and poverty and a *doubling* of the annual average of federally constructed housing in the first six Reagan years compared to the Carter years.

Putting aside armchair, knee-jerk explanations of homelessness, analyst William Tucker, with the aid of mathematician Jeffrey Simonoff, has conducted an extensive and detailed numerical study. Mr. Tucker has considered fifty major cities. He has compared—with statistical regression techniques—the homeless rates with seven possibly causal variables: poverty, unemployment, public housing, city size, weather, rental-vacancy rates, and presence or absence of rent control.

In his formal analysis, there is virtually no significant correlation between homelessness, on the one hand, and poverty, unemployment, public housing, city size, or temperature, on the other. That is, "differences in homelessness among cities cannot be explained by . . . these factors." That leaves the two variables, rental-vacancy rates and the existence of rent control. Both are independently significant, helping substantially to account for differences in homelessness.

Rent control is much the more important. Further, when vacancy rates and rent control are run *jointly* against homeless rates, the vacancy variable adds nothing in accounting for homelessness. In effect, the vacancy element is subsumed in the rent-control factor, for the nine *rent-controlled cities* in the sample of fifty have the nine *lowest vacancy rates*.

So rent controls accounts for "pathologically low" vacancy rates as well as homelessness. Rent control—diminishing immediate financial incentive and increasing general regulatory uncertainty—greatly reduces housing construction and housing maintenance. And when a jump in rent to now bloated market levels is permitted for a vacated apartment, few people move in the short run, and once-expensive housing does not filter down to low income people in the long run. So we produce, not housing, but housing shortages and minute vacancy rates.

Substantial homelessness is man-made. And men perversely make it mainly with rent control.

(January 1988)

Mouse Wisdom:
Housing, Rent Control, and Vouchers

Moody mouse Karl was in one of his moods of sensitive civility. "Homelessness," he said with commendable compassion, "is a distressing problem."

Mouse Adam, who is always sensitive and civil, agreed. "But," he added, "it helps us deal effectively with problems when we have coherent analytic notions of the nature of the problems."

"The nature of this problem is obvious," snapped Karl quite uncivilly. "We need to make available more housing at low prices."

"Granted," granted Adam, "it would be nice to have *lots* more of *everything* at *zero* prices. But that is simply a simple wish, and daydreaming will not produce apartments and other goods. Where are the apartment buildings to come from?"

"Apartment buildings are to be built by people who build apartment buildings—even if they have to be paid to do so," said surly Karl in sarcastic manner.

"It is not helpful to be surly and sarcastic," cautioned Adam. "Little producing and supplying is done for the sheer love of the activity. Business firms that suffer big enough losses long enough will collapse, and resources that the firm would have used will shift to other producers who find it profitable to buy them for their own production activity."

"So producers cannot produce if they are not paid enough," Karl acknowledged. "But buyers cannot buy if they do not have enough money. That's why we have rent controls: we must keep prices of apartments low so that poor people can rent them."

"We can't have it both ways," admonished Adam. "We must let rents be at market levels, or apartments will not be built and well maintained; but low income people are very hard pressed to pay those market prices. If the community is to subsidize housing for the poor, rent control surely is not the way to do it. Artificially low rents increase the number of apartments demanded while decreasing the rate of their construction. Creating a shortage and intensifying scarcity is a strange strategy. A more sensible approach is housing vouchers—cash given directly to tenants, who then can enter the market with supplemented buying power to compete for apartments of their own choosing."

"It doesn't help to have a voucher if there are no vacant apartments to bid for," grumped Karl.

"But there *will* be apartments at market-clearing rents," Adam pointed out. "Unsurprisingly, the cities with very low vacancy rates and much homelessness—such as San Francisco, Washington, D.C., and New York—are cities with rent control. Government-imposed rent ceilings guarantee the creation and perpetuation of housing shortages. Vouchers in a setting of rent control simply add to the demand for *existing* apartments and thereby increase the shortage; but vouchers in an uncontrolled market increase demand to which apartment builders respond with new construction."

"I suppose," confessed a crestfallen Karl, "that builders respond to signals and incentives. They produce only when it is economically feasible to produce. The market works well when it is permitted to work, and it doesn't work well when we don't let it work well."

(February 1988)

Rent Control: Full, Uniform Subversion or Partial, Selective Subversion?

Advocates of conventional rent control—governmentally imposed maximum rents for apartments—deny the obvious and defend the indefensible. Purported motives are to establish low prices and equitable distribution of available housing. The result is to lower money rents but to raise other expenses and non-money rents, to create shortages, and to allocate rental space largely on the basis of chance and favoritism rather than impersonal market bidding. And, as even most of the commissars admit, suppressing the rate of return on housing investment is not a shrewd tactic for increasing housing supply.

But we are blessed with a self-styled "new generation" of rent controllers. And they boast of the sophistication and finesse with which they subvert open market activities.

The modern tactic, as reviewed by Professor Charles Baird, allows rent increases to cover some rising costs and taxes; it exempts newly constructed rental units from control; it permits market-determined rents when apartments are vacated. The supposed sweet reasonableness of the allegedly new controls approach is more asinine than sensible.

First, the approach dilutes, or partially abandons, the controls program. Uneven, inconsistent, partial foolishness is still foolishness, and no foolishness would be better than some. We cannot reasonably persuade ourselves that it is equitable and efficient to ration *existing* housing through constraints and decrees while rationing *future* housing through higher, market-clearing rents.

Second, a Hong Kong rent ordinance sixty years ago exempted new construction. One result was premature destruction of controlled rental housing and replacement with new, uncontrolled housing. The silliness is then extended by controlling demolition-and-reconstruction, with new constraints to cope with the consequences of earlier constraints.

Third, the existence of controls, even if now confined to present housing, cannot be encouraging to prospective investors in the housing business. What government has done to today's existing housing may be done to tomorrow's existing housing, after resources have been committed. Creating fearful uncertainty is not the way to induce investors to invest and producers to produce.

Fourth, any housing which is constructed will not only be priced higher than old housing—which precludes the equity we presumably seek—but it will be more expensive than it would have been in the absence of controls. As population increases and community income rises, prices of old housing will rise little. Those who already have housing will have no incentive to reduce the amount of housing they demand. Indeed, staying where they are will avoid the large rent increase they would face if they moved. So the increasing demand will center on new housing, and the price of new housing in the *fragmented* market will be higher than it would have been with a *wholly uncontrolled* market.

Imposing rent ceilings is a strange way to provide apartment roofs.

(September 1981)

Agriculture and Energy

Farming and Industrial Policy

A Philosopher of the Left, who bears the title of Professor of Economics at a glamorous university in New England, finds the history of American agriculture over the past half century to be a unique "success story." And purportedly it has been a success because of highly active and pervasive government participation in the industry—through price controls, income support, cartelization of production and distribution, and discriminatory provision of financial and real inputs. Indeed, the philosopher/professor is so enamored of this merger of private and government interests and activities that he wants to extend such mercantilistic, fascistic "cooperative strategy" through all of industry.

Well, many have amusing little ways of analysis, generalization, and prescription. There is, of course, much basis for gratification over the technological advances in our agriculture. And doubtless that progress has derived in part from various governmental machinations and subsidizations. But a fuller assessment uncovers warts along with the hogs—porkbarreling which goes against the grain.

The essence of the farm program has been to supplement farm income, making it both larger than that warranted by economic productivity and more stable than that commonly yielded by nature, technology, and markets. The strategy of the long-established governmental approach to agriculture has been to try to keep prices well above market equilibrium levels and to buffer the industry from market generated adjustment to changing demand and cost realities.

Along with numerous cut-price provisions of physical resources, technological information, and consumption and investment finance, the key tactic has been enormous curtailment of market supply, through either reduced production or government purchase of surpluses induced by artificial prices. We find a consequent record—along with rising technological efficiency—of vast oversupplies and rotting reserves from uncleared markets, of bloated consumer prices and tax bills, of falsified signals and massively misdirected resources, of net farm income in constant prices which has suffered great variance around an appalling downward trend for a decade, and of bureaucracy of incredible bulk. If this be a story of continuing policy success, the genteel mind recoils from contemplation of failure.

With all these economic experimentations, political ploys, and sociological shenanigans, with all these intrusions and curtailments and redirections, consumers, taxpayers, and exporters in general have been hurt; farm laborers and owners of small farms have not been greatly affected; and only large landowners and the legions in the Department of Agriculture have benefited.

But, distressingly, bureaucratic windfalls are quite a sufficient explanation for the vitality and expansion of a misconceived government program.

(July 1983)

Crops and Robbers

The name of the grain is wheat, the third most valuable crop (after corn and soybeans) of prodigious United States agriculture. The yield of wheat per acre has an upward trend over time, and since 1978 the number of harvested acres has increased. This bountiful production is currently faced with weakened demand. Not only is domestic demand anemic, but foreign demand has fallen. Wheat exports in 1982 may be 10 percent smaller than in 1981—and for several years almost two-thirds of output has been exported.

Large output and reduced demand may suggest surplus. In fact, government wheat price-support outlays have swelled—in just the first seven months of fiscal 1982, support payments totaled ten billion dollars, far above original expectations. And, to some, accumulation of surpluses calls for government corrective programs, curtailing output by bribes and regulations and hyping sales by subsidies. A conspicuous business magazine accepts such tactics without question: "Clearly," it asserts, "the Administration will have to use a combination of production limits and export promotion to reduce U.S. surpluses."

This is nefarious nonsense. It implies that there is no market process of equilibration, that there will be no market adaptation by producers and consumers, no market reallocation of resources or redirection of purchases, and no generation of a market-clearing price without ad hoc interventions and directives by Big Brother. But there was an efficient market mechanism of adjustment in this country before government assumed the role of Economic Deity.

Indeed, it is the ineptitude of government which creates farm surpluses. A surplus—like a shortage—is a price phenomenon. If the price of a commodity is pegged above the market-clearing level at which buyers are willing to buy just the amount sellers are willing to sell, then, of course, sellers want to sell more than buyers want to buy. The excess supply over demand is, by definition, a surplus.

To correct a surplus, remove its cause. Unpeg the artificial disruptive government minimum price, and let the market perform its function of determining prices which reflect realities of consumer demands and producer costs. As the demand and cost realities change, prices will change—and farmers, who are neither stupid nor lazy—will adjust to the changing prices.

To the extent that government programs have not misdirected farmers, they have adjusted readily to changing circumstances. Changes in wheat prices—up and down—have been followed by changes in the same direction in wheat acreage. Such behavior is predictable because it is sensible.

But good economic sense has a bad press, and political types consider it bad tactics for themselves. So presumably we shall continue to play around with the government game of crops and robbers, subsidizing waste and muffling the voice of the consumer in directing farm production.

(August 1982)

Sugar and Bittersweet Charity

In an open world market, the price of sugar would be about three cents a pound. Most of the world does buy and sell sugar at that price, and the market is cleared: at that price, buyers buy all they want, sellers sell all they want, and the amount demanded equals the amount supplied.

But three cents a pound has been deemed not sweet enough a price for the United States sugar industry. So our government—the guardian of our liberties and the promoter of our general well-being—has largely segregated the United States from the world sugar market. Through import taxes and quotas, imports have been so restricted that the price of sugar here is well over twenty cents, some seven times the price in the rest of the world.

Now, when a given commodity sells at a given time for greatly different prices in different markets, it requires little devious imagination to see the possibility of cashing in. Simply buy sugar in the general world market at three cents and sell it in the protected American market at over twenty cents.

Of course, such initiative is officially frowned on. After all, the reason why the price differential exists is the severe curtailment of imports. To revert to importing all we want would sour the scheme, and our sugar prices would fall back to the world level. Buying more sugar abroad than is sanctioned by government is illegal as well as fattening.

But the *purpose* of restrictions is to keep people from doing what they otherwise would do. And if the incentive to do illegal things is very great, people will break the law. A price differential of 7-to-1 provides very great incentive. So some United States sellers of sugar may be guilty of smuggling, evading quotas and defrauding the government of tariff receipts.

While it is not nice to applaud naughtiness, the incentive for the smuggling stems from the government's subsidy to sugar growers. Price supports and import restrictions purportedly are required for an "orderly" sugar market. These measures of control and subsidization supposedly protect both consumers and producers from wild price fluctuations.

But consumers do not gain from being fleeced. And many industries endure variations in demand for their products. Retail stores commonly do half their annual business during the Christmas season, but they are not bankrupted by low sales of other months. Fresh fruits and vegetables—which cannot be stored as well as sugar—experience large price changes without disappearance of suppliers. Producers and refiners of sugar can protect themselves from unpredictable price changes by contracting for future deliveries at prices agreed upon today.

The government is attempting to root out fraud in the importation of sugar. The basic fraud is the sugar subsidy program itself. The program gives consumers higher prices, it wastefully distorts the operation of the market, and it provides incentive to violate harmful import restrictions. Such is the bitter cost of government's sweet charity.

(August 1985)

Energy Emergencies and the Marketplace

The Reagan Administration has stated its energy policy. It declares that the market, not the government, should guide and coordinate the production and distribution of our nation's energy, even during emergencies caused by suddenly shrinking supplies of world energy.

Inevitably, a stance stemming from elemental economic principles and a reliance on market operations has been criticized as not "really . . . a policy and certainly" not "a plan." In many circles, even a policy and certainly a plan requires government to do things. Faced by abrupt reduction in oil imports, "only the federal government," we are told, "is in a position to set priorities . . . Only with careful planning would such priorities be fair and efficient." So goes a typical newspaper editorial.

Schizophrenically, the editorial acknowledges that the "marketplace accomplishes economic wonders" in usual circumstances. And it is conceded that "the allocation schemes imposed by Washington during the severe oil shortages in 1973 and 1979 only made things worse." Ah, "but the dismal record does not mean that the job cannot be done right. . . ." So, in time of troubles, the faint of heart and the weak of comprehension easily forsake the wonder-working market and repair with whimpers to the bureaucrats who have persistently failed them.

Only the market can cope efficiently with sudden short falls in energy supplies. If less oil is available, then consumption must be curtailed: priorities must indeed be set. But if those priorities are to be efficient, then the oil must be used only for those purposes most valued by the community. The market, not government, identifies these most valuable uses.

Smaller supplies of oil cause consumers to bid up prices of oil and oil products. The quantity of oil products demanded falls, because consumers will shun uses which they value less than the higher prices. Since those higher prices reflect the community's increased value of oil products, consumers unwittingly eliminate uses which they individually value less than does the community. Less valuable uses are given up in order to satisfy more valuable ones. The marketplace thus expresses the community's priorities, and scarce supplies are used efficiently.

Some will want to contravene these economically determined priorities, however, by using government power. They will cry that higher prices are "unfair" and bemoan their unfilled "needs." Government officials then can impose price controls in order to cope with the emergency. With controlled prices, shortages result, and bureaucrats begin to allocate energy supplies. Those with sufficient political muscle are able to obtain more energy than they would otherwise buy in the free market. Their less valuable uses are satisfied at the expense of the community's more valuable ones.

This—arbitrary controls, inevitable shortages, and allocation by decree—is the careful, fair, and efficient political planning which some editorial writers recommend.

(August 1981)

OPEC and the Complications of Cartels

The course of true love has never been wholly smooth among the thirteen nations of OPEC. Still, the cartel, with its price- and production-control maneuvers, was a mighty force in the 1970s.

OPEC is not dead, but it is now a Samson with a crew cut. Its difficulties have steadily grown since 1979. It now reacts to rather than dictates to the world petroleum market. And the reactions are not entirely peacefully orchestrated within the family. Each member would like to maintain sales at high prices; it has become apparent that either sales or prices will have to be reduced; but the members differ on how *much* to adjust sales or price and on how to *distribute* the adjustment costs among themselves.

It is not surprising that the power of OPEC would be diluted over time. The rest of the world has curtailed consumption, developed alternative supplies, and accumulated strategic reserves. And it is not surprising that, with the dilution, members of the group would break ranks on how to make disagreeable adjustments to deteriorating circumstances.

In broad outline, the rise and decline of OPEC is consistent with the troubled history of cartels. Contrary to common mythology, cartels have *not* been readily formed and highly effective over prolonged periods, and the world of commerce is *not* dominated by beady-eyed, cigar-chomping, rapacious cartelists.

It is not easy to organize a cartel, melding highly autonomous organizations into a monopolistic facsimile. There are markets to divide, prices to set, and production quotas to assign. Successful operation is even harder than initial organization. Members must remain persuaded that they enjoy net benefits from submersion in collusion compared to acting as independent agents. The more profitable the collusive efforts, the greater the incentive for outsiders to seek admission or to organize their own club or individually to compete. The more numerous the participants and the more lucrative the tightening of the screws on consumers, the greater the temptation for individual members to cheat—and the greater the fear of each that some *other* member will cheat.

Long-term survival of the cartel has two fundamental requirements: first, cheating by a member on the stipulated prices, outputs, and markets must be detectable; second, detected cheating must be adequately punishable without leading to a break-up of the cartel. Because of competition—overt competition from outside or *sub rosa* competition within—effective cartels cannot expect a long life.

OPEC has cracked its big whip longer than have most. Many initially doubted that it would last as long as a decade. The longevity may be attributed largely to the cartelists being governments rather than corporations, to the tribal emotionalism which stoked stubborn ambitions, and to inept responses by oil-importing countries. But even OPEC has found competition of the market to be a formidable foe of collusion.

(December 1984)

Nuclear Power and the Costs of Saving Lives

We say that human life is of infinite value. But obviously we do not do all that is possible to diminish risk. Less obviously, efforts and resources which are directed to safety are often directed badly. So we commonly talk foolishly and act irrationally. This is a message from distinguished physicist Bernard Cohen.

How much does it cost to save (that is, to prolong) a life? Millions of childhood deaths from disease and malnutrition could be averted each year in the poorest nations at a cost per life saved as low as fifty dollars.

Lives in the United States cost more to save. Still, screening for some types of *cancer* costs as little as $20,000 to $60,000 per life saved; treatment by kidney dialysis runs to some $400,000 per life saved. *Highway* fatalities can be reduced in various ways which vary greatly in expense: the cost per life saved through improving traffic signs is about $30,000; it costs ten times as much to save a life with turn lanes and flashing lights at railroad crossings; all the measures of traffic safety average $150,000 per life saved.

Many ways of saving lives from cancer and automobile accidents, while not inexpensive, are highly cost-effective in comparison to saving lives from radiation and reactor accidents in the nuclear industry. The cost per life saved in management of radioactive waste is as much as $300 *million*—and, while huge costs are borne now, the few lives saved are those thousands of years in the future, by which time there may well be either a cure for cancer or no people.

The safety costs of nuclear reactors are even more astonishing: on reactor safety we are spending $2.5 *billion* per life saved. Further, the greater safety costs imposed on construction of nuclear plants have induced utilities to build more coal-burning power plants. And coal-burning plants are notoriously more harmful to health than are nuclear facilities: when we build a coal plant instead of nuclear, some 900 to 1,000 additional people are thereby condemned to an early death.

If as many as sixty nuclear plants are completed, we will have spent at least an extra $100 billion to save perhaps *fifty* lives—and $100 billion spent on cancer screening and highway safety could save something like *one million* lives.

Why this insanity—this loss of contact with reality—in allocating resources? Well, politicians respond to public concern; irrational concern about nuclear power stems from media coverage; and the entertainment types posing as journalists attract audiences—and thus advertising revenue—by hysterical misrepresentation of esoteric hazards.

Professor Cohen believes we pay too high a price for such sophomoric Halloween charades.

(January 1988)

Property Rights

Different Property Rights and Different Communities

Some things can be costlessly shared: my enjoyment of a sunset does not mean that there is less sunset for you. Even some things produced with scarce resources, such as radio broadcasts, can be consumed by one person without leaving less for others—although that raises problems of determining who is to bear the costs.

Many things are not consumed in common: a banana eaten by me is one less banana available to the rest of you. And even the massive outpouring of the American economy falls far short of providing everyone all of everything he wants. Since we want more than we can have, and since much of what I get is at the expense of everyone else, scarcity implies competition. As put by the great Thomas Hobbes three hundred years ago: ". . . if any two men desire the same thing, which nevertheless they cannot both enjoy, they become enemies." So, inevitably, Hobbes determined, life is a ceaseless struggle for power.

How can this "perpetual and restless desire of power" be channeled and conducted in a manner consistent with gentility and prosperity? "The fundamental economic problem within *any* society," contemporary economist Louis De Alessi points out, "is to evolve— whether by design, accident, or some combination or both—a set of rules for channeling competition and resolving conflict. These rules, embedded in a framework of formal and informal institutions, . . . sanction the range of permissible behavior by specifying the *nature of the rights* that individuals may hold to the use of resources . . . to the *income* that the resources generate, and to the *transferability* of the resources to others. The resulting system of property rights determines how *prices* . . . are set and, thus, how the benefits and the harms resulting from a decision are allocated between the decisionmaker and others."

Every community will have, and be largely defined by, a set of rights to use of property. Most of us happily accept, even when we do not sensibly promote, broad options in using our own resources in producing income and in using received income to bid for the outputs of others who compete for our favor. But most communities of today and of history have been characterized by ground rules which limit options of the populace and concentrate power in Big Brother. With little room for individual use of personal wealth, with few alternatives in what can be done and how it can be done, there is little linkage between productivity and reward—and thus there is little productivity.

Freedom to choose may be rather an acquired taste, as evidenced by uneasy flounderings of some immigrants from societies where choice and initiative are severely limited. Freedom certainly can be lost, through both silliness and subversion. And perhaps even the love of freedom eventually dies when freedom itself is suppressed as private rights to use of property are sufficiently supplanted by totalitarian rules of property.

(March 1988)

Property Rights and Managerial Behavior

There is, we are told, more than one way to skin a cat. And when tactical options are different, tactical choices will be different.

These propositions concerning options and tactics help to explain some behavior of business managers, as analyzed by economists Armen Alchian and Reuben Kessel. It is a story of different adaptations to different opportunities provided by different property rights.

Owners of a business firm hire a manager. The manager did not take the job out of altruistic concern for the well-being of the stockholders. He is interested in pleasing the stockholders, but only as a means of keeping his job and obtaining greater rewards for himself. His fundamental objective and the essential criterion in determining his activities is his own condition: he seeks—as do the owners of the firm who hired him and the customers who buy the products of the firm—to attain maximum personal well-being.

One road to bettering one's condition is more money income. And some business managers will be rewarded with more income by increasing the profitability of their firms. When there is close linkage between market success of the firm and his own income, the manager has much incentive to run a tight ship, calculating shrewdly in directing the firm's use of resources.

But the ground rules—the property rights—can be different. A state-regulated monopoly, such as the local gas company, is confined to a maximum rate of return. And other firms, although not formally regulated, can feel governmental pressure—even if only by amorphous antitrust threat—to restrain profits to levels deemed civilized by populist standards. If there are imposed limits on profit making, then the manager has that avenue to personal betterment partially closed. With significant profit limitations, there is little point in striving for a more efficient operation, and the linkage is weakened between his own productive performance and his own net worth.

Although one path to greater personal well-being for the manager of a regulated or circumscribed firm is narrowed, there are secondary tactics. If he cannot garner greater take-home rewards through increasing the profits of the firm, he can consume wealth in other forms. If the firm has reached the profit ceiling, then he may spend more of the company's money for frosting on the cake—thicker rugs and fancier luncheons in a bigger boardroom. And he can adopt personnel policies which add to his life's fulfillment even if they detract from economic efficiency—not hiring, for example, lieutenants of the wrong religion, nationality, and gender. When more profits and personal income are not at stake, bigotry costs less and is consumed in larger quantities.

We should not be astonished by such perquisites and prejudices. Managers who indulge in them are neither less rational nor more corrupted than their profit-maximizing brethren. It is, rather, a matter of adapting to available options. People act differently, not so much because of differing genes and gentility, but because they operate under different property rights.

(April 1983)

Private Property and Pollution

Everyone who is sensitive, cultured, and very anxious to do good knows that the free-market economists have sold out to Big Business, and that Big Business, in turn, delights in pillaging and raping the landscape, the seascape, and the atmosphere in its frenetic search for an extra buck. But Professor Dwight Lee provides quite a different—and vastly more sophisticated—picture.

The problem of environmental pollution, Professor Lee explains, is fundamentally an economic problem, that is, a problem of scarcity. Pollution is a cost of living and producing; reduced production is a cost of cleaner and more attractive environment. There is an unavoidable trade-off between man-made goods and environmental purity. How much of the one are we to sacrifice at the margin to obtain more of the other? What is the optimal combination of production and pollution?

We seek a community solution which reflects individual preferences. Individuals must be able to *compare* their relative assessments of benefits and costs; and they must be able to *communicate* in such manner as to provide both the *information* and the *incentives* required to direct scarce resources into their highest valued activities.

The policy problem in dealing with pollution is *not* the result of the use of private property in pursuit of private advantage; the problem stems from too *little* reliance on private property. We have excessive pollution, not because of private property and the market, but because inadequately specified private rights to use of property dilute and limit the workings of the market. And the actions of the polluters reflect, not unique or extraordinary greed, but rational individual adaptation to a situation of deficient effective assignment of property rights.

The role of conveying accurate information and efficiently coordinating activities of self-interested individuals is performed splendidly by open markets to the extent that *private property* prevails. For well-defined and enforced ownership rights in resources make possible mutually beneficial *exchange*: you can sell only what you own and buy only what is owned by someone else. And uncoerced exchange will be conducted at market-clearing prices, which reflect the worth of goods not only to their owners, but also to others in the market.

Automobiles are private property, as are the gasoline and maintenance services, which keep them rolling. People rationally buy and sell such assets. But operating a car creates pollutants which are emptied into the air—and air is not privately owned. Small wonder that, in tooling down the road, we accept the gains of automobile transportation but ignore the pollution costs. We weigh the costs of the car, the gas, and the maintenance against their benefit, but we do not have to buy the air, so we treat pollution as being free.

In the absence of saleable property rights, there are no markets and no prices to induce and guide efficient use of resources. The costs of pollution are not fully weighed, and individually rational activity in a defective institutional arrangement results in excessive pollution.

(January 1983)

Fun, Games, and Property Rights

Scarcity is one of the few things we have in abundance. All our straining, striving, competing, and colluding will not yield an "economy of abundance." Any economy must be an economy of economizing.

Choices have to be made on which things to produce and how big a slice of the social pie a given individual will receive. But how are the decisions on use of scarce resources to be made? Who decides what, how, and according to what criteria?

One of society's critical questions is: Who will be permitted to attend the Rose Bowl football game? Who gets to see the game, and how do they get to see it? On such a momentous matter—and there are tens of thousands of people and hundreds of thousands of dollars involved—one could hope for efficiency in ticket distribution. The actual manner of distribution doubtless serves some purposes—otherwise the procedure would be changed—but economic efficiency is not one of them.

There is, according to a newspaper account, a Tournament of Roses Association and a Board of Directors of Pasadena. The Association manages the Rose Bowl and the Rose parade, but the city directors vote on matters concerning the bowl and the parade. Neither the members of the Association nor the directors *directly* share in the profits or losses of the Association. So for them there is no personal payoff for efficiency.

Reward for efficiency is not the only way to receive pay. Each of the city directors is given four tickets to the parade, the game, and a luncheon, and they are permitted to buy another one hundred tickets at face value. These tickets are not supposed to be resold at a higher price, but some do end up in the hands of others at much higher prices. The story does not relate what the Association managers gain—

except the continuing goodwill of the city government and the con-tinuing reputation of good guys who charge less than market-clearing prices for seats.

What are the consequences of breaking the linkage between managerial efficiency and managerial reward?

First, there are the frustrations of the ticket shortage. Many who are willing to pay more than the low stipulated price cannot get a ticket.

Second, there is the indignity of the helter-skelter, first-come-first-served scrambling for the tickets sold by the Association and the two involved athletic conferences—another manifestation of the shortage which reflects pricing tickets arbitrarily low.

Third, since all 101,000 tickets could be sold at higher prices, total sales revenue is less than it could be.

Finally, while the managers have no incentive to maximize receipts, they can use resources which are not theirs to enhance per-sonal prestige and power.

These are not evil or irrational people. But the ground rules under which they act make very strong the ties which bind the old boys.

The existing property rights do not conduce efficiency, but they are not likely to be changed by those who are comfortable with them.

(January 1988)

Mouse Wisdom:
Old Movies and the Color Green

"You know," mouse Karl assured an unknowing mouse Adam, "I am a sensitive soul and an artistic artiste. And," he added, "I am currently offended."

"Whatever your sensitivity and artistic credentials," responded Adam, "you are often offended. What's the problem this time?"

"Computer colorizing of film!" exclaimed Karl. "Some old black-and-white movie classics have been artificially colorized. And some Hollywood stars and directors have decried such colorizing as 'moral-ly unacceptable' and 'sinful,' a 'cheesy symbol of greed.' I am proud to take my stand with those of Hollywoodian virtue."

"I confess," confessed Adam, "that I have associated the image makers and script readers with vanity more than virtue. And I find it about as hard to take them seriously on this issue as when they furrow their little brows and speak ever so seriously on political economy, physics, and foreign policy."

"How gauche!" recoiled Karl. "This is a very strong moral issue. Works of art are not to be mutilated. You ought not to be able to buy a Rembrandt painting, cut it to fit a frame, update its background with polka dots, and then hang it in a gallery as a Rembrandt."

"I do have enormous respect for the work of Rembrandt," Adam said, "and it would be utterly reprehensible to mangle or destroy it. But quite aside from the problems of judging Rembrandt masterpieces and movies by comparable criteria, the analogy is highly imperfect."

"Well," conceded Karl, "Rembrandt pictures do not move, and moving pictures do. But messing with works of art is not to be condoned in any case."

"There *is* a basic difference in the two cases," Adam insisted. "There is only one copy of any Rembrandt picture, but we can make any number of movie prints. And if we color some of those prints, we still can have copies of the original black-and-white version. Colorizing does not *destroy* the original work; instead, it provides an *alternative* to the original."

"No one," pouted Karl, "should prefer such an alternative."

"Even for you, that is being pretty precious," said Adam with some impatience. "Commercial products are made for the paying public, and the public is to express its own preferences. That public has already paid off the directors and actors who made the movie. Those individuals have been handsomely compensated for their work, and they do not own—and never have owned—the film. Those who now do own the film can reasonably try to market their asset most profitably. To make the most profit is to satisfy best the desires of customers—and it appears that those customers like colorization. It is not shameful desecration to provide alternatives to a market in which people can make their own choices. It is not inherently sinful to increase market options. Professor Allen taught me that."

"I conclude," said a now wiser Karl, "that William Allen is a better economist than is Woody Allen."

(July 1987)

Mouse Wisdom:
Private vs. Public Sports Facilities

"I easily relate to professional jocks," confided mouse Karl as he pulled himself up to his full two inches and admired his two-ounce physique.

"Such a macho specimen," his mouse friend Adam gently responded, "should find of special interest a study by Professor Dean Baim, at Pepperdine University, of privately and publicly owned sports arenas and stadiums."

"Private and public, indeed," snorted Karl. "The presence of a professional team is advertising for the host city, provides variety to its cultural life, solidifies community spirit, and contributes to the local economy. So the city should make its own investment in arenas and stadiums. Private fast-buck types should not get a slice of the municipal pie."

"Your premise about the broad worth of sports teams to the community probably is well taken," Adam agreed. "But your conclusion that, therefore, the arenas and stadiums should be built, owned, and administered by government is analytically a *non sequitur*—and empirically badly founded."

"Here we go with the old dogma," groaned Karl. "For you, private property is always nicer than governmental."

"It is not mindless dogma," corrected Adam. "It is a conclusion stemming from careful review of the real-world situation. Professor Baim has compared public and private arenas and stadiums by several criteria—and the facilities which are privately owned or operated are consistently superior."

"What are the criteria and comparisons?" asked a wary Karl.

"Construction costs, for one thing," replied Adam. "After correcting for inflation, the cost-per-seat of *publicly constructed arenas* has been nearly 50 percent greater than those privately contructed. The difference is even *greater* for *stadiums*, with public construction costs approaching two and one-half times more than private. And private facilities typically take better care of patrons and do so more economically, illustrated by providing appropriate parking. Further, the facilities—especially the relatively versatile arenas—are used more fully during the year by private managers."

"The numbers may happen to make private ownership look good," grumbled Karl, "but you surely are not claiming that private managers are purer in heart."

"No," agreed Adam, "but the ground rules, the options, the incentives differ for the two groups of managers. Private directors and decisionmakers, in contrast to those in government, see a direct, strong linkage between their performance and their reward: it pays them personally to be efficient."

Karl grunted his last grump: "Economics is not everything. Don't forget the broad community advantages of having a local team."

"On that consideration, too, private ownership is attractive," Adam responded. "Teams have been much less likely to leave facilities they have owned: 'loyalty' to a community is not enhanced by having to rely on renting a public arena or stadium."

Karl conceded. "Rah, rah, rah," he softly said.

(December 1985)

Productivity, Competition, and Wage Determination

Politics and Productivity

Customary politics and good economics are like oil and water. For economics reveals the costs we must bear to obtain what we want; but politics conceals them by pretending that government can disgorge goodies without cost. Sugary promises of something for nothing sell much better than bitter analyses of uncomfortable costs. No wonder popular politics stinks when sound economics sinks.

Good economics has certainly sunk to the bottom in this year's presidential campaign. Consider how candidates play to Americans' fears about their future wages.

One aspirant charges that our country "is caught between cheap labor at home and slave labor abroad." Workers are oppressed by their employers, he insists, so government must assert workers' rights if wages are to rise. That is, the key to higher wages is government intervention in labor markets. And the key to government intervention in labor markets is the candidate's election. The message is simple: "Vote for me, and I will give you higher wages."

It is a bogus message. Government cannot grant a higher level of wages. That is because higher wages do not depend on somehow obtaining a bigger slice of the existing economic pie. Labor compensation now receives almost three-fourths of national income, but after-tax corporate profits receive less than 4 percent. In order for wages generally to rise, the size of the pie obviously must grow. But it is a pie of output, and making it bigger requires increasing the productivity of work. The only way for people in the aggregate to earn—and consume—more is for them to produce more.

Employers and employees share the common interest of increasing productivity—a mutual interest which political types try desperately to conceal. They prefer to cast employer and employee as incompatible adversaries. This preference reflects the fact that there are so many more workers than employers: more votes can be had by defending legions of workers against an enemy more imagined than real.

But a glance at our economic history suggests how wage gains have come from mutual efforts of workers and businesses. Encouraged by the prospect of greater earnings, businesses increase their technology and capital goods. Then, armed with new techniques and tools, workers are able to produce more output per hour of work. And as businesses bid more intensely for increasingly productive labor, they bid up the general level of wages.

As a result, changes in *real hourly labor compensation* closely track changes in *output per hour of work*, whether hourly output is rising or falling. If real wage rates are to grow, then the productivity of work also must grow. And productivity growth requires encouragement of more investment in search of profit. But that is less likely when politics does not mix with sound economics.

(April 1988)

Employment and Wages, Competition and Fairness

The editorial writer was speaking about employment and wages.

There is something wrong with "the system," he said, for there are more workers than jobs: "there is never a surplus of jobs," and the unemployment rate is invariably greater than zero. Even those who have jobs, he added, are not likely to be paid what they are worth, for the market is "always a buyer's market," tilted in favor of the employer. Daddy Warbucks can decide by whim how many and whom to hire and on what terms, while the poor but honest worker can only accept whatever is offered.

The unemployment rate *is* greater than zero. The way the measurement is made guarantees that. An officially unemployed person is one who declares himself to be part of the labor force—he wants a job and purports to be looking for one—but does not have a job. But both the notion of "the labor force" and the notion of "unemployed" are based heavily on estimates, preferences, and tactics of people. A person may falsely declare himself to be a job candidate to qualify for welfare aid. He may be interested in a job but price himself out of the market with an unrealistic assessment of either his productivity or of

demand for his sort of services. He may be sensible but feel inadequately informed about market options and is currently searching for
information—and the more generous is unemployment compensation,
the longer he is inclined to search.

So there is always some unemployment—thank goodness. If
everyone is always to be employed, a worker could not quit a job for
any reason, including investment of time and foregone current income
to seek a better job.

The problem of unemployment is not jobs being fewer than
workers. On *some* terms, a job is *always* available in an open market.
But a wage and the hours of labor required to earn it can be so un-
rewarding that a person is rational to decline the job offer and remain
unemployed.

The more valuable the worker, the higher the bid for his services.
The high wage offer reflects rational concern of employers for their
well-being, not a delicate sense of altruism or fairness. If you are technologically efficient in performing services which the community
values highly, and if relatively few other workers are so productive,
you will prosper. It is competition among the hateful employers that
raises wages, for they must bid against each other for labor to supply
demanded products and thereby earn rewards. And it is competition
among the lovable fellow workers that holds wages down by providing alternatives to employers.

But editorial writers rarely applaud efficient coordination of free
people through open market calculation and competition—or realize
that without open markets, there will be neither freedom nor efficient
coordination. Competition in serving the community through market
activity based on productivities and preferences is so gamey and unfair! Editorial writers of sensitivity deny scarcity and condemn competition—and whimper about unfairness.

(April 1985)

Weeds and Workers

Myths multiply in economics like weeds in a garden. Indeed, myths,
unlike weeds, are often cultivated. An example is the popular notion
that American workers are suffering from a falling standard of living.

A glance at a few statistics seems to support the belief. Real average hourly earnings—that is, hourly earnings adjusted for inflation—were about 6 percent lower in 1986 than at their peak level in 1972. And real annual wages and salaries per employed person were slightly lower in 1986 than they were in 1972.

But economist William Dickneider points out that each of these three measures of earnings ignores the fringe benefits that have become an important part of workers' compensation. Indeed, during the last few decades, the relative size of supplements to wages and salaries more than tripled, rising from about 5 percent of total labor compensation in 1950 to some 17 percent in 1986. So American workers have been receiving a much larger fraction of their pay as health insurance, retirement benefits, and other employer-provided supplements.

By ignoring these substantial supplements, the measures of workers' pay present a greatly distorted picture of earnings. When supplements are excluded, real annual earnings per employed worker averaged a bit less in 1986 than in 1972. During this period, however, real supplements per employed person increased almost 50 percent. When these benefits are included in workers' pay, today's earnings are the highest ever.

To be sure, the negative real growth of national output from 1979 to 1982 took a bite out of living standards of American workers. Since 1982, however, real average labor compensation has been rising again. Despite the renewed growth, the increase is small compared to that of the 1960s, when its growth was about three times faster than that recorded since 1982.

No doubt, the slower increase in workers' earnings has its roots in the anemic growth of labor productivity. In order to receive more hourly pay, employees must also produce more output per hour of work. But from 1972 to 1982, output per hour of work slowed considerably, both here and abroad. While not fully recouping its historical vigor, our productivity growth picked up after 1982. Not surprisingly, the growth of average real labor compensation also increased, but it too has not regained all of its past strength.

Although the standard of living of American workers is not rising as fast as it once did, it is not declining, contrary to the belief of many. Still, the weeds of myth persist. And with their persistence, they entangle our economic thinking and our political agitation.

(May 1987)

Labor Unions

Union Wages, Union Woes

Labor unions are in big trouble. During the last decade, their membership has plummeted 16 percent, their ranks thereby falling from 25 percent of the labor force in 1975 to less than 18 percent today.

As the primary reason for this decline, many cite the so-called deindustrialization of America. Manufacturing industries, such as steel and autos, were once union strongholds, they argue, but foreign competition has sapped their vitality. As union manufacturing jobs have declined, non-union service jobs have replaced them. Falling union membership is thus described as an indicator of America's withering industrial strength.

Not so, say two economists at the University of Pennsylvania. Professors Peter Linneman and Michael Wachter present evidence showing that unions have helped greatly to produce their own woes.

The economists studied changes in our economy's employment and wages between 1973 and 1984. During this time, union wages compared to non-union wages rose to an all time high. As the union relative-wage premium soared, union employment contracted in almost all industries. It fell in construction, mining, durable and non-durable manufacturing, retail and wholesale trade, transportation, finance, insurance, and real estate. The only major exceptions were areas—government and other services—where the union wage premium did not increase.

Over the same period, non-union employment increased in all industries except non-durable manufacturing. The economists conclude that "the shift from goods to service-producing sectors cannot be an important part of the 'unions-in-decline' story. The so-called deindustrialization of America appears to be a union-specific phenomenon...." Indeed, they deduce that more than half of the decline in unions' share of total national employment was due to increases in union wage premiums during this time.

Further, the upward trend in union wage premiums seems to have continued, contrary to the popular view that unions have made significant wage concessions since 1980. In actuality, recent collective bargaining has had "little visible impact" on the wage premium. Instead, so-called wage concessions have only postponed or reduced increases in union wages.

The observed relationship between union wages and union employment demonstrates the fundamental law of demand: higher wage rates reduce the amount of labor demanded, and lower wage rates increase the amount demanded. As union wages have risen relative to non-union wages, union employment has predictably declined while non-union employment has risen.

The ability to sell any good or service depends on the price charged. By stubbornly ignoring this elemental fact, labor unions continue to generate much of their misery.

(November 1986)

Government Unions and the Right to Strike

"We who are pure in heart," purred mouse Karl to his friend Adam, "usually can find a silver lining in a disturbing cloud. Although labor unions generally have not prospered in recent years, public employee unions have done very well."

"Which is cloud and which is lining may be subject to debate," mused mouse Adam. "True, private sector unions have been losing membership and gaining only small wage increases, in contrast to unions of government workers. And apparently an increasing share of strikes has been by public employees."

"Workers are workers," Karl bristled. "The right to strike is an essential ingredient of a free society. In equity, it must be as much a right for the public worker as for the private."

"I suggest," suggested Adam, "that 'equity' has many facets. Public and private unions exist in different circumstances, so it is not outrageous to permit them different legal strike privileges. Even when denied the right to strike—a denial which is less and less effective— public workers have some advantages."

"Government employees are dedicated public servants," sniffed Karl.

"Doubtless," Adam dryly doubted. "But federal pay is higher than, and state and local pay is rising relative to, private pay, and public job security is greater. And there are basic problems in justifying government worker strikes."

"You want public employees to be second-class citizens," charged Karl.

"No, I don't," assured Adam. "But consider some critical considerations. First, government must be sovereign, the final repository of public authority. Government itself is to be severely contained by constitutional construction and community consent, but it cannot permit its own operations to be shut down by coercive pressure of union officers.

"Second, economic survival is a different process for public and private workers. In the market, consumers have options: buy or not buy, or buy from this seller instead of that. Sellers prosper only by successful competition in pleasing buyers while adequately containing cost. But government goes on collecting heavy taxes irrespective of consumers' demands—even when some service is not provided at all because of a strike. And if a government wage settlement cannot be financed with current tax revenue, just increase taxes or (in the case of the federal government) create more money out of thin air.

"Finally, there will be pressure—both from the community and within government—to acquiesce in budget-busting wage agreements. For government has made itself the sole supplier of many important services. And when taxing and monopolizing government does surrender to union demands, bureaucrats are comforted to find that their domain now has more workers getting more pay."

"So," said a cowed Karl, "government differs from the market, so the position of government workers differs from that of business workers, so it is not astonishing that the rights to strike should differ."

(September 1986)

Mouse Wisdom: Wages, Stress, and Strikes

The two mice who live in my office have had another discussion. Karl was upset by a strike of the cat controllers.

"I don't blame them," Karl said to Adam. "Cat controllers endure a lot of pressure keeping track of all those beastly felines."

"You mean the controllers don't think they are paid enough to compensate for that stress?" asked Adam.

"That's right, and they are right," snapped Karl.

"Did someone compel cat controllers to take those jobs?" Adam continued.

"No," said Karl, "but that has nothing to do with their unsatisfactory wages."

"Well," Adam mused, "the amount of stress cat controllers must endure is unattractive to most mice. But many jobs have undesirable attributes when compared to others, as individuals have different aptitudes and inclinations. People allocate themselves and terms of work are adjusted until labor markets are cleared. Disagreeable—as well as agreeable—attributes of jobs and alternatives of workers are reflected in wage rates."

"That's why the controllers are striking," exclaimed Karl. "They want wages that will compensate them for the pressure they bear."

Adam tweaked his whiskers. "The fact that controllers have voluntarily chosen their jobs proves that their wages do compensate them for their stressful work. If a mouse worker believed that his wage did not make up for his best sacrificed job, or for his foregone leisure, or for his enduring unattractive work, he would not accept the job."

Karl disagreed: "I still think that cat controllers deserve higher wages."

"We all think we 'deserve' higher wages," responded Adam. "You are always complaining that you should be paid more at the cheese factory, but you continue to work there because your wage is sufficient for you to let your employer pollute your life with work. Wages are prices of labor services, and prices are not determined by what sellers think they 'deserve.' Like other prices, wages are determined by the quantity of services workers willingly make available and the quantity demanded by employers."

"But," said Karl, "the strike shows that cat controllers will not willingly make their services available at the wages they now receive. By your own reasoning, Adam, I am correct. Controllers are withholding their services because their wages do not compensate them for their stressful jobs."

"That's not correct," answered Adam. "The strike is a *collective political* action designed to withhold services that workers would otherwise continue to offer as *individuals*. If individual mice thought their wages were insufficient, they, as individuals, would withhold their services. There would be no strike, but there would be a *shortage* of cat controllers because employers would want to hire more services than were offered at that wage. Because of that shortage, employers would bid up the wages of controllers until workers offered the quantity of services demanded. A strike was called because individual mice continued to work—a choice they made because the wages paid were enough to compensate them for their stressful work."

Karl, pretending to be busy reading the paper, did not respond.

(September 1981)

Minimum Wages, Comparable Worth, and Incomparable Foolishness

Mouse Wisdom: Trying Badly to Do Good with Minimum Wages

"I'm happy to see that UCLA undergraduates have spunk," said a happy Karl to his fellow mouse, the wary Adam.

"Spunk can be an asset," agreed Adam, somewhat warily, "provided that it is manifested in activity more useful than burning down the administration building."

"What a student has done," chortled Karl, "is tell Professor Allen that she is not persuaded that minimum wage legislation is sinful."

Adam was now more annoyed than wary. "Maybe neither you nor the student listens well to Professor Allen," he said. "Analysts are not in the business of converting people to dogma. Dispassionately, they demonstrate what economic analysis can contribute to understanding of certain aspects of the world. And elementary analysis strongly suggests that minimum wage stipulation fails in achieving the goal for which it is supposedly adopted—and in its failure, it makes the problem worse."

"How can directly correcting the problem make it worse?" shrieked Karl. "The essence of the problem of poverty is small income. Higher wages mean bigger income. So we must stipulate by law a minimum wage."

"It is true," agreed Adam, "that selling a given number of hours of labor at a higher wage rate yields more income than selling the same amount of labor at a low wage. But if the problem of income involved nothing but arbitrarily raising the wage, then why not make everyone rich by putting the minimum wage at $1,000 an hour? Or maybe $1,000,000?"

"Now you're being a ridiculous rodent," scolded Karl. "If employers had to pay a worker at least $1,000 an hour, there would be very few hired."

"Precisely," said Adam. "Not many people are so productive as to be worth such a wage. Unhappily, a good many are not worth even $3.35 an hour, which is the currently imposed minimum wage. At that wage, they are priced out of the market. They cannot be rationally hired, for they would be paid more than the value of what they produce. And employers who persist in spending more on inputs than the inputs are worth will not long continue as employers. So," concluded Adam, "the immediate issue is whether a worker is better off unemployed at an artificially high wage of $3.35 or competitively obtaining a job—and gaining work experience—at, say $2.50."

"I see your point," grumped Karl. "A minimum wage requirement steals from the handicapped worker much of his already poor power to compete in the market. But I still would like to have people earn more than two or three dollars an hour."

"So would I," Adam said. "And so I would like to see people become more productive and valuable, through education, experience, and mobility. It is great productivity which enables us—individually and collectively—to live well. Policies which reduce productivity harm us all even when inspired by compassion. And minimum wage laws hurt mainly those we were trying to help—the young, the untrained, the inexperienced, the socially unattractive, who are least able to bear the costs of waste."

(December 1984)

Loose as a Goose in an Economy of Uncertainty

Workers' wages may go up because they are forced to rise, perhaps by minimum-wage law, or because they are induced to rise, because of increase in demand for labor or decrease in labor supply.

It makes a difference whether the higher wages are imposed on the market and enforced by outside institutions or generated by market participants in adjustment to market changes. In the first case, we are coerced into disequilibrium and unemployment; in the second, the market is cleared.

From the late 1930s, when the New Deal introduced the federal minimum wage law, until the early 1980s, we were blessed with persistent government attempts to confound and supersede the market. People of low productivity—largely the young and especially the black young—were priced out of the labor market. Over the past few years, wages have been pushed and pulled up through the market, as the supply of young workers has fallen while the labor demand of an expanding economy has increased.

But while the wage-increasing process—government decrees or market bids—differ in important respects, in another regard the two cases are very similar. When employers are confronted by rising wages, they can be expected to adjust to the new labor market situation.

It is not enough for the seller to provide good products and attractive service. He must do so while closely controlling costs. And if one portion of his purchased inputs becomes more expensive, he will economize. Economizing calls for input-substitution at the margin, replacing some of the now more highly priced factors with lower-cost alternative production techniques.

Economizing cannot mean total offsetting of greater costs while keeping the quantity and quality of output unchanged. Instead, we economize so as to minimize the adverse consequences of greater costs, making the best of a worsened situation.

Feasible tactics for economizing vary among firms, but managers have much incentive to be ingenious. With wage rates now higher, some workers will be fired; some will be used for fewer hours; and some will be used differently. All this may entail such devices as dropping store hours of marginal profitability, opening later and closing earlier; reducing labor hours through substitute products and production procedures, using more labor-saving machinery, and relying more on customer self-service; replacing workers of little experience with people of more training and maturity who require less supervision and are less inclined to change jobs frequently; and encouraging labor availability by offering child care facilities and transportation.

It does not help to curse either changes in the market or attempts by people to roll with punches. We have our being in a world of incessant and uncertain flux. It behooves us to hang loose in a flexible economy in order to make do as best we can.

(October 1986)

Poverty and the Minimum Wage

Doing nothing can be better public policy than doing something. Behold the minimum wage. Many posing politicians support increase in the minimum wage because they believe—or say that they believe—it will raise incomes of hardworking, poor Americans. According to a United States senator, it is the most "important poverty program that Congress could pass without adding to the budget deficit."

But, contrary to cultivated mythology, the minimum wage is not basically and effectively a poverty program. Indeed, few workers receiving the minimum wage are governmentally designated as poor—a conclusion supported in a recent study by two economists at the United States Congressional Budget Office.

The study was based on the March 1985 Current Population Survey of American Households. It revealed that only 10 percent of hourly-paid workers in 1984 earned no more than the minimum wage. And of these low-paid workers, fewer than 20 percent belonged to families with incomes below the poverty line.

Put differently, fewer than 2 percent of employees received the minimum wage or less *and* also lived in poverty. Indeed, only a minute handful of the relatively few people employed full time, year-round at no more than the minimum wage—two-tenths of 1 percent of all paid workers—were below the poverty level.

An important reason for the low incidence of poverty among minimum-wage workers is the fact that most of them live in families in which other working members earn substantial income. Conspicuously, teenagers account for almost one-third of those receiving the minimum wage or less. And teenagers generally are marginal workers: they move into and out of the labor force, do not work full time, and depend on the earnings of other family members.

All this reveals that the minimum wage has little relationship to poverty. If Congress increases the minimum wage, the employees whose pay is thereby raised typically are *not* poor: *few* will be pulled out of poverty. But *many* who would have found jobs and gained income and work experience if the minimum wage were not pushed up again will be priced out of the labor market and end up with no work at all.

Some members of Congress might believe—or say—that they can fight poverty by legislating higher minimum pay. But this policy could not, at best, reduce poverty much, for few minimum-wage recipients live in poverty; and, at the same time, many people of low productivity—both those who have been employed and those newly looking for employment—will be robbed of the opportunity to compete for jobs.

To handicap further by political decree those already most handicapped in the labor market because of little training and experience is to evince appalling poverty of the poverty program. If that is the best politicians can do, they should—in sense and in compassion—do nothing.

(September 1987)

The Negative Value of Comparable Worth

"Equal pay for equal work," required by law, is not a perfectly simple formula. Equal work must be carefully specified—the same current and prospective amount of the same quality of work, supplying the same product demand. Still, the principle of equal pay for *equal* work is sensible.

But now there is strident insistence—usually in the context of the battles of the sexes—on "equal pay for work of *comparable* worth." And the comparable worth principle is *not* sensible.

Assigning numerical weights to jobs by personnel committees selected by Big Brother is manifestly absurd on its face. Bureaucrats, job evaluation sociologists, and labor union lawyers cannot usefully pretend to compare precisely truck drivers with laundry workers or electricians with secretaries. What determines value is not the characteristics of either the work or the worker; instead, value reflects consumer valuation of the product. What a good is worth is simply what it can sell for.

The comparable worth proposal is an analytic aberration. Whatever appeal it may initially have on uncertain criteria of equity and fairness, the ultimate failure of comparable worth is that it cannot work.

First, comparable worth will not clear the labor market. If the committee sets too low a wage for a job, the position cannot be filled—there is a shortage. If the wage is set too high, there are too many applicants for the job, some of whom would like (but are forbidden) to offer their services at a lower wage—so there is a surplus. Even an initial accidental clearing of the market would not last. Jobs A and B have been specified as equal, but if now the A-wage is raised to forestall a developing shortage, that would necessitate raising the B-wage, too, thereby creating a surplus in that market.

Second, comparable worth will hurt employment, especially employment of women. Increasing costs reduce output—except in government, where taxes may be increased—and the least productive and most overpriced workers are fired first. Further, changed prices of productive services lead to new least-cost combinations of inputs, with capital being substituted for more expensive labor. Finally, artificially raising wages in traditional "women's" jobs reduces incentive for women to move into "men's" jobs. While female mobility *out* of women's jobs would be reduced, male mobility *into* those jobs would be increased. Increasing competition for a smaller number of women's jobs is a peculiar way to help women.

Most fundamentally, the essence of the comparable worth strategy is to replace the impersonally efficient market with bumbling political machination and payoff. The best efforts of workers would be diverted from investing in economic productivity to gaining government favor. And the community in general, no longer able to record the preferences which guide the use of its resources, would have lost freedom along with efficiency.

(March 1985)

The Marketplace and Women's Earnings

The wage gap between men and women who work full time is offered as proof of discrimination against women. But sex discrimination is not the reason why women, on average, earn only some 60 percent of what men earn.

Profit is required for business survival—and sex discrimination is not profitable. If women are willing and able continuously to do the same amount of the same kind of work as men, an employer would be foolish to pay men more when he could hire equally productive women for less. Companies that paid their male employers higher wages would have higher production costs and would be less able to compete with companies that did not discriminate. Employers would demand more lower-wage women and fewer higher-wage men, causing women's wages to rise and men's wages to fall. The marketplace eliminates, not perpetuates, sexist employment practices.

Much evidence supports this conclusion. If the earnings gap were due to sex discrimination, then *self-employed* women would escape that discrimination and receive higher earnings. But the wage gap is even bigger for the self-employed. Further, women in all *age brackets* and at all *education levels* would earn less than men if discrimination were the reason for lower earnings. But, as reported by the Federal Reserve Bank of San Francisco, earnings of men and women are identical for college graduates just entering the labor force.

The earnings differential between men and women appears to be due to differences in job qualifications and career interests, not to discrimination. Marriage and child rearing reduce steady *participation* of many women in the labor force, and that absence from the labor force causes a meaningful depreciation of job skills. Each year's absence appears to reduce a person's wage by 3 to 8 percent. Other data confirm the relationship between wage and labor force participation. Changes in the male/female earnings gap are closely related to changes in the birth rate. When the birth rate rises and more women leave the labor force to rear children, the wage gap increases ten years later, when many of those women have returned to work. And when the birth rate falls, the wage gap shrinks ten years later. But for single women who have never experienced this deterioration of job skills, there is no wage gap.

Greater absence from the labor force is not the only cause of lower wages for women. Earnings are reduced also by the *kinds* of jobs many women seek. Women often seek occupations which are most compatible with traditional roles of marriage and motherhood. Not only are some monetary earnings there traded for more family time, but the depreciation of job skills during absences from the labor force may be minimized in these kinds of occupation.

The male/female wage gap is not due to sexist marketplace that pays women less than they produce. And forcing employers to pay higher wages will reduce total female employment and reduce women's incentives to move into non-traditional jobs. The marketplace is a friend, not a foe, of women workers.

(July 1984)

Poverty, Politics, Piety, and Income Distribution

An Old Truth About the New Poverty

Today's poor differ from those of yesterday. A greater proportion of the nation's poor is now comprised of people whose incomes are less dependent on job earnings. In particular, the *elderly* and *female heads of families* now represent a larger fraction of the poor.

These individuals are often called the "new" poor. Because they participate in the economy much less than others do, their incomes—and thus their poverty rates—are commonly thought to be little affected by faster economic growth.

But this is not the picture one gets by examining the evidence. Though less than for the general population, the correlation between economic growth and poverty is significant for the elderly. And for female heads of families, the connection is even stronger. How can changes in economic growth substantially influence the poverty rates of these groups when their participation in the economy is so low?

The explanation may lie in the dynamics of poverty. The poor are largely a revolving pool of different people, not an unchanging stagnating group. As some lose income and enter this revolving pool, others simultaneously acquire more income and leave it. These flows into and out of poverty include the elderly and female heads of households.

Poor elderly families obtained only 3 percent of their incomes from marketplace earnings in 1983, but earnings provided almost 30 percent of the incomes of elderly families that were *not* poor. By enabling more of the elderly poor to obtain employment, greater growth permits some of these individuals to increase the fraction of their incomes provided by earnings. So, too, does greater growth enable more elderly citizens to retain employment. As a result, higher rates of real growth increase the number of elderly leaving poverty, as they reduce the number of those entering it.

The same dynamics of poverty also explain why economic growth affects the poverty rates of female-headed families. Although earnings contribute about 30 percent of the income of poor families headed by females, earnings make up almost 70 percent of the income of similar families that are *not* poor. As with the elderly, economic growth influences the employment of women, and thereby determines if they have relatively less earnings (and are poor) or relatively more earnings (and are not poor). Focusing only on the low employment and earnings of the poor ignores the mobility between poor and non-poor groups, whose patterns of employment are very different.

Like other citizens, the elderly and women who head families are continually entering and leaving a revolving pool of the poor. When they leave the pool, they participate more directly and fully in the community's prosperity. And prosperity reduces the population of the poverty pool. More growth means less poverty. That is an old truth that still applies—even to the new poverty.

(December 1985)

Poverty, Politics, and Promises

Poverty has many dimensions. Some speak of a "poverty culture," created and nurtured by little ambition, skill, and self-reliance. Thriving in such a culture are permanent poverty and its ugly sibling, welfare dependency.

Others speak of brief spells of poverty. Divorce, job loss, and other adversity thrust poverty upon individuals who cope with resourcefulness and resolve, and soon recover from their temporary affliction.

With its many dimensions, poverty is affected by many factors. But one stands out: economic growth. Much of the reduction in poverty during the last few decades can be attributed to the general advance in the economy.

From 1950 to 1960—well before the avalanche of government poverty programs—the percentage of individuals in poverty fell from 30 to 22 percent. This was an average decline of nearly one percentage point per year. Between 1960 and 1970, the poverty rate continued to fall, reaching less than 13 percent in 1970. The average annual decline again was about 1 percentage point. After 1970, the decline began to slow. The rate even increased in 1974 and 1975. And after rising again near the end of the decade, the poverty rate, at 13 percent in 1980, was slightly higher than in 1970.

That the poverty rate would fall in the fifties and sixties and rise in the seventies is not surprising. During the first two decades, real gross national product grew by an average yearly rate of about 3.5 percent. But during the 1970s, real growth dropped to a yearly average of 2.8 percent.

During each of these three periods, a strong, *negative* correlation exists between changes in the poverty rate and changes in real GNP. That is, the poverty rate fell when growth was strong in the first two decades and then rose when growth was weak in the 1970s. Indeed, during the seventies, almost three-fourths of the variation in the poverty rate is explained by variations in real growth.

The relationship between economic growth and poverty has been equally strong in the 1980s. As weak or negative growth pushed the poverty rate up during the recession of the early eighties, so have recent increases in real GNP begun to pull it down. But at 13.5 percent, the rate requires much continued growth to fall back to, and then beyond, its previous low of 11.1 percent in 1973.

Politicians should remember this connection between higher rates of economic growth and lower rates of poverty. For by promising more and more health care, child care, job protection, and other programs for middle-income America, they jeopardize economic growth. Such reckless political promise might be an avenue to political power. But is is also a road to poverty.

(October 1988)

The Political Legend of Low-Pay Jobs

"There is persuasive evidence that the standard of living of the average American worker is declining steadily, and Congress and corporate leaders must act soon to reverse the trend." So writes a newspaper columnist. Under the weight of analysis, however, the "persuasive evidence" crumbles like a squeezed cookie.

The biggest cookie of evidence in a study by Barry Bluestone, of the University of Massachusetts, and Bennett Harrison, of MIT. The study concludes that higher-pay jobs are giving way to lower-pay jobs. Allegedly, higher-pay employment in manufacturing, construction, and transportation is being replaced by lower-pay employment in the services sector of the economy.

The argument has been heard many times. Indeed, it has become an unctious sop to organized labor in which politicians try to justify greater government intervention to shore up waning union strength. But the popularity of the claim does not prove or disprove its validity. That requires evidence.

Consider the evidence summarized by Warren Brookes, editorialist for the *Detroit News*. Mr. Brookes argues that the Bluestone-Harrison study is grossly biased, partly because of the periods used in its analysis. By comparing the period 1973–1979 with that of 1979–1984, the study included in the later period the traumatic years of 1979–1981, which saw "two recessions, the worst inflation in modern history, and a massive 7 percent, two-year decline in average real wages." These events, observes Mr. Brookes, caused the share of higher-pay jobs to decline temporarily in the early eighties. Since 1982, however, economic recovery has been adding proportionately more higher-pay jobs, pushing their share in the economy back toward the level of the last decade.

If one looks, not at the Bluestone-Harrison periods but at the four-year presidential budget periods, a strikingly different conclusion is reached. During President Carter's budget years, more than 40 percent of all new jobs were in the lowest of three pay categories, while jobs in the highest-pay category actually declined. During President Reagan's first budget period of 1981–85, however, the opposite occurred: close to half of all new jobs were in the highest-pay category, and only 6 percent were in the lowest-pay category.

Our economy is *not* replacing higher-pay with lower-pay jobs. As columnist Robert Samuelson put it: "Generally speaking, the mix between well paid and poorly paid work is the same as in the 1970s. Creating the impression that it's otherwise is an exercise in statistical myth making designed to advance a political agenda."

Here, then, is the final evidence we have about low-pay jobs: politics has once again parented and nurtured an economic legend.

(May 1987)

Marx and the Growth of Wages

Karl Marx was not a good prophet. More than a century ago, he predicted that labor income would steadily fall in industrialized nations. Both average *pay rates* and *employment* would decline. Fewer people working and paid continually less per hour would result in the suffering that Marx believed would inevitably bring the overthrow of economies based on private property and markets.

The actual history of capitalism tells a different story: wages and working conditions have improved, not worsened, in these economies. In the United States, individual and total wages have risen substantially over the decades because both real wage rates and employment have increased. Since 1929, for example, employment has risen proportionately more than population; per capita work force compensation, adjusted for inflation, has expanded more than 2.5 times; and total wages as a fraction of national income have increased from 60 percent in 1929 to 74 percent today.

Why hasn't the gloomy prediction of Marx come true? A ready response cites the increased role of government. "Marx was not . . . 'wrong' in his economic vision," argues a popular Marx apologist. "The economic laws of motion which his model of capitalism revealed may still be visible in American capitalism," he continues, "but they are faced with a set of remedies which spring from political and social attitudes quite beyond his imagination."

The political remedies often praised for stemming the Marxian tide of trauma include minimum wage legislation, unemployment compensation, and laws encouraging labor unions. If the government had not made these changes, it is argued, American workers would long have known Marxian misery.

However desirable these government-instituted changes may be judged on other grounds, Professor Jack Hirshleifer, of UCLA, concludes that they have *not* increased wages of American workers. True, the minimum wage, unemployment insurance, and unions can raise the pay rates of *some* workers. But it is true, also, that these higher rates of pay reduce total *employment* without increasing the real determinant of wage rates, the *productivity* of labor. With productivity unchanged and less employment, total wages would be smaller, not larger.

Wages have grown rapidly during our nation's history because the productivity of labor has increased. As technology advanced and as businesses added to their stock of equipment and facilities, an hour of work became more productive. By *competing* against one another to obtain greater *quantities* of this labor made more valuable by more capital, businesses bid up the *wages* they pay.

With more employment at higher wages, the standard of living of American workers has increased enormously. The rising employment and wages have been due mostly to the very economic institutions Marx condemned: private rights to property and voluntary exchange in the marketplace.

(May 1986)

The Scarcity of Ecclesiastical Clarity

To acknowledge *existence* of a problem is not magically to imply the most appropriate *resolution* of the problem. Indeed, pointing to a problem does not imply even that there necessarily is a resolution attractive to all. And we surely cannot expect happy resolution when we misspecify the nature of the problem and mismeasure its dimension.

There is the problem of poverty. There always has been in the dual sense that the community has—and always will have—less of all good things than we want and that the distribution of income is uneven. Clergymen and secular politicians sometimes accept the unavoidable fact of scarcity, but commonly, in the name of Christ, they are eager to invoke the power of Caesar to remedy unequal income distribution. For inequality is considered to be inequity, and inequity is deemed to be iniquity.

Eminent economist Thomas Sowell has considered the document of the National Conference of Catholic Bishops entitled *Pastoral Letter on Catholic Social Teaching and the U.S. Economy*. Dr. Sowell finds the clergymen overeager to proclaim pietistic conclusions without benefit of economic analysis, while buttressed with simplistic delineation of the issue. Here consider selected aspects of the size and shape of the problem.

The bishops note that the top 20 percent of *families* receive eight times the income of the bottom 20 percent—and purity of heart is sufficient to understand that that is inequitable and iniquitous.

But Dr. Sowell notes, first, that there are 28 percent more *people* in that top 20 percent of families. Adjusting simply for the different numbers of persons reduces the 8-to-1 ratio to close to 6-to-1. Further, the top 20 percent of families supply nearly four times as many weeks of work per year. Adjusting for the different amounts of work reduces the income ratio to just over 2-to-1 for families and to well below 2-to-1 for persons.

These elemental corrections do not include subsidies to the poor, and they say nothing about the qualitative differences in the work done. It is not obviously inappropriate on grounds of morality that different productivities be differently rewarded—and if we are to produce much, high productivity must be relatively well rewarded.

Producing things is often considered ungenteel and best ignored by the pure of heart. How much more refined to wait for manna from heaven. But, realistically, to have much to distribute, some will have to produce much.

It is not apparent to us sinners that there is cause for moral outrage in the most productive people receiving twice as much income as the least productive. And if, by ecclesiastical decree, the pie is to be divided into equal shares, the pie to be shared will be much smaller. We then will be equals, not only in the eyes of the deity, but also in poverty.

(April 1988)

Production and Distribution

Wealth production is one thing. Wealth distribution is another. While production and distribution are different, the two are intimately related. What we produce and how well we produce will be determined in large part by how the resulting output is divided among producers and other members of the community.

People produce and invest today to reap rewards tomorrow and the day after tomorrow. Those who work very hard and very effectively in doing things which other people value very highly will receive very large rewards. Perhaps in your ideal world we should be motivated only by sheer love of constructive activity or by unadulterated love of humanity. Some such love does exist, but it is not sheer and unadulterated: most of us most of the time are inspired and guided more by prospective payment than by pursuit of philanthropy.

In all this, there is a two-way functional relationship. What things are produced and the combination of those various goods is a reflection of the pattern of spending by the community. By expressing preferences through voting with dollars in the market, people make it worth the while of producers to supply a particular pattern of outputs.

At the same time, that pattern of spending is a reflection, not only of preferences, but of the distribution of income, and income distribution is determined by relative productivities. What is produced is affected much by income distribution; and income distribution is affected much by what is produced. Money is spent on production; and money is earned by producing.

So, when society's institutions and ground rules permit, people will sensibly respond to incentives in choosing among options available to them both as consumers and as producers; and such response will yield economic efficiency, with scarce resources well used in serving the demonstrated income-weighted preferences of the community.

And yet, some clerics at the highest bureaucratic level stubbornly ignore the nature of man and of his world. Economist Thomas Sowell notes that "throughout the Pastoral Letter [of the National Conference of Catholic Bishops], real income—which is production—is treated as having occurred *somehow*, with the only real question being how it should be distributed. There is no real concern evident as to how today's distribution decisions might—at least might—affect future production, and therefore the material well-being of all." Indeed, the bishops' "substantive analysis in no way differs from an analysis of the distribution of manna from heaven."

People are paid for their guided productive efforts, and those efforts will be great and sensible if the producers can then use their income as they please. This may strike some as grubby. But until men better resemble non-fallen angels, it would help if clergymen who purport to give worldly guidance better resembled no-nonsense economists.

(April 1988)

Inequality: Economic and Political

In a largely open, private-property economy, income is distributed basically by *value of productivity*—how *much* you contribute to the production process and how highly the community *values* your contribution.

It is a brutal, even though purposeful, arrangement. The race to prosper is manifestly "unfair"—we do not begin the competition with equal beauty, ambition, energy, and intelligence or with equal cultural background or with equal family fortune or with identical interests and talents. Some are more productive than others in those activities which the community deems most useful. And so incomes are highly unequal.

Of course, the private-property, enterprise society is not the only kind with inequalities. And the prospect of a collectivist utopia in which liberty has been foregone but inequalities still persist should give pause even to the most innocent. The fact that the inequalities would reflect preferences of the politbureau instead of producer productivities and market preferences would hardly make them more attractive.

The proportionate differentials in income distribution appear to be comparable in the United States and Russia. A scholarly review has concluded:

> . . .the differentials between, say, the extreme income percentiles [in the USSR] may be no less than the USA. Secondly, the relative opulence of the Soviet elite may seem less tolerable against a background of greater poverty. Thirdly, the manner in which this minority is nurtured by the state, and indeed protects itself, may be found disagreeable by many. Finally, the promotion of elitism in the face of a highly egalitarian ideology implies disconcerting hypocrisy on the part of the Soviet leadership.

Journalists—including Hedrick Smith of the *New York Times*, and George Melloan of the *Wall Street Journal*—impressionistically fill in the Soviet picture. We are told by such non-romantic observers that, while "the police state repression is real, . . . the egalitarian values they espouse are mainly mythical. . . . for all the party's egalitarian cant, there are few societies where the demarcation between the weak and the powerful, the haves and have-nots, is more clearly drawn." It is judged that "in the land of the proletariat, people are far more rank-, class-, and status-conscious than in the West."

Indeed, the exclusive powers and privileges of rank, class, and status account for more of the living differences than do unequal money income. ". . . the benefits enjoyed by the Soviet elite depend on influence, connections, and access that money cannot buy. The system has institutionalized a double-standard in life-styles for the elite and for the masses. . . . And the elite take these advantages for granted, with an arrogant disdain for the common man that often surpasses the haughtiest rich of the West."

If equal economic rewards are both desirable and feasible, the point cannot be illustrated by Soviet history.

(August 1981)

Mainly Macroeconomics:
Income and Monetary Analysis

Introduction

The foundations of economic analysis are in price-and-allocation theory. But there are interesting questions and serious problems which must be considered on a large scale—matters of government spending, taxation, inflation, fiscal and monetary policies, exchange rates, the balance of payments. We can deal with some issues only with the aid of the big aggregates and big averages of the economy—although we must keep well in mind that real, live, individual people are behind those aggregates and averages. Great masses of data are likely to remain mere summary measures and mechanical indicators if we do not ask how the world looks—its options and constraints, its incentives and perils, its payoffs and penalties—to the particular people who make decisions.

A commonly used aggregate is "national output and income," measured generally as gross national product. GNP can be subdivided into its spending components and into its components of income dispersal. The *spending* on the output of the economy over one year determines and measures the marketplace *value* of that output, and all of that received spending is disposed of in various forms of *income*—taxation. Thus:

GNP = C + I + G + X, from the standpoint of income-creation, and

GNP = C + S + T + M, from the standpoint of income-disposal,

where "C" is consumption spending, "I" is investment spending, "G" is government spending, and "X" is foreign spending (exports) on currently produced domestic final output; and "S" is saving, "T" is tax collections, and "M" is imports.

The GNP figure is imperfect and inadequate, conceptually as well as operationally. In addition to physical difficulties in accurately gathering the mass of data, there are questions of what to *try* to include and what we *do* measure in this summation of economic activity.

And in using the measurement for analysis over time, there are corrections to be made for changes in prices, varieties and qualities of goods, population, and income distribution. Still, there would be absurdity in throwing away usable information because it does not perfectly measure all we should like to measure.

Such national income accounting has sometimes been used—and misused—as a basis of discretionary fiscal policy. Simple models seem to demonstrate that government can diddle with its own spending (G) and collection of taxes (T) so as to attain targeted values of GNP. Doubtless, government spending and taxation can affect national income, but the models provide only limited guidance in real-world policymaking. They do not well incorporate considerations of what the government will buy, through what taxes and borrowings it will finance the spending, what will be the side effects on money supply, interest rates, and community expectations, and how long will be the lags between policy conceptualization and implementation and repercussion.

Discussions of large budgets deficits (G larger than T) also have exhibited some of the perils in moving from accounting tautology to analytic theory to policy prescription. Many have blamed the deficits, which began to balloon in 1975 and reached an impressive peak in

---

TABLE 1

Federal Outlays, Receipts, Deficits, and Defense Spending as a Percentage of GNP

		Outlays	Receipts	Deficit	Defense
Truman:	1946–52	16.4%	16.3%	0.1%	8.5%
Eisenhower:	1953–60	18.1	17.5	0.6	10.4
Kennedy-Johnson:	1961–68	18.4	17.3	1.0	8.3
Nixon-Ford:	1969–76	19.3	17.7	1.7	6.3
Carter:	1977–80	20.7	18.3	2.4	4.7
Reagan:	1981–88	22.9	18.6	4.3	6.0

SOURCES: *Economic Report of the President*, February 1988 and earlier editions; *Economic Indicators*, December 1988.

TABLE 2

Annual Rates of Change:
Money, Velocity, Price Level, Output, and Spending

	$\dot{M}$	+	$\dot{V}$	=	$\dot{P}$	+	$\dot{Q}$	=	$\dot{PQ}$
1966–81	6.4		3.0		6.8		2.6		9.6
1981–88	8.6		−1.6		3.8		3.0		6.9
Hypothetical	3.0		0		0		3.0		3.0

SOURCES: *Economic Report of the President*, February 1988; *Economic Indicators*, December 1988.

1986, on T being cut while G was being bloated by increased defense spending. In actuality, both government receipts and outlays have increased much faster than GNP, with outlays leading receipts—but not because of a massive explosion of defense spending. As proportions of GNP, both outlays and receipts are now at the highest levels since World War II, and defense spending is the lowest of any period except the Carter years. See table 1. Most politicians and editorial writers— and even some economists—have yet to learn the source of the deficits, what are and are not the problems of deficits, and the relative significance of the size of *deficits* and *budgets*.

Matters of national output, national income, and price level can be approached through monetary analysis as well. Instead of breaking down aggregate expenditure into components of C, I, G, and X, we can state it as M times V, the amount of money multiplied by the average number of times a dollar is spent on output during the year. GNP = MV. And the expenditure on output determines the value of the output, which can be noted as price times quantity, or P times Q, an index of price per unit multiplied by a measure of the units of output.

So spending on output (MV) necessarily equals the value of output (PQ). And the *sum* of the proportionate (percentage) changes in the money supply ($\dot{M}$) and monetary velocity ($\dot{V}$) approximately equals the proportionate change of the price index ($\dot{P}$) *plus* the proportionate change in the real amount output ($\dot{Q}$), both being equal to the proportionate change in the value of output ($\dot{PQ}$), which is GNP in current dollars.

During the inflationary period, 1966–81, money expanded at an annual rate of well over 6 percent, velocity rose at 3 percent, so expenditure went up nearly 10 percent. It was not to be expected that production would rise that fast; indeed, output expanded at less than 3 percent. With spending up at close to 10 percent and output up at less than 3 percent, prices inexorably soared at nearly 7 percent. See table 2.

Since 1981, the spending rate has been dominated even more than before by money, for velocity has changed less than before, actually falling a bit. If the change in velocity were *zero*—and it rarely has deviated greatly from zero—then money and spending would move together proportionately. And if money (and spending) increased at just the same rate as output—typically about 3 percent—inflation would be zero.

In the earlier period, money and prices increased at nearly the same rate, for the change in velocity was nearly offset by that of output. In the 1980s, V and Q have not changed proportionately, and neither have M and P. The Federal Reserve cannot control velocity, but it can closely control money. If money were to be increased at about the same rate as output expands, then the rate of inflation would approximate the rate of change of velocity. (Since $\dot{M} + \dot{V} = \dot{P} + \dot{Q}$, then $\dot{M} + \dot{V} - \dot{Q} = \dot{P}$. If $\dot{M} = \dot{Q}$, then $\dot{V} = \dot{P}$.) This would mean that P would fluctuate over the years within a range of something like –1 and 3 percent per year. This is a much smaller range than that of the past twenty years, when money, instead of steadily growing at a rate of about 3 percent, has erratically bounced between –5 and 20 percent.

All of the micro and macro analytics find a home in the realm of international economics. The bases of trade are the bases of trade, and the gains from trade are the gains from trade, whether the traders reside in the same country or in different countries. And in both domestic and foreign trade, we gain from what we get, not from what we give.

What a country has available for its own consumption and investment "absorption" (A) is mainly its own production: we live better when we produce much. But some of that domestic output is exported to foreigners, and some foreign output is imported. So A = GNP – X + M. If imports are greater than exports, then the nation absorbs more of the world's output than it produces: we live better also by being subsidized than by subsidizing.

Output, Employment, and Indicators

GNP: *Measuring Output and Economic Well-Being*

Smog is a comfort to those who like to *see* what they breathe. And statistics of gross national product are a comfort to historians and policymakers who like to *measure* the community's economic activity. Many are willing to forego the assurances of visible air, and a few are almost equally disenchanted with the measurement of GNP.

Certainly, the GNP measure is imperfect. Coverage is incomplete both conceptually and operationally. GNP is a money summary of total output over an accounting period. But some productive activity is not included in the statistical compilation, for the activity does not involve market transactions. The work of the do-it-yourselfer and of the homemaker are not valued in the market and thus are not part of the constructed GNP figure. Similarly, illegal activities and illegal camouflaging of legal activities are not reflected in market records. Nor is value imputed to leisure.

There would be problems with GNP measurement even if it were inclusive and accurate. In 1929, GNP was a bit over $100 billion; in 1984, it was close to $3.7 trillion. Was the later output thirty-seven times greater? And how about national economic well-being?

A change over time in raw, uncorrected GNP numbers does not tell us much. One correction pertains to *price* changes. The value of production is determined by prices, as well as amounts, of outputs. From 1929 to 1984, the price level rose almost sevenfold; corrected for that inflation, the GNP measure was about five times greater—not thirty-seven times greater— in 1984 than in 1929.

Prices are not the only variable. There are *quality* changes: 1929 airplanes and record players were very different from their 1984 counterparts. And there are output *composition* changes: in 1929, there was no television or pantyhose—and introduction of at least one of those things has improved economic well-being.

Still another consideration is *population*: 1929 output was divided among 122 million people; in 1984, there had to be 237 million slices— almost twice as many. Even if average income per person increases, there is the matter of *income distribution*. If all the increase in income were to go to one-tenth of 1 percent of the people, some could wonder if general economic well-being had been much improved.

So the GNP does not tell us perfectly accurately all we should like to know. Neither does a thermometer, a scale, or a blood pressure reading. But what they do tell us can be partially corrected and useful-ly combined with other information. The world is hard enough to understand and to improve without throwing away useful informa-tion. Get rid of smog, if you like, but continue to compile GNP data.

(March 1985)

The Causes of Unemployment

As measured in this country, the unemployment rate is rarely below 3 to 4 percent, and at the depth of the Great Depression, it rose as high as 25 percent. Why is there ever unemployment of workers?

Usually, the answer runs in terms of bad (or at least inadequate) psychology or economics. Some complain that the core of the un-employed are lazy, unambitious, irresponsible. Others contend that unemployment is a result of insufficient aggregate demand—and so the cure of unemployment is forced inflation of the economy. For some people and some circumstances, such answers have some validity— but much more is involved.

First, many who are officially counted as unemployed are heavily and rationally investing their resources in looking for work. They are sampling the market, seeking information on employment alternatives. That information is valuable, but it is not obtained either freely or instantaneously, and generally, the faster it is to be acquired, the more costly it will be.

We should hardly want to have the measured unemployment rate kept at zero, for preclusion of unemployment would mean virtual preclusion of quitting one job in order to get a better one and of searching for a best job by those entering or reentering the work force. Such preclusion would greatly restrict freedom as well as dilute efficiency.

A second sort of cause of unemployment are laws and arrangements which inhibit adjustment of prices of labor services. Long-term labor contracts—with or without benefit of union pressure—can get in the way of market adjustments. If demand for labor falls but the price of labor is pegged, the quantity of labor workers want to sell at that price is more than employers will buy.

Other workers are unemployed, not because demand has fallen while the wage rate is maintained, but because wages are raised to artificial levels in the face of constant demand. One can price himself out of the labor market by stipulating a required wage of $1,000 per hour. Or one can be priced into unemployment by government making it illegal for his services to be bought or sold below a stipulated minimum wage.

Finally, one can rationally, and thus predictably, decline employment because of sufficiently attractive alternatives which have been provided—provided, in large part, by those too anxious to do good. A considerable amount of a variety of welfare is available for the unemployed. Few would want to sweep away all amounts of all types of welfare aid. But there is an inherent problem in welfare programs, a problem of work incentive.

Suppose a person receiving $6,000 a year in aid now has the option of taking a job at $7,000. Foregoing the $6,000 in order to obtain the $7,000 is, in effect, a staggering tax on his earned wages of over 85 percent! Actually, the tax is bigger than that, for he will have to pay income tax on his wages. It is an unreasonable test of the work ethic to ask a person to accept employment when the work-tax will approximate 100 percent.

So we will continue to have some unemployment—partly because market information is costly, prices are not fully adjustable, and welfare imposes a tax on accepting a job.

(May 1981)

Stingy Nature, Foolish Policy, and Employment

We live in a stingy world, so it is silly to contend that there are not enough jobs. There is more than enough to do to keep us fully occupied. And yet, even in boom periods, there is some unemployment. How can there be unemployment when there is always work to be done?

There are always *some* available tasks on *some* terms. But those are not necessarily the activities and employment conditions workers like, so the employment offer is rejected. Is the person turning down the job irresponsible or unrealistic? In some instances, yes; but that is not a broadly useful generalization. You may be a bum—but that is not established by your refusal to be my full-time lackey at one dollar per year. You have better alternatives than that, so you are sensible to decline my offer.

Finding those better market options poses problems, however. You cannot immediately and costlessly obtain information on all those potential jobs. Your information will never be perfect and complete, but you can make it better and fuller by investing some of your time, energy, and money in searching for additional market information. And part of your rational investment in the information search may be foregoing the job of my assistant at one dollar per year.

But even an intelligently conducted search may not yield employment opportunities you deem very attractive. You can't find the sort of job which destiny and your mother had planned for you. That is a familiar story in "command" societies, where Big Brother is not very sensitive to either your destiny or your mother. And it is a story often found also in "market-performance" societies. Our neighbors will reward us in the market for producing those things they like. They will reward us especially well if not many others are as good in producing these things. But we cannot expect to be paid much for doing things which the community does not value highly, no matter how pure our heart or how refined our education.

There are employment problems in addition to the costliness of information and the necessity to adapt supplies to market demands. There are self-imposed barriers which prevent people from freely exchanging labor services for wages. Mr. A is willing to pay Mr. B a certain number of dollars for a certain amount of a certain kind of work; Mr. B agrees to the terms. But the two people—both adults in this Land of the Free—can be prevented from carrying out the mutually useful deal. They may be prevented by a minimum-wage law or by employment taxes and other costs determined by government; they may be stymied by union-membership requirements and contracts. In such cases, the market has not *failed*; it has been *subverted*.

Subversion of the market is not confined to reducing the *amount* of work we do, but also to reducing *how well* we work. Governmental penalties, subsidies, protections, constraints, and directives lower our productivity, forcing us to adapt to a world we have made even less bountiful than the world bequeathed by stingy nature.

(March 1982)

On Measurement and Interpretation: Glasses and Doughnuts

From what perspective and with what emphasis are we to view various variables of the marketplace? Is the glass half full or half empty?

In a recent ten-year period, our real output increased 35 percent—an annual rate of 3 percent, which approached twice the rate of increase of the working-age population and was three times the rate of increase of the total population. Further, employment rose by 21 percent, more than the proportionate increase in the working-age population. So it is apparent that the decade was one of appreciable expansion of employment, productivity, and per capita real income.

For contrast, consider a ten-year period when the number of people unemployed rose 65 percent and the unemployment rate increased almost 30 percent. Obviously, this was a difficult, if not disastrous, time of collapsing economic activity.

Actually, both sets of data pertain to the *same* period, 1971–1981. How can the same decade be one of high and rising employment and also one of high and rising unemployment? Evidently, whether it was among the best of times or one of the worst is largely in the statistical eye of the beholder.

It is common to attach great weight to the rate of unemployment. That rate is a statistical construct comparing an estimated number of people without a job who profess to be seeking a job, with an estimated number of people in the so-called civilian labor force.

The official unemployment rate is a tricky tool of analysis. The reported rate can be deemed misleadingly small, for it does not reflect those who have become so discouraged in seeking employment that they have dropped out of the labor force and are no longer counted, and it does not indicate the part-time employees who want full-time jobs.

Conversely, the rate is bloated by those who find it rational, given the welfare rules, to claim to desire employment but who actually do not want a job or who decline jobs while waiting for better offers. And the rate can be increased through expansion of the labor force by those now seeking employment for the first time or by those rejoining the competition for jobs.

From 1971 to 1981, jobs increased robustly, employment expanding twenty-one million. But the measured labor force went up even more, by twenty-four million. So unemployment rose three million, and the unemployment rate went from a moderate 5.9 percent to a large 7.6 percent. The labor force rose proportionately faster than the work-age population. And the labor force became a bigger fraction of population because of more participation by women: the proportion of the male population in the labor force actually fell a bit, while the proportion of women increased a whopping 20 percent.

The *real* performance of the economy—job creation and production—was pretty good. The *statistical measurement* of unemployment camouflaged the positive aspects of that performance. But some find the hole more fascinating than the doughnut.

(October 1982)

Public Works:
The Oversold Solution to Unemployment

With a high unemployment rate, politicians are scrambling to create the image that they are taking corrective action. It has become good copy, in particular, to propose federal funding of public works jobs to rebuild roads, bridges, sewers, and other so-called infrastructure components in order to reduce unemployment. The gut issue evidently is not maintenance of the nation's capital, but whether the creation of public service jobs can decrease—or give seeming promise that it will decrease—the unemployment rate.

Public works programs would, in themselves, create specific jobs, of course. But expansion of public jobs is likely to cause employment to contract elsewhere, so there is no net increase in employment.

Other employment will contract because federal expenditures on public service jobs must somehow be financed—a financing which will reduce spending elsewhere. If the federal government is to increase spending for pubic works, then it must either reduce other government expenditures, raise taxes, or deficit spend.

If *federal expenditures are reduced* for other programs, such as national defense, then fewer people will be employed producing guns. Or if transfer payments to individuals are reduced, then fewer people will be employed producing the butter which would otherwise have been demanded. In either case, decreases in federal expenditures in one area in order to make room for increases in public works will not provide a net increase in national employment.

Similarly, if *taxes are increased* in order to fund the expansion in public works, then taxpayers will have less income to spend. Demand for and employment in the production of consumer goods will contract. This contraction will occur whether the increased tax is directly on consumers' incomes or is an increased excise tax on a particular good, such as gasoline.

If, instead, the expansion of public works is financed by enlarging the already-swollen federal deficit, then the government will either have to borrow or create new money in order to pay its bills. If it *borrows* from the community, the government would intensify its competition with businesses and households for scarce credit and crowd out borrowing for private investment. Private spending of private funds for private purposes would be displaced by government spending of funds sequestered from the people.

If the increased deficit spending were financed by greater *money creation*, however, then spending would not be decreased in other areas, and there could be a temporary, modest rise in employment as public works jobs were increased. But soon the rate of inflation—which is a form of taxation—would increase and threaten future productivity and employment. A bit more employment today is then obtained at the expense of less employment and more misery in the future.

For today's relatively high rates of unemployment, there is no panacea, no easy way out. But neither candor nor competence is what the public commonly gets from its elected officials. It is more popular to promise the quick fix—even when there is none.

(December 1982)

Reducing Poverty: Trickling Down or Climbing Up?

The poor have been called "the other America." While most citizens taste the fruits of progress, those of "the other America" are thought trapped in poverty. And their faces are many: the sick, the aged, the handicapped, female heads of families, the unemployed, the uneducated.

The poor are thus perceived as forgotten Americans left behind, castaways of an economy which has failed to make room for them. When the economy grows, the poor benefit only from crumbs that trickle down from the sumptuous table of those more fortunate. So government poverty programs are believed to offer the poor their only hope. Those who stress vigorous economic growth to help the poor are called callous advocates of a derivative policy that can never fill the bellies of the impoverished.

Yet, reductions in our nation's poverty are closely associated with robust economic growth, *not* with increases in federal poverty programs. How can economic growth strongly benefit the poor if, as is believed, they are mired in a poverty from which government welfare is the only escape?

The answer is simple: the common perception of poverty is wrong. Most of the poor are *not* permanently trapped in that condition, but are comprised mainly of different people over time. The poor are more accurately described as a revolving pool of different individuals, not a stagnating class of hopeless victims. Some become poor and enter this pool; others simultaneously acquire more income and leave it. And most do not long remain in this revolving door of poverty.

This is the conclusion of the University of Michigan's Panel Study on Income Dynamics, which has been studying a representative sample of five thousand families. By tracking the same families from 1968 to 1979, the panel discovered that "only a little over one-half of the individuals living in poverty in one year are found to be poor in the next, and considerably less than one-half of those who experience poverty remain persistently poor." More specifically, the persistently poor—those remaining poor for eight or more years during the ten-year period—accounted for only 38 percent of the poverty experienced during this time. Further, those who were poor in all ten years accounted for only 10 percent of the poverty of this period.

Poverty is not commonly a permanent or long-lasting affliction. Most poverty is a temporary setback, whose major causes the panel identified as marriage or divorce, illness or death, birth of a child, and temporary unemployment. Most who are poor will recover after a short period, a recovery that is faster and less painful in a growing economy.

For most of the poor, therefore, economic growth does not mean a trickling down of a few crumbs of affluence; it means greater opportunity to be more productive and climb back up the income ladder. That is why economic growth has been poverty's most formidable foe.

(January 1985)

Misleading Indicators

We have great difficulty figuring out where we have been and understanding where we are. Still, many are not deterred in trying to find ways of foreseeing where we are going.

Interest in the future is not confined to idle curiosity. If we were to know pretty well what prices and interest rates and national income will be a year or two from now, we could partially protect ourselves against bad developments and cash in on some of the good; and through public policy, we might mitigate prospective catastrophe and conduce prosperity.

To be able to predict is to enhance our power to control. But how to predict future activity of the economy? Well, there are purported "leading indicators." Each month, the Department of Commerce calculates an index of twelve economic variables. The index is supposed to change direction before turning points in economic activity, giving us warning of forthcoming booms and busts.

Some take such devices seriously. Maybe the devices do help more than they mislead. But they are to be handled very gingerly.

Predictably, the dozen variables represented by the index do not always point in the *same direction* or change direction at the *same time*. If they did, just one variable would be enough. But, with a divided jury of variables, we have the problem at any time of deciding which components of the index are to be taken most seriously.

The aggregate index can give *false* signals of imminent turning points in the economy. It can give *ambiguous* signals. And it can give signals subject to *misinterpretation*: an increase in prices of materials may reflect a discouraging supply shock rather than expanding demand. Some of the difficulty in using the index stems from *incorrect data*—it has proved prudent to revise the calculation in each of the first two months after its initial pronouncement, and the revisions can be so great as to reverse the direction of change of the index.

Finally, even when the figures prove to be accurate and give a clear and correct signal, the *lead time* of the warning can vary enormously. If the lag between the turning point of the indicator and the turning point of the economy is just a month or two, there is no warning at all: the turning of the index is not taken seriously unless the new direction is followed for at least three months. And if the lag approaches two years, then the warning is simply a uselessly vague indication that "eventually" economic activity will change.

It is hardly surprising that the index of leading indicators commonly indicates poorly. Many things can affect the future. What will the Federal Reserve, Congress, foreign fiscal and monetary authorities and suppliers, unique combinations of circumstances, and new business practices do to us next? But if fine-tuning control of the economy depends on prediction, and if prediction relies on measuring and interpreting leading indicators, we should put little reliance on fine-tuning.

(April 1986)

The Government Budget
and Its History

Deficits and the Historical Record

The conventional federal budget is an accountant's nightmare—or joke. It does not include all government transactions; it does not distinguish current expenses from capital investments; it does not well indicate the thrust of fiscal policy and its impact. Yet, it is commonly presumed that it should be balanced.

In some circles—including conspicuous Republicans—balance *per se* is the critical objective, with little regard for either the *level* at which the budget is balanced or the *manner*—increased taxation or reduced expenditure—in which a deficit is eliminated. If deficits strike such terror and take precedence over all other policy considerations, it is in order to ask how they actually have been pernicious.

The latest—if not last—federal surplus was in 1969. Look at the record of the succeeding dozen years.

The budgetary problem has *not* been starvation of government by a niggardly community. Receipts increased at an annual rate of over 10 percent—while the price level was rising at less than 7 percent—and were much more than three times as great in 1981 as in 1969. But rapidly increasing receipts surely will not balance the budget or even reduce the deficit. In that period, government outlays went up even faster, at an annual rate over 11 percent.

This massive increase in the budget and its deficit stemmed, more specifically, from non-defense spending. Exploding at an annual rate of 14 percent, it was almost five times larger in 1981 than in 1969. Non-defense spending is now equal to 17 percent of gross national product; only nine years ago, it was 13 percent. Reducing the proportion back to just the 1973 level would reduce government spending by enough to balance the budget.

What is the damage done by deficits? Supposedly, they raise interest rates and reduce growth. But that has *not* been the case.

The deficit and interest rates have tended strongly to move in *opposite* directions. From 1968 to 1969, the deficit fell $28 billion—but both long-term and short-term interest rates greatly increased. From 1974 to 1976, the deficit soared by $61 billion—but long-term rates fell slightly, and short-term rates fell greatly.

Meanwhile, real output of the economy moved with the ratio of the deficit to GNP: as the deficit became bigger or smaller relative to GNP, production rose or fell.

Interest rates are causally correlated, not with deficits, but with the price level; and the rate of inflation, in turn, is a function of the rate of money growth. The rate of money expansion has been erratically falling for nearly two years, the inflation rate has been greatly reduced, and interest rates are far below the peaks at the end of 1980.

It may be too much to ask politicians to get economic analysis straight. But surely they could get a lackey to look up the historical numbers. If they can't *understand* the world, they could at least *observe* some of its behavior.

(September 1982)

Fiscal Degeneration

Big and growing federal budgets and budget deficits have become a degenerate way of life. It was not always so.

Over the first century and a half of our independent history, federal spending was a small and quite steady part of national income. It was universally presumed that the budget should be generally balanced. There were occasional bulges in government spending and in government debt during wars, but budget surpluses following wars invariably reduced the debt.

The pattern was shaken by a depression decade of deficits in the 1930s, followed by World War II. There was no whittling-down of the debt after the World War II, but at least the debt did not appreciably increase from 1945 through 1960. Indeed, as a proportion of gross national product, the debt was cut by more than half in that period, which included seven years of surplus.

It has been a basically different kind of story over the past quarter of a century. Since 1960, there has been only one year of surplus as government spending has risen tenfold—not only proportionately much more than GNP, but absolutely more rapidly than tax receipts.

Compare the decades of the 1870s, the 1920s, the 1970s, and, finally, the 1980s. In the days of Little House on the Prairie, federal spending was just over 4 percent of GNP, and each year of the 1870s saw a budget surplus. Half a century later, in the Roaring Twenties, federal spending was still about 4 percent of GNP, and, again, each year was in surplus. But after another fifty years, in the 1970s, the proportion of government spending had expanded five times, to over 21 percent of GNP, and each year of the decade showed a deficit, the average annual deficit equaling more than 2 percent of GNP. The situation has deteriorated further in the eighties, with federal spending nearly 24 percent of GNP and every year in deficit, the average shortfall being 4.5 percent of GNP.

Not only have we been on a quarter century binge of ever-increasing *amounts* of collective spending by Big Brother, but we have acquiesced in a broadening array of *kinds* of spending, not all of which have contributed to a prosperous, strong, and tranquil community.

Why the drastic change? Government has long existed, government borrowing to pay for spending has long been possible and sometimes practiced, so there has long been the possibility of profligate government spending and massive borrowing. Changes in genes and hormones cannot explain why we now do willingly and wildly what we previously had done grudgingly and little.

What has changed is the attitude of the people and their government representatives—the dogmas they hold, the mores they adopt, the proprieties they embrace—with decreased and still decreasing weight given to personal independence and collective responsibility.

(November 1985)

Spending and Deficits

Everyone talks about the federal budget deficit. They are against it. Most in high places want to reduce the deficit by increasing tax rates in order to increase tax collections.

Indeed, the tactic of tax increase in order to serve the strategy of deficit reduction is well nigh axiomatic. Policy by axiom—and selling the policy to the public by slogan—is enormously convenient: it seemingly relieves one of the obligations to investigate and to think.

The only hints of analysis dropped to us from our public servants pertain to interest rates: big deficits mean high interest rates, we are told, and high interest rates crowd private investors out of the credit markets. Only occasionally does some isolated commentator—and it is lonely at the bottom—point out that there is but a very low correlation between deficits and interest rates; that, instead, interest rates are increased mainly by inflation; that inflation stems from lousy monetary policy that creates too much money; and that investors can be crowded as much by high taxes as by high interest rates.

The beleaguered commentator can wonder, if deficits are supposed to increase interest rates, how rates have fallen greatly over recent months in the face of a large deficit which is anticipated to grow much larger. And he can wonder, if we are concerned about the fate of business firms and the employment they provide, how one can find it shrewd to counter a major recession with major increases in taxes.

But let us not be beastly or even picky. Suppose we have decided—whether or not shrewdly—to increase tax receipts in order to diminish the deficit. What are the chances of success? Well, have *past* increases in receipts reduced deficits? Not always. Indeed, not usually.

In the thirty-seven year-to-year observations since World War II, federal tax receipts and the budget deficit have moved in the *same* direction—almost always both increasing—on nineteen occasions, about half the time. The record is even more sobering if a lag is noted: in twenty-three of thirty-six annual instances—two-thirds of the time—a change in receipts was followed a year later by a deficit change in the *same* direction. When we *increase* tax receipts, we *spend* even more and get a *bigger* deficit. In the past decade, the average annual increase in receipts has been nearly $50 billion, and the average increase in the deficit has been over $12 billion. Over those ten years, receipts rose at a remarkable 11.5 percent annually and were three times as great in 1982 as in 1972; but government outlays rose still faster, at more than 12 percent.

The wretched record is clear. So is the silly psychology which gives rise to the continuing record: government will generally increase its spending more than the public increases the taxes provided to government.

(December 1982)

Budgetary History and Diagnosis

We are not likely to prescribe wisely unless we first diagnose well. It is almost universally diagnosed that we have a major problem with the federal budget; and it is widely believed that proper prescription calls for greater tax collections, which, in turn, requires higher tax rates.

All that must be correct, for we hear a constant chorus of politicians, journalists, business executives, and even some economists, saying so. But the common chorus is incorrect.

The major mistake is focusing entirely on the conventionally measured *imbalance* of the budget rather than the *size* of the budget. The excess of government spending over collection of nominal, customary taxes does have some significance. But *all* of the government spending is financed *somehow*, and all of the spending sequesters resources from the community or redistributes resources within the community. So the most critical budgetary question pertains to the magnitude of this sequestering and redistributing. How much of the community output is absorbed by or channeled through government?

That critical ratio of federal spending to gross national product has risen in *every* administration since World War II. At the height of the wars in both Korea and Vietnam, about 20 percent of gross national product was represented by government outlays; the peak in the peaceful Reagan years was close to 24 percent, and the Reagan average was nearly 23 percent. Government revenue has risen almost as persistently, although more slowly.

Cumulative budget deficits were barely greater than zero during the Truman and Eisenhower administrations despite Korea, and they were only 1 percent of GNP during the Kennedy-Johnson-Nixon years, despite Vietnam. The fat began to fall into the fire in 1975, with the deficit spending equaling between 2 to 6 percent of GNP in the past fourteen years.

Underscore two points. First, the nominal deficit did not grow to impressive proportion because of tax cuts and faltering government revenue. The ratio of revenue to GNP was higher during the Reagan administration than during any other since World War II—indeed, it is the largest taxation ratio of any administration in our history.

Second, the striking increase in government expenditures relative to GNP has not stemmed from burgeoning defense spending. The proportion of GNP devoted to defense fell steadily from over 13 percent in the Korean period of the early 1950s to less than 5 percent in the late 1970s. The ratio began to rise in 1979, but has averaged less than 6 percent in the 1980s. The defense ratio has been smaller during the Reagan administration than during any other since World War II except for the Carter period.

Those who proclaim that we have been in an era of large budget deficits because taxes have been cut and defense spending has been bloated should know these things. Surely some of them do.

December 1988)

The Nature and Significance of Government Deficits and Debt

Mouse Wisdom:
The Government Budget Always Balances

"I often find the world so confusing," grumped a commonly confused mouse Karl, "that I don't know whether to laugh or cry."

"Given the nature of the world," suggested the meditative mouse Adam, "whenever in doubt, it is more appropriate to cry."

"Tell me which I should do about the government budget deficit," persisted Karl.

"I see no reason to laugh about the deficit," Adam replied. "But there is little reason for hysterics, either. The deficit is a problem, but the problem is smaller in size and different in nature than many politicians and journalists seem to suppose."

"It seems serious to me," Karl confided seriously. "Everyone knows that the deficit creates inflation, raises interest rates, and threatens governmental bankruptcy."

"I don't know what you mean by 'governmental bankruptcy,'" said Adam. "The government will always pay its bills. And it is not inevitable that the so-called deficit will have a perceptible effect on either the price level or interest rates. If you insist on reveling in fiscal concerns, you would do better to worry about the *size* of the budget rather than the *imbalance* of the budget. Indeed," added Adam, "in a significant sense there never is a budgetary imbalance."

"Gasp!" gasped Karl. "No budget imbalance? Everyone knows that the federal deficit in recent years has been $200 billion and more!"

"Everyone seems to know many things which are not so," observed Adam dryly. "Look at it in this commonsensical way: the government acquires things—resources and products of resources; the government cannot have more than it gets from the people; the community does not give these things to the government—Big Brother pays for what he gets; and the funds with which the payments are made, like the things that are bought, come from you and me— raising the means to make the payments *is* taxation, even if accountants and statisticians label as 'taxation' only certain of these means."

"I can see that what government gets, it gets from the public," said Karl cautiously, "but I have supposed that everything is proper and in good order—whatever that means—as long as conventional taxation covers government spending. Fiscal prudence means simply that people give government enough in ordinary, explicit taxes to pay for all that government wants to spend."

"That is mainly just bookkeeping camouflage," replied Adam with some bitterness. "Government spending is government spending, whether government directly gets the funds it spends by handing to the public a tax receipt or a bond or newly printed money. The cost of what government gets from the people is neither diminished nor delayed by any legerdemain of financing procedures. The size of the budget is seen, not in the amount of traditional *taxes*, but in the amount of government *spending*, that is, in the amount of the people's wealth and of the people's income sequestered by and channeled through government. But, big or small, no matter how financed, the government budget is always balanced."

(March 1987)

Government Bonds, Taxes, and Societal Squabbling

We have been taught that a deficit in the government budget is the excess of expenditures over tax receipts. But tax can mean different things, and different meanings of tax imply different meanings of deficit.

In a real and fundamental sense, any government sequestering of resources from the community—regardless of just how the sequestering is done—is a tax on the community. When government *spends* and acquires things from you and me, it is thereby *taxing*. So the government budget always balances.

To acquire funds for its spending, government can coerce contributions from the public and it can cajole people to contribute through buying government bonds. In important respects, we are led astray by accountants and statisticians counting only the coerced contributions as taxes.

When government bonds are sold today, first interest on the debt and then principal of the debt will have to be paid in the future. Conventional, explicit taxation can thus be delayed. But with the commitment of *expected* explicit taxes, *current* wealth is reduced by the amount of the present value of those future commitments. That current reduction in wealth is itself a current tax, even if we do not generally call it a tax.

Although the real budget is necessarily balanced, there is a *nominal* deficit when spending is not financed by current explicit taxes. And a large nominal deficit is not of trivial concern.

One problem pertains to future redistribution of income. Practically, deficit financing implies greater tax payments in the future. But we do not know today exactly *who* will have to pay *how much* of tomorrow's explicit taxes. What we can reasonably presume is that the assignment of tax obligations will *not* perfectly coincide with the holding of the bonds which are to be serviced and paid off. Taxpayers and bondowners are not identical groups. Indeed, observes Armen Alchian, one of the world's eminent economists, "if . . . the government bonds each of us held matched exactly the tax on each of us to pay interest and principal, we could cancel. . . [the government debt]."

In contrast to private debts, Professor Alchian continues, "when the government issues debt, no one knows definitely who is liable for exactly how much of the repayment. . . . That impending redistribution, to be determined in the future, will cause divisiveness and political instability as we or our children argue and fight, like heirs disputing an ambiguous will. *That* is . . . the principal danger of a large government debt."

If current government spending is financed by current taxes instead of government selling of bonds, then the fight over who pays how much of the taxes takes place currently. So there is struggle over the paying of explicit taxes, whether the paying is done now or later.

If we are to minimize community conflict, we must reduce government spending and government taxing and the associated government wealth redistribution.

(March 1987)

The Government Budget and Deficit Difficulties

A large and growing share of national output is channeled through government. What government absorbs, it gets from the community. Whatever the immediate sources of the funds government spends, that expenditure to acquire the public's wealth—that reduction in wealth left in private hands—is taxation. With government absorption simultaneously matched by private cost, the real government budget is always balanced.

But only the private cost represented by conventional, explicit taxes is listed in the government budget. When those explicit taxes are less than government expenditures, there is a nominal deficit. And that nominal deficit—while tending to obscure the perennial balance in the real budget—has significance of its own.

One problem is that tax payments to government are not in the same pattern and proportion as debt interest and principal payments by government. Some people pay more in taxes than they receive in interest and principal, and some pay less. So government financing redistributes wealth, and such redistribution can create community heartburn.

There are additional difficulties with the nominal deficit. There could be large deficits with small budgets, and large budgets can be balanced. But experience—including experience of the last two decades—indicates that large deficits are most likely to be associated with large budgets. And there is much reason, both economic and philosophic, to fret about persistent increase in the governmental share of the national economy.

Further, large deficits, current and expected, call for funding considerations and practices that, in anticipation and in action, are unsettling. The hopes and fears—especially the fears—of wonderment about government borrowing, taxing, and inflating evoke uncertainty, inhibiting long-term planning and adding a risk-premium to interest rates.

Still another danger of nominal deficits is inflation and further bloating of interest rates. Recurring large deficits lead to larger tax collections. Tax receipts can rise because of increased explicit tax rates and also because of nominal national income increased through higher prices. Inflation—which pulls up interest rates along with other prices—stems from creating money too rapidly. And one way too much money can be created is through the Federal Reserve "monetizing" the debt.

The feds monetize the debt by buying government bonds. Thus far in recent history, monetization has not been massive—but the temptation and the potential are. First, monetization reduces the interest-bearing debt held by the public. Second, in substituting money and bank reserves for debt, monetization generates inflation, which reduces the real value of the remaining publicly held debt.

Unhappily, government can gain—although the community loses—through lousy fiscal policy abetted by clumsy monetary management.

(March 1987)

The Deficit Debate and Getting It Straight

Many ascribe to the federal budget manifold woes and perils which are either much exaggerated or properly to be imputed to other causes. Help in setting some of the discussion straight has been provided by Thomas Humbert, of the Heritage Foundation.

Of course, we are supposed to do something about perceived problems. But policies are adopted today because of conditions anticipated tomorrow. And the record of forecasting tomorrow's deficits has been sobering.

Over the thirteen years between 1971 and 1983, the Office of Management and Budget provided an annual average *projected* deficit of $33 billion; the *actual* deficits averaged $56 billion—a 70 percent error. Forecasting errors which are both huge and erratic cannot be a satisfactory basis of rational policy. The moral is, Mr. Humbert notes, "policy should not be guided by forecasts, especially in turbulent times, but by fundamental principles designed to create a stable climate for long-term economic growth."

There would be a problem in using budget forecasts even if they were consistently accurate. For the *federal* deficit is not a good indicator of *total* government borrowing. *State and local* governments have a combined surplus these days of over $50 billion, offsetting more than one-fourth of the federal deficit. Nearly another fourth is irrelevant to government borrowing in the market, for it is new debt acquired by agencies of the government itself. On the other hand, there is the cost of off-budget debt, much of which defies accurate measurement. Net borrowing by government may be only some two-thirds the size of the conventionally measured federal deficit.

At any rate, don't big deficits create inflation, raise interest rates, and crowd out private borrowers? If incessant reiteration provided the test of truth, deficits would be dastardly, indeed.

Deficits are *not* nice. They complicate monetary management, engender distracting uncertainty about government policies, and are commonly associated with expansion of government in the economy.

But a growing mountain of analyzed experience makes it increasingly clear that large deficits and anticipated large deficits contribute little to high and rising interest rates or to high and rising inflation or to crowding private investors out of credit markets. These things do happen, but they happen because of excessive *spending* by government and excessive *money creation* by government.

So we badly forecast a variable (namely, the federal deficit) which is both poorly specified to quantify the market activity in question (namely, government borrowing pressure in the credit markets) and inappropriately chosen to explain the phenomena in question (including inflation, interest rates, and private investment). We use lousy data for the wrong measure in misconceived analysis.

Otherwise, the chitter-chatter about the deficit is splendidly done and highly useful.

(June 1984)

Budget Strategies and Procedures

Sensible Deficit Strategy: Steady as She Goes

Karl, the worrisome mouse, loves to worry. "I am worried about the federal government deficit," he confided to his calmer friend Adam.

"Much of my own concern about the conventionally measured deficit," said Adam, "is that it will inspire dumb policies to reduce it. But if we sensibly resolve the condition basically by containing the rate of increase of government spending, fiscal life should go on quite serenely."

"But," whimpered a still worried Karl, "do we really have that policy choice? Ever so many people—some of whom supposedly are knowledgeable, bright, and honest—insist that the big deficits were caused by tax cuts and can be corrected only by tax increases."

"The summary record is clear," said Adam sharply. "Over the twenty years between 1965 and 1985, despite much upward and downward diddling with tax rates, revenue increased quite steadily at a robust annual average rate of 9.6 percent; but spending rose even more rapidly at 11 percent. Revenue and especially spending went up faster than national income, and both the budget and the deficit increased relative to GNP."

"But what of the future," cautiously asked Karl. "Even if too much spending caused the deficit, to eliminate the deficit maybe we have to increase the rate of revenue growth."

"That is simply incorrect," corrected Adam. "Tax receipts go up at about the same rate as GNP. The rate of GNP increase is equal to the rate of inflation plus the rate of output expansion. Now, suppose we confined the growth of government spending to the rate of inflation. Then, revenue would rise faster than spending by the rate of increase in real output. We could have about 5 percent inflation and 3 percent production growth over the next several years. That would mean government spending going up at 5 percent annually and tax receipts at 8 percent."

"And what would that do to the deficit?"

"The deficit would then be eliminated in just six years," replied a gratified Adam. "The deficit will be corrected over some period if revenue rises at a faster rate than spending. If the increase in spending is held to the rate of inflation, then the gap of the rate of revenue increase over spending increase would equal the rate of output increase. I want the real, inflation-corrected increase in spending held to zero, and I want the rate of output expansion to be substantial. But increasing tax rates, while doing little or nothing to raise tax collections, would reduce the growth rate of output and thereby delay elimination of the deficit."

"Might we get what you want?" hopefully asked Karl.

"We are already in the process!" exclaimed Adam. "For the last three years, government spending has been rising at a rate of just over 4 percent, only a little more than inflation, and revenue has been rising at 7.5 percent, a little more than GNP. So the prescription is essentially: instead of doing something dumb, hold her steady as she goes."

(December 1988)

Budget Deficits, Constitutional Mandates, and Character

There is much concern—some of it legitimate—about deficits in the federal budget. And so there is much talk about how to reduce deficits. One approach—mechanical rather than political in nature—is to decree deficits into non-existence by means of a balanced-budget constitutional amendment.

We do well not to let an unreasonable stipulation of perfection in an imperfect world preclude progress. But the proposal for a balanced-budget amendment may have more than its share of problems.

One problem pertains to the very objective. To specify simply that the budget must be balanced is not to specify a goal which is necessarily very attractive. Our more appropriate concern is with the *size* of the budget rather than with the *balance* of the budget—with the budgetary level defined in terms of government *spending* rather than *tax collections*. A budget can be a disaster—both economically and politically—because of how much is spent and what the spending is for, even when it is balanced.

Roy L. Ash, former Director of the Office of Management and Budget, reminds us of intimidating technical problems in decreeing budget balance—problems of measurement and procedure in implementation and in avoidance of circumvention. What measure is to be balanced? Along with the conventional budget, there are massive off-budget expenditures, in part by the Postal Service. There are the huge trust funds, including Social Security. And there are "tax expenditures"—exemptions, deductions, and credits which are alternatives to direct government spending—and there are costs imposed by the state on the private sector as substitutes for expenditures by government.

A different category of complications relates to any "emergency" override provision. Can such a safety valve be formulated so as to make it immune to Congressional abuse? Mr. Ash notes that "we can't constitutionally mandate that politicians must not be creative." Too much interpretative and procedural flexibility would vitiate the constraining purpose of the amendment; too little adaptability could conduce confusion and clumsy paralysis.

Even when the requirement of budget balance is combined with a rule for determining maximum taxation, implementation rests on definitions, calculations, and estimates—along with Congressional integrity—which leave effective constraints largely uninteresting.

Finally, if the provision of the balanced-budget amendment were (unsurprisingly) violated, who would do what to whom? What could be the channels of redress and remedy?

It is a disgrace that there is occasion for ingenious proposals to impose responsible fiscal policy by constitutional mandate. The policy problem stems ultimately from cowardice, venality, and demagoguery. Given the disgrace, it is a frustrating shame that an appropriate amendment—which first seems straightforward—is so complicated in formulation and uncertain in effect. Lack of character in high places makes life harder than it need be.

(August 1982)

The Line-Item Veto: A Marginal Improvement?

How to contain government spending? One proposal is to give the President line-item veto authority for appropriations bills. Some bills appropriate tens of billions of dollars in dozens of spending categories for several government departments. But the President faces an all-or-nothing choice: he either approves the entire bill or he vetoes the entire bill.

It may seem reasonable to permit the President to be selective in approving or vetoing individual items in a massive, heterogeneous appropriations bill thrown together by log-rolling legislators. Forty-three states have given that power to their governors. But objections have been offered to the item veto proposal.

It is complained that the great bulk of the budget is effectively beyond the reach of veto or of any other kind of discretionary control: payment of interest is not legally optional, and most entitlement payments seem not politically optional. Use of the item veto might nibble off only one percent of the budget. Still, a billion here and a billion there does add up. Indeed, as a Heritage Foundation study notes, an annual 1 percent cut in the budget beginning in 1974 would have reduced 1985 spending by over $100 billion—equal to half the deficit. At any rate, it is a peculiar argument against adopting a procedure to say that the procedure would not encompass enough!

Other objections to the veto proposal are mutually incompatible. It is said that Presidents—despite their persistent request for item veto authority—do not really want it and would rarely use it. At the same time, we are told, granting the authority would greatly and maybe undesirably shift power from Congress to the President. The first concern largely negates the second: authority little used cannot be power greatly shifted. Used well by appropriate criteria, the proposed veto power would not permit more spending; at worst, it would not be used to have less spending.

A third complaint is that the proposed procedure would be used, but not in ways intended. On the one hand, a grandstanding Congress might load bills with pork for the President to cut, but if the political price of cutting is deemed too great, spending would be allowed to increase. On the other hand, a blackmailing President might use the threat of selective veto to cow a cowardly Congress for his own purposes, which are likely to be expensive.

So the item veto authority would not reduce spending greatly or quickly, and it is conceivable that it would perversely lead to Congressional or Presidential irresponsibility which would increase spending.

Still, the budget is a growing mess. Modifying the budget-making procedure with the delegation of a Presidential item-veto authority could be of only marginal help. But in a messy world, most improvements are marginal. Some improvement is better than none, and potential gain is better than assured continued deterioration.

(June 1985)

Taxation: How Much, What Kind, Who Cares?

Crowding Out: Interest Rates and Taxation

A rose by any other name would smell as sweet, and a tax increase is no less malodorous for being called "tax reform" in the interest of fairness. When more taxes are collected out of a given level of national income—whether collected fairly or unfairly—the phenomenon *is* a tax increase. Even a jackass (to use a Presidential term) can understand that.

What was the basis of last summer's overweening concern with tax unfairness, correction of which just happened to entail an enormous increase in tax collection? The President rhetorically asked: "Would you rather reduce deficits and interest rates by raising revenue, . . . or would you rather accept larger budget deficits, higher interest rates, and higher unemployment?"

The line of thought—if such it is—seems to be: first, increasing taxes reduces the government deficit; second, reducing the deficit reduces interest rates; and, third, reducing interest rates increases investment, output, and employment.

That is not very elegant economics. The first point—linking tax increases to deficit reductions—is a combination of baseless hope and political cowardice. The second—linking smaller deficits to lower interest rates—diverts attention from the major determinants of interest rates to a relationship which is very weak and highly uncertain. The third—linking reduced interest rates to expanded economic activity—is a grossly inadequate specification of the conditions of prosperity.

Still, we do want a more robust economy, and, other things given, it would help greatly to get interest rates back down to civilized levels. So, with exaggerated generosity and patience, give the Presidential and Congressional case more than its due. Suppose we presume that raising taxes actually would reduce the deficit and that reducing the deficit would reduce interest rates. After all, the government must pay its bills, and if government spending is greater than tax collections, then it must borrow; but when government borrows, it must compete with private borrowers; in the credit-market competition, interest rates are bid up, and private business is "crowded out."

This has a plausible ring. But, at best, it can be only a partial story. The private sector can be crowded out of investment as surely by high taxes, which reduce cash flow to cash trickle, as by high interest rates, which inhibit borrowing. Internal financing is at least as legitimate as external financing; private saving is at least as attractive as private debt; a dollar earned and not taxed away is at least as good as a dollar borrowed.

Reducing a government deficit by the alternative strategy of reducing government spending avoids crowding out through the tax channel. But increasing taxes to pay for continued government spending increases absorption of private cash while failing to alleviate government absorption of the community's real resources.

(October 1982)

Income Tax Law, the Marx Brothers, and Mephistopheles

As it has evolved, income tax law is a monument to foolishness and deviousness, suggesting the combined handiwork of the Marx brothers and Mephistopheles.

The legislation of 1981—which elated some innocents and terrified others—promised limited relief and marginal modification, but the ridiculous, jerry-built structure was not endangered. Now, suddenly but belatedly, a good many people of widely differing orientations have agreed on the nature of desirable reform.

The essence of the "new" idea—which a few have long advocated—is to tax all incomes uniformly: there would be the same tax rate applied to incomes of any amount from any kind of source, with no special deductions, credits, or exemptions (except for personal exemptions, probably larger than those now in effect, to buffer the very poor). The uniform, or flat rate would approximate today's minimum marginal rate.

The appeal of this proposal is more than aesthetic: numerous significant advantages are inherent.

- One, it could vastly simplify the mechanics of preparing tax reports.

- Two, it would obviate convoluted and expensive tax-strategy considerations in spending and investing, which concentrate on saving taxes on current income rather than on producing more income.

- Three, it would provide the full work, saving, and investment incentives of zero marginal tax rates.

- Four, it would equalize absolute taxes for people with equal incomes and equalize relative taxes for people with different incomes.

These four improvements of simplification, productive incentives, and uniformity would discourage tax evasion, counteract the growing fear of and contempt for government, and make feasible more than ample financing of government at a minimal rate. There are still additional advantages.

- Five, it would eliminate unlegislated tax increases through inflationary bracket-creep.

- Six, it would reduce the expenses of tax collections—and the massive, unique interpretive and implementational authority of the Internal Revenue Service.

- Seven, it would neutralize the proclivity of Big Brother to use tax tactics in social engineering strategy.

Is there any chance that the good sense embodied in the flat-rate proposal will be made effective? Sure—about the same chance that the Marx brothers would be converted into deacons of decorum and that Mephistopheles would be metamorphosed into a disciple of virtue.

Good sense presumably is a necessary condition for good tax structure, but it certainly is not sufficient. Making good sense effective would shear too much status, wealth, and power from too many—tax lawyers and accountants, the masses inhabiting tax shelters, government officials. So, instead, it is the great bulk of the taxpayers—including some who believe they garner net gains through the dozens of loopholes which provide billions of dollars of benefits—who will continue to be sheared.

(August 1982)

Mouse Wisdom: Proportional Tax Cuts and Differential Incentives

Karl likes to believe that he is a no-nonsense mouse. He confronted Adam, his poised and patient companion—although Karl rather confuses poise and patience with wimpishness.

"I understand," said Karl in a no-nonsense manner, "that some of your economist friends have cutely said that the way to soak the very rich is to lower their marginal tax rate."

"We are not out to 'soak' anyone," corrected Adam. "Government is not intended to punish anyone except criminals—and it is not yet illegal to have a relatively large income."

"OK," snapped Karl. "But don't try to con me into supposing that common percentage cuts in tax rates don't favor the wealthy. Reducing a marginal rate on high incomes from 70 percent to 50 percent and reducing a rate on low incomes from 14 percent to 10 percent is the same *proportional* cut in each case. But that reduction of 20 percentage points for the rich is much more *money* than the 4 percentage points for the poor."

"Of course," agreed Adam. "But Professor James Gwartney, of Florida State University, points out that that is not the end of the story. We are talking about *marginal* tax rates. With a 70 percent rate, Daddy Warbucks keeps only 30 cents after paying his tax on an additional dollar of income; with the new 50 percent rates, he keeps 50 cents. Being able to increase take-home pay by two-thirds—from 30 cents to 50 cents—out of every additional dollar of earnings is a great incentive to earn more (and to shelter less) income. By contrast, Tiny Tim increases his disposable income from 86 cents to 90 cents out of another dollar, which is less than a 5 percent improvement. Daddy's net income situation has been greatly changed, but Tiny has not been much affected."

"So," Karl grudgingly acknowledged, "the same proportional *cut* in marginal *tax rates* means a much greater proportional *increase* in *after-tax* income for the wealthy. That is a matter of arithmetic. But what of the taxation consequences?"

"The consequences have been predictable—and by some predicted," Adam said. "In the 1920s, the 1960s, and again in the 1980s, cuts in the marginal tax rates for the top of the income scale have been followed by such large increases in taxable income that the tax payments by the wealthy have actually increased. From 1981 to 1983, individuals' total income tax payments *fell* 11 percent in constant dollars, but the very top earners paid a little *more*."

"Amazing," said an amazed Karl. "Maybe some economists are not completely crazy, after all."

"In fact," added a poised Adam, "good economists have been saying for a very long time that people respond to incentives. And they are right in saying today that people are motivated by after-tax earnings. Let them keep appreciably more of another dollar earned, and they will earn—and pay taxes on—many more dollars."

(July 1985)

Individual Choice and User Fees

Those who get what they want should pay; those who do not want should not be forced to receive and should not be obliged to pay. That is a sound principle in a world where we cannot have all we want and thus must pick and choose. The principle of rational economizing is sensibly applied to government as well as to the private market.

One government device—discussed by Robert W. Poole, Jr. in his book, *Cutting Back City Hall*—is "user charges." The fee-for-government-service is an explicit payment for the service by the beneficiary. Public services are made available at a price paid by the specific consumer of the service, not financed out of general taxes as part of a nebulous package dumped on the community at large.

In the genuine marketplace, people pinpoint their expenditures. They buy only those things in those amounts on which they *choose* to spend their money at prices *known* to them. Since they know what they are buying and the terms on which they buy, since they can choose what to get and what to forego, their wealth is used in accordance with their own preferences.

In short, consumption in the open market is rational, and resources are used efficiently. For, in a free society, rationality and efficiency have meaning only in connection with what individual members of the community prefer.

Surely, there are some services and facilities provided on a broad communal basis—services and facilities which yield benefits so generally that they are appropriately financed by the general public. We all benefit from provision of national defense against foreign aggression and communicable diseases. In such instances, we cannot expect to define and enforce property rights so precisely as to identify particular beneficiaries of the services and charge only them to finance the services.

But it is not easy to identify a large number of so-called public goods— goods which, in their nature, benefit the community at large, no matter how they are financed. Most services of government—even fire and police protection, and certainly garbage collection, ambulances, and golf courses—can be (and increasingly are) provided to *readily identifiable, specific, voluntary users*, who, therefore, can be charged on the basis of how much of the service they consume. User fees are charged to users—and only to users. The criteria and the procedures—and thus the efficiency—of the free market are applied to and utilized in the government sector through the use of "public prices for public products," treating citizens as consumers with a variety of demands.

Government doubtless will always be with us. We non-anarchists believe that government *should* always be with us. But we are not obliged to insist stubbornly that government be largely unaccountable and typically wasteful, blithely and badly providing a huge package of services, many of which are not much wanted, or are not wanted in the proportions provided, by any given individual citizen, but still with everyone assessed a large and growing tax payment, no matter how little he likes the government product.

A free society is one in which the members of the society have freedom. One giant component of freedom is based on the axiom that those—and only those—who get, should pay.

(March 1981)

Mouse Wisdom: Sneaky Taxes

"A great idea," bubbled excitable mouse Karl to sober, sensible mouse Adam. "Congress wants to give workers health insurance, unpaid leaves for new parents, day care for children, advance notice of plant closings, and other benefits."

"These goodies are not gifts," said Adam soberly. "Who will pay the immense cost? The federal budget remains saturated with red ink, and new taxes are as popular as a cat at a cheese tasting party."

"The solution is obvious," answered Karl. "Clever politicians want to require businesses to provide them."

"Sounds like a sneaky way to raise taxes," Adam sensibly surmised.

"Nonsense!" snapped Karl. "Employers would be required simply to give workers the benefits they deserve."

"But you ignore the productivity of labor," admonished Adam. "Workers can be paid either in money wages or in benefits. If money wages are reduced to make room for increased benefits, total pay does not rise. But that is not what politicians propose. By mandating all these benefits, they will push workers' pay above their productivity and thereby increase employers' costs of production."

"So what?" responded Karl. "Businesses have lots of profit; they ought to use some of it to provide more benefits for workers."

"Including money wages and benefits," explained Adam, "labor compensation represents nearly three-fourths of national income. In contrast, after-tax corporate profits represent less than 4 percent of total income. In 1987, that amounted to $137 billion. Compare this figure with the likely cost of the mandated benefits. A health insurance bill now before Congress could itself cost businesses $40 billion a year. That's close to one-third of all after-tax profits earned last year!"

"That *is* a big sum," admitted a surprised Karl.

"Government could not take such a huge chunk of profit without devastating national production and employment," continued Adam. "The mandated benefits would be a tax immediately on labor and consumers and indirectly on corporate profits."

"Is that what you meant when you said the required benefits would push workers' pay above their productivity?" asked Karl.

"Yes," affirmed Adam. "The cost of labor would rise, so goods and services would cost more to produce. Because of the higher cost of production, each affected business would increase its price and reduce its output."

"That would harm almost everybody," Karl keenly conceived.

"Indeed, it would," answered Adam. "Higher prices would hurt consumers; reduced production would weaken demand for labor and cause employment and pay to fall; and higher production costs would cut profits and hurt stockholders."

"So, as consumers, workers, and stockholders, we all end up footing the enormous bill," concluded a crestfallen Karl.

Adam sadly smiled: "As I said, it is a sneaky way to raise taxes."

(August 1988)

National Defense

"The Great Arsenal of Democracy"

At least prior to this era of possible push-button devastation, battlefield resolution was achieved by bomb and bayonet—and by those who dropped and wielded them. But even in those primitive days, the bombs and bayonets—along with ships, tanks, airplanes, and provisions for troops, civilians, and allies—had to be produced.

In World War II, the United States had to do a great deal of the producing, as well as a considerable share of the fighting. The economy was obliged to make a mighty effort after having lurched and stumbled for more than a decade. In December 1940, President Roosevelt called upon the nation to be "the great arsenal of democracy." How and how well did it respond?

Output had to rise at the same time that millions of our most productive men were channeled into military service. In 1940, the armed forces had only a half million people; in 1944 and 1945, there were 11.5 million. But civilian employment did not concomitantly fall. Instead, from 1940 to 1945, it *increased* over five million.

It was possible to expand the military and the number employed by a total of some sixteen million on an annual basis partly by reducing unemployment by seven million, to a minimal level. It was a disgrace that the economy had an unemployment rate of 15 percent in 1940, but it was also convenient to have a large pool of idle resources to draw on just when output had to be expanded. The remaining nine million increase in the armed forces plus employment came from a much larger proportion of participants in a somewhat larger population: in 1945, nearly 70 percent of those in the age range of sixteen to sixty-four years were either employed or in the armed forces, compared to only 55 percent in 1940.

The great productive effort is reflected in a growth in real output of more than 50 percent from 1940 to 1945—while employment rose only 11 percent. Not only did the *amount* of output increase enormously, but the *composition* of output was shifted toward war purposes. Real private investment was cut almost in half; consumption, in this so-called total war, went up one-fifth, but it was reduced appreciably as a proportion of total production; the massive change was in government absorption of national output, which increased fivefold.

The U.S. economy, despite some bumbling and misdirection, performed magnificently. The arsenal of democracy made victory possible. But it was neither easy or quick. It required four years after 1940 for real output and government use of output to reach a peak. A generation ago, that was good enough. In the future, we may not have four years to get organized, gear up, and grind out the product. And with resources initially more fully employed than in 1940, there will be less available room for output expansion. Perhaps one moral is that from now on we must be fully prepared all the time.

(May 1982)

Defense and Opulence

It is contended that we must choose between substantial national defense and substantial national opulence. Indeed, some assert that opulence is the best defense—supposedly, the plump chicken is the one whose neck is least likely to be wrung. But we are reminded by Professor Charles Van Eaton, of Hillsdale College, that since World War II, good economic performance and large defense budgets have co-existed.

In the short run, prosperity and defense expenditure certainly are mutually consistent. Money national income consists of and is measured by total spending—including spending by government—on output. Spending is spending, and more military spending this year will not reduce this year's income.

This is not the whole story, of course. First, we are not indifferent to the composition of this year's output. For a given national output, the bigger the government budget, the smaller the private budget. And for a given government budget, the more spent on defense for us all, the less is available to congressmen to divide among their respective projects.

Further, the size of the private sector share is one determinant of the amount of *saving* and the direction of *investment*. More military spending, while creating income today, could, through adverse effects on long-term productivity, reduce output tomorrow.

But the burdens of our defense have not been devastating to the economy. Indeed, by obvious indicators of national economic health—the price level, unemployment, output—we have done best in recent decades when the military budget was relatively large.

Beginning after the Korean War, compare two thirteen-year periods, 1954 to 1967 and 1967 to 1980. From the mid-fifties to the late sixties, defense outlays as a proportion of gross national product ranged annually from some 7 to 11 percent, the average being about 9 percent. From 1967 to 1979, the ratio of defense to income fell each year, from 8.9 percent to 4.6 percent, recovering a bit in 1980, with the average just over 6 percent.

By all our measures, the economy performed better in the earlier period, when the proportion of income directed to defense averaged almost 50 percent higher. Real GNP rose 64 percent compared to 46 percent; unemployment was 5.1 percent compared to 5.7 percent; and prices rose 33 percent compared to 126 percent.

This is not to say that increasing defense spending as a proportion of GNP will surely increase output, reduce unemployment, and subdue inflation. Nor is it to say that, even if one invariably found such correlations, increasing defense spending is surely the best way to promote economic strength. But evidently investment in military survival can be compatible with prosperity. We may even hypothesize that inadequate military investment will not enhance the probability of survival and that failure to survive will not contribute to our prosperity.

(July 1983)

The Deficit, Taxes, and Defense Spending

Many academic, editorialist, and politician types, while entirely comfortable with rising taxes, purport to be terrified by spending on national defense. Sometimes they seem convinced that, despite our enormous gross national product, we cannot afford to protect ourselves adequately in an unfriendly world. Sometimes they like to presume that the defense budget tail wags the economy dog, and they sneer at "artificial" prosperity based on military spending. And of course, in conjunction with inadequate taxation, the increase in such spending over the last five years supposedly is the central cause of the federal budget deficit.

A major newspaper—parroting many others—has recently played the latter theme. The deficit, it is asserted, stems from two key sources: overexuberant tax cuts on the revenue side, and overexuberant defense expenditure on the spending side.

But if we are to fret about the deficit, it would be nice to get straight what is causing it. And there is much craziness in ascribing it most basically to tax cuts and military spending.

What has actually happened to the budget? Compare the first half dozen years of the 1970s—1970 through 1975—with the early 1980s—1980 through 1985.

In the first part of the seventies, the annual federal deficit averaged just over $20 billion; in the eighties, it has been seven times greater, averaging almost $150 billion. But this explosion of the deficit did not at all stem from curtailed government receipts. Receipts averaged 18 percent of GNP in the earlier period; in the later period, they were a greater proportion, averaging 19.3 percent.

The sevenfold increase in the deficit from the early seventies to the early eighties stems entirely from the spending side of the budget—spending which averaged 19.6 percent of GNP in the former period and a huge 23.7 percent in the latter period. From 1970 to 1985, government receipts, along with GNP, rose at a robust annual rate of about 9.3 percent, but spending expanded still faster, at more than 11 percent. We did not tax too little; we spent too much.

But did we spend too much on defense? No one can say for sure. But at least note that in the days of relatively moderate budget deficits, in the early 1970s, defense spending equaled 6.3 percent of GNP, whereas in the big-deficit 1980s, defense spending is only 5.8 percent of GNP. Further, defense spending is now a much smaller part of the total budget. In the early seventies, defense averaged almost one-third of federal spending, and in the early eighties, it has averaged only one-fourth.

Do you suppose that journalists and historians and congressmen really do not know such things and have no notion of how to find out?

(September 1985)

Age and Social Security

Age, Income, and Policy

With each passing day, I grow older. And, for good or ill, I have been doing that for quite a long time. So while I may have little enthusiasm for advanced age, I do not scorn the aged. But one can reasonably ask basic questions about public policy toward those with silver hair in their golden years.

This is critical policy. As Randall Pozdena, of the San Francisco Federal Reserve Bank notes, Social Security retirement programs and Medicare account for nearly 40 percent of total federal expenditures. On both philosophic and fiscal grounds, we are obliged, in determining priorities, to review the economic condition of the beneficiaries of such programs.

As reflected in Federal Reserve surveys in 1977 and 1983, the condition of the elderly has improved over the past decade or so, and is now pretty good. This is partly because of *market* phenomena. About half of non-human wealth in the United States is in the form of residential real estate; such real estate is held mainly by older households; and, since 1972, housing prices have risen considerably more than the general price level. At the same time, inflation reduced the real value of most mortgage debt.

There are also *policy* phenomena, including massive increases in Social Security benefits. Those basic benefits rose in real terms from 1970 to 1983 by 120 percent—while non-agricultural real hourly wages of those who pay the bulk of the Social Security taxes actually fell a bit.

Both the *wealth* and the *income* of the relatively elderly rose between 1977 and 1983. In the latter year, nominal net worth was greatest in the economy for those in the 65 to 74 age group, nearly double the national average.

Income for those over sixty-four has increased substantially over the past decade relative to all households. And poverty among them has fallen by 20 percent, and is now lower than for any other age group.

It would be silly to say that the most mature have few legitimate economic concerns. The problem goes beyond disparities of wealth and income found within every age group. In addition, the elderly—who are ending, or have ended, their economically productive years—are especially vulnerable, and less adaptable, to uncertainties of inflation, interest rates, health, reliability of government programs, and other slings and arrows.

Still, one can wonder about the comprehension and courage of politicians who blithely speak of even more grandiose retirement programs. Perhaps community aid should be directed more to the weak and incompetent than to the elderly as such. And perhaps wealth would be greater for the entire community, and intergenerational friction smaller, with greater emphasis on private use of private means for income protection.

(December 1987)

Social Security Myths

As in Western Europe and Japan, the United States Social Security system has persistently become less secure even as the Social Security taxes have become more severe. Awareness of the crisis is growing. Still, the public has acquiesced in a strikingly docile manner to misconstruction and misdirection of the Social Security program. Surely, people have been so patient because government has matched incompetence in policy substance with skill in promotion skullduggery.

The Social Security crisis is real. But it is cloaked and camouflaged in pervasive mythology. The Commissioner of Social Security agrees that "the issue is misunderstood by the public due to almost fifty years of misleading information provided by the government. . . ." He adds that from its beginning in 1935, "Social Security was shrouded in myth."

Contrary to myth, Social Security is not an *insurance* system, with individually owned policies, actuarially determined premiums, and contingency payoffs based on the scheduled premiums.

Contrary to myth, Social Security is not a *pension* system, with individually received benefits equal to what the recipients had invested, with interest, in the scheme.

Contrary to myth, Social Security is not a *trust fund*, with people paying into their respective personal accounts, which thus accumulate until drawn on by the account owners.

Contrary to myth, Social Security is not funded through *contributions*, with individuals choosing whether or how much to save through this program.

Contrary to myth, Social Security is not basically and uniformly a *good retirement* plan, yielding more benefits than could otherwise have been earned with the same money put into private retirement funds.

Contrary to myth, workers do not look upon Social Security taxes as the *equivalent of deferred income* and thus as constituting no burden.

Contrary to myth, Social Security has never been intended to provide *sole*, *full retirement* benefits, and it is not adequately funded for even the partial, but enlarged, wage replacements in retirement which were stipulated in the 1970s.

Far from being an individually funded insurance and pension arrangement, with each person accumulating—by government mandate, to be sure—his personal nest egg, we have a pay-as-we-go arrangement, with today's workers subsidizing today's retirees. And, persistently, politicians buy today's votes by increasing benefits to be paid tomorrow and tomorrow and tomorrow by tomorrow's workers. But the demographic future foresees a continuation in the dramatically declining ratio of workers to retirees. So we have been cavalierly committing relatively fewer and fewer workers to bear greater and greater burdens in smaller and smaller anticipation that they, in turn, will eventually be beneficiaries.

Thus we have concocted an enormous fiasco exquisitely designed to breed fiscal chaos and community divisiveness.

(March 1983)

Little Brother:
State and Local Government

Tall Taxes and Stunted States

Cities and states—like individuals and families—generally are facing obligations of the moment. They have bills to pay right away, and there is only limited room for immediate maneuver. But with sense and responsibility in handling our affairs, the long run can be more than simply an unending series of short-run accommodations. We have considerable control over our fate, and how well we prosper is determined in large part by what and how much government does and the way those activities are financed.

Higher taxes obviously can temporarily mitigate the fiscal problems of cities and states, but over time they tend strongly to retard economic growth and thus harm people, wealthy and poor alike. These perverse results of higher taxes were recently described by Richard Vedder, an economist for the Joint Economic Committee of Congress and professor of economics at Ohio University. Professor Vedder lays bare the strong, positive relationship between higher taxes and lower economic growth.

In classifying all states as having high, moderate, or low taxes, he discovered that states with relatively *low* taxes had the *highest* rate of economic growth. More precisely, states with the lowest per capita taxes saw their real per capita income grow more than one-third faster—a significant differential—than states with the highest taxes.

Not only the *level* of taxes is associated with growth, but—perhaps more important—also the *kinds* of taxes. States which grew most rapidly had by far the *lowest* levels of *income* tax and *property* tax per person, and they had the *highest* level of per capita *sales* taxes.

The reasons for the correlation of this configuration of taxes and their incentives and disincentives with economic growth are not mysterious. Income taxes—especially steeply progressive income taxes, which take higher proportions of greater incomes—penalize efforts to work more and to save more. After New York lowered its progressive income tax rates in 1977, its economic growth increased and its unemployment fell in relation to the national average. Property taxes penalize those who make investments in businesses. A state's higher income or property taxes reduce the rate of return on investments which people make in themselves or in their physical assets. Productive resources then have a greater incentive to migrate to other states where tax rates are lower. On the other hand, states that emphasize sales taxes, rather than income or property taxes, penalize consumption and raise the incentive to save—saving which then is made available for greater investment.

Tax cutting is not a panacea—a quick, automatic road to riches. But higher income and property taxes certainly are not a long-run road to prosperity—and since 1980 such state and local taxes have been rising rapidly.

(February 1983)

Government:
Ignorance, Stupidity, and Psychology

Dealing with any government agency—aloof, arrogant, autonomous—is a potential source of massive heartburn. Dealing simultaneously with two agencies—with overlapping and intermingled jurisdictions and each eager to defend and expand its bureaucratic turf—can more than double your pain.

In two long feature stories, the *Los Angeles Times* has told a disheartening—and, indeed, despicable—story of state and county government converting a minor problem of procedure into seemingly unresolvable ruin.

Calvin Barginear and his family laboriously accumulated enough money from their garage and towing business to buy thirty-six acres of land near the Pacific shore in California. They intended to subdivide the property into twelve lots, keeping one and selling the others. In 1980, they received from the Los Angeles County Regional Planning Commission tentative approval for the land division. Final approval required permits from the California Coastal Commission. But the Coastal Commission would not give permits, because, in revising its land-use plan, the county neglected to include the Barginears' subdivision, supposedly because it presumed that the Coastal Commission would honor subdivisions which had already been approved. The Commission insisted on full protocol, the county refused to play the game, and, eight years later, the Barginears are financially finished and likely will lose all their land.

The reason why this administrative misunderstanding was not quickly resolved was neither ignorance nor stupidity. The dispute, the proposals, the rebuttals degenerated into lamentable legalism, but the basic facts—like the desirable nature of the land-use proposal—were never in question. And people sufficiently ambitious and alert to get into such agencies are clever enough to satisfy clear-cut, mechanical questions in a civilized manner.

No, the bureaucratic boys and girls could have gotten together in good will and good judgment, in analytic sense and sense of propriety, to make things right. The formal rules are not so rigid, the administrative machinery is not so confined, that these petty servants of the public could not have served sensibly.

The explanation of the fiasco is not ultimately to be found in the law: it is to be found in the realm of psychology—abnormal psychology for most of us, but entirely normal for government types. Little people with too much power were not sufficiently sophisticated to give ground, to compromise, to accommodate, to cooperate, to correct clerical oversights, to keep promises—in short, to seek reasonable solutions and to do what was required, in concern and compassion, to ensure justice.

Supposedly, we are to be comforted by the suggestion that state and local government—Little Brother—is relatively "close" to us. But there are some things—including hair shirts and government—one does not want to be close to.

(March 1988)

Government and the Community: On Getting Things Done

I try to be patient and brave. Chin up, stout fellow, eyes front, stiff upper lip, and all that. But, made of frail flesh, I can gracefully tolerate only a finite amount of commonly found editorial economics and journalistic analytics.

An economics writer with a London newspaper is visiting the United States. He has written an essay for a Los Angeles paper on the peculiarities of American local government finance. Like some Englishmen before him, he feels that Americans are not taxed enough.

"Voters here, as elsewhere in the industrial world," he tells us with proper British condescension, "have been tricked into believing that taxation is by definition wasteful; that by cutting taxes government will somehow unleash an explosion of private-sector energy that will quickly fill the vacuum left by the state; that it is better to pay a private contractor to take away your garbage even if it costs you twice as much as the public service." As an additional example of private-sector inadequacy, he notes: "It is pointless to fill the pothole outside your own house if your car is going to fall through the pavement in the next block."

The writer might consider the following over tea:

First, only anarchists would believe that "taxation is by definition wasteful"—and I am acquainted with no anarchists.

Second, while government is required by society, it does not follow that *more* government is better. There must be taxation, but do not flippantly deny that taxes can be collected ineptly on too large a scale, with government expenditures done badly on wrong things.

Third, while there *are* legitimate government projects, learning specific community preferences and pursuing them efficiently is not easily done. Political processes cannot match market mechanisms in registering demands and organizing production.

Fourth, the widespread "tax revolt" of the late 1970s had to use crude political procedures, so it was not implemented with refined precision. But it was a revolt against a genuine and genuinely fearsome ham-handed aggrandisement by Little Brother. From 1947 to 1975, the ratio of state and local expenditures to gross national product came close to tripling—a much faster rate of increase than for federal expenditures.

Fifth, the journalist really should look at the record of "cutting back city hall," as Robert W. Poole, Jr., entitled his book. He would find that—explicably and thus predictably—in a great number of cities over a huge range of size, some sort of private-industry collection of garbage has been dramatically more economical than municipal collection. And even street repair can be done better by private firms contracted by government than by workers employed by government.

This is hardly the entirety of the issue of state and local finance. But it provides a belated beginning of journalistic education.

(September 1986)

MONEY, INFLATION, CENTRAL BANKING

Monetary Analysis: Prices and Interest Rates

Inflation, Output, and Employment

Some suggest that full employment is easily attainable and perpetually retainable. All we need do is spew out much more money. If the embers of inflation are stirred, that would help stimulate the economy. And since money can be created out of thin air, only a simpleton or a subversive would oppose a sufficiently robust "full-employment" policy.

In actuality, over substantial periods, changes in the amount of money have little to do with real production and the employment of resources it requires. In the fifteen-year period, from 1965 to 1980, total monetary expenditure tripled, mainly because the amount of money expanded 145 percent. The price level went up 140 percent—nearly the increase in money. But real output rose only 60 percent—much less than the expansion of money but half again the rise in employment.

In the long run, real output depends mainly on real resources, and the amount of money impinges more on *prices* than on production. But a bulge in money and spending can hype the economy to some extent for a brief while. How?

One explanation for the quick fix turns on miscalculation. With rising inflation, employers and workers are briefly fooled into believing that only the demand for their particular output and service has increased. Jobs are more readily offered and accepted. But when increases in other prices and wages are finally perceived, the spirit of expansiveness evaporates, and unemployment goes back up.

A different explanation—reviewed by economists Dan Birch, Alan Rabin, and Leland Yeager—does not require misdirected euphoria. Rather, it begins with the elemental recognition that an increase in the rate of total market expenditure is matched by the sum of proportionate changes in output and in prices. Increased spending is split between greater production and inflation. But prices—which are adjusted piecemeal in many decentralized input and output markets—do not quickly move to their ultimate higher level. And, with sluggish prices, the short-term impact of greater spending is mainly on output, so employment rises. The increase in output does *not* stem from inflation; indeed, it is *possible* because inflation has *not* absorbed all the increased demand.

But this rationally expanded rate of activity in response to greater spending cannot be maintained. There are real resource limitations. As inventories of first sellers and then suppliers are depleted, production is increased, and inputs are no longer so readily available, continuation of expanding spending raises costs and prices. After its brief flurry, the rate of real activity falls back to a sustainable level. And the more sensitive the community becomes to inflation expectations, when money increases, the briefer and smaller will be the impact on output and the quicker and faster will be the rise in prices.

Converting the economy into a money-junkie, relying on an indefinitely prolonged series of quick fixes, is a disgraceful prescription for economic health.

(January 1983)

Monetary Instability, Uncertainty, and Productivity

For well over two hundred years, economists have realized that the *amount* of money in the economy is not nearly as important as *changes* in the amount. The economy can readily adapt to a constant money stock, and the size of that money stock makes little difference. But when the amount of money changes, there are repercussions; the repercussions are varied, with some prices, interest rates, outputs, and employments changing faster and changing more than do others;

these lagged and dispersed changes can hurt many people even as they may benefit a few.

We are learning more of an additional complication. Not only are changes in the amount of money significant, but *variability* of the money change also can affect our real economic activity. Over a period of years, the money stock may rise by x percent; but it makes a difference whether that increase comes about steadily and quite predictably or erratically and surprisingly.

Much of the linkage between *changes in money* and *performance of the economy* involves *uncertainty*. If changes in money are highly erratic, people respond in ways of self-defense that tend to increase costs and reduce effectiveness, thereby lowering national income. And if changes in money are large enough to generate increasing *inflation*, then greater inflation itself will create additional uncertainties which discourage production, for higher inflation means more variable inflation. Over the past five years, we have made for ourselves a worst of both worlds: money has commonly been increased too fast and always increased too unevenly.

There are many changes. A world of innovation and mobility and effectively registered community preferences is obviously a changing world. But adaptation to advances in knowledge and to shifting desires is very different from adaptation to unpredictable changes in the amount of money and in fluctuating degrees of inflation. Deliberately changing one's tactics during a game is one thing; being confronted with arbitrary changes in the rules and their interpretation or in the dimensions of the playing field is something entirely different.

When we manage the money supply badly—aberrantly increasing it much too rapidly and then much too slowly, usually with inflation of a widely fluctuating rate—we unnecessarily add to our burdens of uncertainty in an already hard world. Much of what we do today is based on anticipations of tomorrow, and greater uncertainty makes the game more difficult. Unavoidable risk is not to be avoided, but we are not obliged to magnify our distractions and misdirections by lousy policy. With a highly variable amount of money, and perhaps highly variable inflation as well, we try to find refuge from the greater risk and muddled market signals by adopting shorter planning periods and reducing venturesome investment.

In our attention to coping with aggravated uncertainty, efficiency is diminished and we produce less well. It is not shrewd to produce less than we can in a world where, at best, we can never produce all we want.

(July 1984)

When Is a Million Dollars Not a Million Dollars?

Although purportedly the best things in life are free, I understand money, too, is nice. So those of us who are wealthy in only beauty, grace, and charm can be intrigued by proffered prospects of accumulating a million or so dollars.

Such prospects used to be confined to buying Florida swamp land or the Brooklyn Bridge low and selling high. Now, there are, in addition, Individual Retirement Accounts—known to financial sophisticates as IRAs. IRAs are being vigorously peddled, by banks, savings-and-loans, brokerage houses, maybe barber shops. And we are told that, if you start soon enough to put the maximum permitted annual amounts into such accounts, you can ultimately draw out a million dollars—or even two or three million.

We are not told incorrectly: the ads are not promoting swamps or bridges. However, nothing but the truth is not always the whole truth, as some have warned. Salesmen are more inclined to give the good news than the bad.

To accumulate those million-dollar retirement nest eggs, the deposits must be compounded at high rates of interest. If $2,000 is deposited each year with an interest rate of 15 percent, the amount will total $1,000,000 after thirty years. But the rate of interest will be as large as 15 percent only if there is substantial inflation.

If anticipated inflation were zero, the interest rate might be a civilized 5 percent. But with anticipated inflation, there will be a premium incorporated in the interest rate. A swollen interest rate of 15 percent implies an inflation rate of about 10 or 11 percent.

So suppose that, over the next thirty years, inflation will be 10 percent and the interest rate 15 percent. Your IRA account grows to the magic $1,000,000. But, with the inflation, that $1,000,000 thirty years from now will have the purchasing power of only $57,000 in 1982 prices. With inflation at 11 percent, the real value of your savings would be a modest $45,000.

Consider the alternative of just a 5 percent return on your IRA account when the price level is steady. Annual deposits of $2,000 compounded at 5 percent for thirty years will total only $139,000, far less than one million. But with a constant price level, the $139,000 would be worth $139,000—some two and one-half to three times as much as the real size of your kitty in the inflationary cases.

It would be jolly good fun to be a millionaire, even at today's prices. But after thirty years of 10 percent inflation, most of the glamor of a million dollars would have been dissipated. We would be vastly better off with a lower rate of return in a world of no inflation than with a high rate of return as a consequence of inflation. Pray for low interest rates, for we will have low interest rates if, and only if, we have low inflation.

(February 1982)

A Tragedy in Three Acts:
Money and Interest Rates

Senator Snort takes it as an article of faith that pumping up the money stock will reduce the market rate of interest. After all, the interest rate is the price of borrowed money, and increasing the supply of money supposedly will lower its price as surely as increasing the supply of tomatoes will lower the price of tomatoes.

Economists have long understood that a large increase in the rate of monetary expansion *will* quickly depress interest rates. They have understood also that the reduction in rates will be temporary as well as quick, with the rates soon rising above their initial levels.

As reviewed by Professor Michael Melvin, of Arizona State University, the immediate negative impact on rates of an increased growth of money is determined by a *liquidity* effect and a *financial* effect.

The increase in money upsets the original balance among money, income, prices, and interest rates. The community suddenly has excess money—the liquidity effect—and the market rate falls to reestablish equilibrium between the amount of money the community demands and the now larger amount in existence. Further, banks have excess reserves—the financial effect—and their first act of adjustment is to invest those reserves in securities. The increased demand for securities bids up their prices, and rising security prices mean falling interest rates. The increase in money growth itself stemmed from market purchases of securities by the Federal Reserve. So expansive action of both the governmental central bank and the private commercial banks have negative impacts on interest rates.

But that is not the end of the play. In fact, it is only a brief first act. In Act II, rates recover. First, banks begin to shift from adding securities to their portfolios to increasing loans. So security prices weaken. And when banks lend, they create still more money, which increases spending; more spending generates more national income as both prices and output rise. Through this *income* effect, the demand for money is increased, and interest rates are bid up.

The climax is in Act III, when developing inflation engenders anticipation of further inflation. With inflation presumed by both lenders and borrowers, the *expectations* effect will bloat current interest rates.

In basic outline, this plot—with interest rates falling in Act I, recovering in Act II, and soaring to new heights in Act III—is very familiar to the economic literati. But Professor Melvin documents a twist which has developed in just the last decade: the liquidity effect of Act I has almost vanished. The community used to take several months to adjust to an increase in money expansion, so it would take six to twelve months for rates to rise back to their initial levels. Now, people are more experienced with inflation. A bulge in the money stock will reduce rates only minutely and for only a few days: by the second month, rates are higher than originally.

More money expansion continues to mean higher interest rates— and now we reach the tragic third act quicker than before.

(July 1983)

Monetary Policy: Living and Learning

Live and learn. But living is only a necessary, not a sufficient, condition for learning. For all of us, learning is hard, and some seem actually to resist the losing of their virginity of ignorance. Rarely has the learning been harder and the resistance more stubborn than in the area of monetary analysis and its application to policy.

Still, even Mortimer Snerd feels in his bones that the amount of monetary spending on goods is relevant to the money prices of those goods. And Mortimer is receptive to the idea that monetary spending is dominated by the amount of money. Putting it together, Mort can almost grasp the conclusion that increasing money fast enough—so that spending expands faster than the amount of goods being bought—will raise prices; and the way—the only way—to subdue inflation is to curtail the increase in money.

That is what we have seen over the past quarter of a century. In the late 1950s and early 1960s, money expansion was very modest, and the price level barely rose; from the mid-sixties through the seventies, money expanded much faster than output could be increased, and inflation was horrendous by civilized standards; during the last few years, the trend of money growth has greatly fallen, and inflation has fallen from some 14 percent in 1980 to about 4 percent now.

As the price level follows the rate of money creation, interest rates follow the price level. When past and current inflation leads to general anticipation of further inflation, market rates of interest are bloated. Lenders will not lend unless the loan contract includes a premium which compensates, at least in large part, for expected fall in the purchasing power of the dollars to be later repaid.

Inflation has fallen greatly. Interest rates, too, have fallen—but not as greatly. Expectations of inflation have been reduced—but interest rates have not come down correspondingly. Why not?

Professor Allan Meltzer, of Carnegie-Mellon University, holds that market rates of interest can embody a second kind of premium. Along with a premium of *anticipated inflation*, there is now a premium of *risk*.

The average rate of money expansion has, indeed, fallen over the last several years. But it has been an extraordinarily bumpy ride, with large, erratic short-term bounces above and below the declining trend. In light of the history of our monetary management, the trend itself is uncertain; with huge gyrations around the trend, lenders and borrowers are twice cursed.

To compensate for this additional uncertainty, lenders add a risk premium to the long-term loans they make. These higher rates spread to short-term loans as borrowers offer to pay more in an attempt to escape the increased rates on longer loans. Higher interest rates—higher than those which would stem from anticipated inflation alone—spread throughout financial markets.

Some of us have learned as we have lived that low inflation-adjusted interest rates require money creation at a rate which not only is *small*, but also *steady*.

(February 1984)

Spurious Causes and Corrections of Inflation

Inflation and the Cost-Push Mirage

Inflation is a chronically increasing price level. It is caused by additions to the nation's stock of money—additions which persistently exceed the growth of the supply of goods and services. Excessive growth of money causes excessive growth of spending; and it is over-exuberant spending which pushes up the price level.

Still, many believe the mythology that inflation is caused by rising costs. Business managers often justify their own rising prices on the ground that costs are increasing. Indeed, some innocents mock the idea that money growth, rather than costs, causes inflation. "That's okay in theory," they delicately sneer, "but real world experience shows that it is rising costs that push up prices."

The contest is not between theory and practice, but between good theory and bad theory. Perceptions of inflation may have been gained from experience, not a textbook, but they are theory, nevertheless: they still represent general explanatory propositions.

This cost-push theory of inflation, however, is *bad* theory precisely because it is not supported by real-world evidence. It does appear that rising costs are pushing up prices, but that impression is an illusion. It is an illusion caused by the way *inventories* of goods delay the effect of money supply increases.

When increased money growth causes total spending to rise more quickly, sales of particular businesses, such as fast food restaurants, will increase. But sales fluctuate from day to day and week to week, so managers of these businesses cannot immediately know that this sales increase will last.

As sales continue to rise, restaurants will use up their inventories of meat. Larger orders will then be placed with suppliers, and inventories of meat packers, too, will begin to shrink.

The price of meat has not yet changed because inventories have absorbed the initial impact of the increased spending. But as more orders to replace depleted inventories work their way down the chain of distribution, orders for cattle also will rise faster. The available amounts of meat are inadequate to meet the rising amounts demanded at existing prices. As a result, prices of cattle will rise as packers bid more intensely for scarce supplies. Higher prices for cattle then cause meat packers to raise their prices; and higher meat prices cause fast food restaurants, in turn, to charge more for their hamburgers.

As higher prices work their way up the distribution chain to the consumer, they create an illusion that higher costs are pushing up prices. But both costs and prices are being pulled up by the increased spending caused by a more rapidly growing money stock. Because the effects of more money and more spending are delayed by inventories, hasty conclusions about the cause of inflation can be deceptive. It may seem that costs are pushing up prices, as it may seem that there is water on desert land. But both are mirages.

(December 1981)

Oil Prices and Inflation

It is not always easy to keep straight the distinction between *long-continuing* and *temporary* changes and between *forces* of change and *measures* of change. Many confuse such distinctions when considering inflation.

Inflation is measured by a price index. The index is a weighted average of prices of many goods. In recent months, the price of oil has fallen and, with a lag, so have the prices of gasoline and other oil products. So the calculated price index tends to get smaller—or increase less rapidly than before—and one is tempted to conclude that inflation has been reduced and that it has been reduced by the fall in oil prices.

But there are problems in analyzing prolonged movement in the general price level in terms of a one-time change in the price of a particular good, even a good as important as oil. First, no *one* price dominates the price index. Second, a short-term wiggle in even the entire price index does not usefully define the state of inflation. The notion of inflation pertains to a *persistent* trend in the price level.

A sudden decrease in oil supply can have an impact on the price level, to be sure. But if the supply does not continue to fall, the new rate of increase in the price index will not continue. After a once-and-for-all jump, the earlier trend in prices will resume, at a higher level. And a one-time fall in oil prices, while directly contributing to a smaller calculated price index now, will not continue to lower the index unless the price of oil continues to fall.

Actually, the effect of a lower oil price on the overall index tends to be offset by increased prices of other goods. If people spend fewer dollars on oil products, they will have more income to spend on everything else, thereby bidding up other prices.

The "oil shocks" which raised oil prices in 1973 and 1979 were *not* the basic reason for the ongoing inflation of the 1970s. And the current "oil shock," which has lowered oil prices, will *not* provide ongoing moderation of inflation in the 1980s. The *calculation* of today's *price index* is an arithmetic exercise; the *causation* of *price trends* is a subject of economic analysis.

What causes persistent price increase, price stability, or price fall is persistence in the relation of the rate of spending and the rate of production of the goods being bought. If real output rises at 3 percent annually and spending on that output also rises at 3 percent, the price level will be steady—no inflation or deflation.

But it is much easier to create money out of thin air and generate spending than it is to create products out of scarce resources. Generally, spending has expanded faster than output, so generally we have had rising prices. If we continue old habits of creating money too fast, we will continue to have inflation—even if oil prices stay low.

(April 1986)

Credit Controls: Confusion and Silly Futility

In the spring of 1980, in an atmosphere of seeming panic and certain confusion, President Carter exercised power to control selected credit. Although the controls program actually adopted was only a smidgen of what the President could have done, and it was pursued but briefly, the unforbidden fruit was tasted. And what was tentatively tasted once may be consumed extensively at a later date of even greater panic and confusion.

Most basically, it was argued that credit controls were needed to break the inflationary spiral of prices and interest rates. But rising demand for credit is a *result* of inflation, not a cause, as consumers and producers seek to "buy now" in the face of rising prices. Higher interest rates *reflect* inflation, as financial markets—both lenders and borrowers—adjust to the continuing decline in the buying power of the dollar.

It is *government*, not the public, which—with massive ineptitude and cowardice—has generated inflation. The public has done its best to adapt to an inflationary circumstance. Then government frowns on the resulting "speculation," "overconsumption," and high nominal interest rates. But instead of correcting its own inflationary errors and thereby providing a stable setting in which people will efficiently work and save and consume, Big Brother—with massive ineptitude and cowardice—continues the inflation but takes away some of the community's options of adjustment, including incentives to save.

The new credit policy was more than a largely misconceived attempt to limit the *amount* of lending. It sought also to *re-direct* lending. Consumers were to be able to obtain financing for houses, automobiles, furniture, and large appliances, but not for non-durable goods. And, in a time when supposedly saving is to be encouraged for investment, small investors were faced with *reduced* yields on money market funds.

Problems inherent in federally allocated credit are enormous, including conspicuously the issue of equity, along with efficiency, in who gets credit, in what amounts, on what terms. Contemplation of the inevitable administrative red tape and bureaucracy is enough to make gentle women faint and strong men cry. The government cannot regulate banks alone, for then loanable funds would be channeled into other financial institutions. The rationing authority would have to control every financial organization, every loan, every investment, every credit sale on all stock and commodity markets, and ultimately credit transactions between private individuals in order to allocate investment funds in accordance, not with community preferences, but with bureaucratic priorities. Like wage and price controls, credit allocation cannot work. For, as with wage and price controls, both the way and the will exist to circumvent it.

It is not market misdirection of credit which has caused a falling off of investment in plants, machinery, irrigation, housing, and other worthy endeavors. Rather, the problem is that government-engendered inflation has diminished the flow of savings, and taxes and regulations have distorted the pattern of investment. The solution of problems of government interference and ineptitude is not *more* inept government interference.

(July 1981)

Mouse Wisdom: A New Friend and Familiar Foolishness

There have been many economic debates between Adam and Karl, the two mice who live in my office. Recently, Karl had returned from shopping and was furious about the high price he had to pay for a whisker brush. After Karl had fulminated about high prices and extolled the alleged virtues of price and wage controls, Adam was about to respond when a large spider appeared from behind a dusty volume.

"My dear fellows," began the spider, "history is a prolific teacher of the destructiveness of price and wage controls. I know from personal experience, for I have lived many lives. Before beginning the numerous transmigrations which have brought me to my present spidery state, I was a scribe during the reign of the Roman Emperor Diocletian. The Edict of Diocletian in 301 A.D. was a chilling example of the pervasive problems which controls create."

"What do you call yourself now?" asked Adam.

"My name is Waldo," replied the spider. "But let me tell you of the havoc wreaked by Diocletian's Edict when he foolishly tried to control prices and wages by government commands."

"Please continue," encouraged Karl, who was eager to defend price controls.

"Not long after Diocletian assumed the throne," Waldo said, "prices and wages increased to unprecedented heights. Much like modern day politicians, the Emperor blamed inflation on the greed of merchants and speculators."

"Right on!" exclaimed Karl. "Greed, avarice—that's what makes prices high."

"No," responded Waldo. "The inflation which Emperor Diocletian condemned was caused by excessive minting of new coins. For many years, to finance massive and growing government expenditures, emperors had issued more and more coins, causing the money supply to grow faster than the goods on which those coins were spent. Like a fly in a spider web," said Waldo, "the more coins minted by emperors to cope with rising prices, the more entangled they became in inflation."

"But what about the Edict?" asked Karl. "Surely the price and wage controls cured inflation?"

"I remember well the disaster of the Edict," answered Waldo. "Diocletian fixed the prices and wages that could be charged. Death was prescribed for those caught selling or buying at prices above the maximum official levels."

"So," smirked Karl, "the Edict did work."

"No, it did not," answered Waldo. "There were informers, supervisors, and controllers everywhere. But even this iron corset of control could not alter the fact that the money supply was too fat. Given the amount of coins available to spend, people wanted to buy more goods than were available at those controlled prices. Goods were hoarded rather than sold, production fell, shortages abounded.

"People simply had too much money to spend at the low, decreed prices. The lesson," continued Waldo, "is that price and wage controls cannot cure inflation: they bring only regimentation, shortages, less wealth, and loss of much personal liberty. I know; I was there."

(January 1982)

Money, Velocity, and Inflationary Experience

Monetary Causes and Economic Consequences

Suppose you get your jollies from keeping track of key economic data. And suppose it is around 1965 or even as recent as 1968. What might you conclude about such problems as inflation, employment, and interest rates?

You might be forgiven—sort of—for concluding that inflation, employment, and interest rates were *not* problems any more. There were people, including high government economists, who believed that we knew so much about controlling economic aggregates that we had entered a permanent era of essentially steady prices and full employment and low interest rates.

General experience of the period gave support to high optimism. Over a period of twenty years—1948 to 1968—the average annual rate of inflation was just 1.9 percent. Indeed, if one of those years is thrown out—1950 to 1951, the start of the Korean unpleasantness, when prices abruptly rose 8 percent—the average inflation rate was a mere 1.5 percent. Only seven times in those two decades was the rate more than 2 percent—but three of those times were between 1965 and 1968, with the malevolent approach of major inflation.

How to account for that substantial period of nearly stable prices? It was a reflection of the small average and fairly steady growth in money. In the twenty years prior to 1967, only once did the amount of money increase as much as 5 percent; in only three other cases did it rise more than 4 percent. But the rate of money growth picked up during the last three years of the period and then jumped to nearly 8 percent during 1967 and 1968: that inaugurated the period of inflation.

Meanwhile, real output and interest rates behaved just about the way described in the textbook—if it is the right textbook. For the whole period, national product rose at a robust 4 percent annually, and unemployment averaged less than 4.5 percent. True, in six of the twenty years, output expanded less than 2 percent, but in each case the amount of money barely increased: it is possible to raise the money stock too slowly as well as too rapidly. And interest rates were low: through 1965, short-term rates remained below 4 percent, and long-term rates were below 5 percent. As money began to rise too fast at the end of the period, both prices and interest rates started to take off.

What is the moral of it all? Obviously, in the 1950s and 1960s, we did *not* establish a permanent Garden of Eden with respect to prices, employment, and interest rates. We *did* demonstrate that consequences stem from causes. We had happy consequences so long as we minded our monetary manners. But the jungle of inflation, rising unemployment, and bloated interest rates quickly began to reclaim the garden when we irresponsibly abandoned the proper cultivation of money control.

Liberty is not the only good thing which requires eternal vigilance.

(September 1984)

A Mountain of Money and Prices

A fog of uncertainty and confusion envelops current beliefs about money and the price level. What does monetary theory tell us, and what can monetary policy do, about prices? Use of an analogy can help us rise above the cloud of misunderstanding.

Imagine two automobiles, starting together, but taking separate roads to a mountaintop. Because the roads are different, the rates at which the cars climb the mountain can differ considerably at any given moment even if both cars eventually reach the top at nearly the same time.

Like the two cars, money and prices have long been climbing. Milton Friedman has presented data of the past century: as the quantity of money per unit of national output has increased, so, too, has the price level in similar proportion.

Overall, the ascending paths of money and of prices have been strikingly similar. In only a few segments of time—the periods of World War I, the Great Depression, World War II, and recent years—have the paths clearly deviated. But even when money and prices basically have moved together in close step, they have climbed at quite different rates in particular years. Professor Friedman cautions that

". . . all of us tend to focus on quarter-to-quarter or year-to-year changes. . . ." And so, cursed with historical myopia, we commonly concentrate on short periods when the rates of ascent differ, ignoring the clear pattern of their rising together over the long pull.

Because the growth rates of money and prices often move in different directions at a given time, it is tempting to conclude that money and prices are unrelated. In the last few years, money growth has greatly speeded up while the growth of prices has greatly slowed down. So many wrongly—and sometimes eagerly—conclude that the link between money growth and inflation has been broken, if it ever existed.

Although the growth rates of money and prices have moved in different directions in recent years, money and prices have still been "climbing the mountain" together. Indeed, the price level and money per unit of output continue to show a strong positive relationship.

Two important lessons await at the mountaintop.

First, appropriate price stability depends on keeping the growth of the money supply equal to the growth of the nation's productive activity in the long run. If the quantity of money per unit of output does not increase over the years, the price level will not change much.

Second, deliberately increasing or decreasing the growth rate of money is not, in Dr. Friedman's words, a "magic fine-tuning tool that can be used to guide the economy precisely along a preselected path. . . ." Changes in the growth of money do not produce short-term results that are sufficiently predictable for such manipulative purpose. Instead, monetary policy should be used for what it can achieve: a price level much more stable than it has been over the last one hundred years.

(March 1987)

Prices and Prosperity

In 1979, the consumer price index rose more than 11 percent; in 1980, it ballooned 13.5 percent; in 1981, it went up another 10.4 percent. This was a ridiculous performance, begat by absurd government policies. Five years later, in 1986, prices rose only 1.8 percent, and memories of inflation faded. But in 1987, the rate of price increase doubled to 3.6 percent, and the 1988 inflation rate may approach 5 percent.

Murmurs of inflation fears are increasingly heard. How frantic should the fearful be? After all, inflation of 5 to 6 percent is a far cry from inflation of 13 to 14 percent.

Still, it is impossible to kill inflation. At best, it will be only dormant. Lousy policies which created inflation before can do it again—and there is no assurance that the rate will not rise again far above 6 percent. Even 6 percent is hardly trivial: at that rate, the price level would double in a dozen years.

But what if some inflation is a price (pardon the expression) which must be paid for appreciable expansion of national production—and of the employment required to produce the product? Inflation itself does not add to our resources or their productivity, but most might find inflationary full employment—if that is the best we can do—to be preferable to noninflationary stagnation.

Many have supposed that inflation and prosperity go hand in hand. But theory does not tell us and experience does not confirm that we must have inflation in order to prosper—or that inflation is invariably accompanied by a high rate of national output.

Look at that recent inflationary decade from 1972 to 1982. Over those ten years, prices more than doubled, rising at an annual average rate of 8 percent, but output rose at an anemic rate of just under 2 percent. But in the next five years, 1982 to 1987, inflation was less than half as much—a bit over 3 percent—and the output rate was nearly twice as great—almost 4 percent.

In fact, *low inflation and high output* are a common combination. In the decade between 1958 and 1968, inflation was a still smaller 2.4 percent, while production growth was a still bigger 4.4 percent. In the Roaring Twenties, 1921 through 1929, output surged ahead at 6 percent while the price level actually fell nearly 1 percent per year. And over a substantial period just before World War I, 1894–1912, inflation was a puny 1.6 percent, while output growth was a robust 4.8 percent.

It is sufficiently obvious for even politicians to see that inflation is neither necessary nor sufficient to have a booming economy. Inflation is a price we need not pay to prosper.

(August 1988)

Inflation: Money and Output

"Dearie me," moaned mouse Karl, who is given in moments of stress to rather coarse language, "I am confused about inflation. I have heard you say," he said to mouse Adam, "that inflation stems from creating money too fast, and I understand that the annual rate of money expansion used to be close to the rate of inflation. But for the last several years, money and prices have not gone up at the same rate, so we can no longer rely on a monetary explanation of inflation."

"The subject of inflation is certainly not simple," said Adam with solicitude. "But we can go far in comprehension by sticking to fundamentals. You have indicated some historical data, but your analysis is inadequate."

Karl was wounded but defiant. "Data," he primly said, "show that the old relationship between money and prices has collapsed. In the fifteen year period betwwen 1966 and 1981, the amount of money rose at an annual rate of 6.4 percent, and the price level went up at a rate of 6.8 percent. But in the following five years, money expanded considerably faster than before—at 8.8 percent—and yet prices went up much more slowly—at 3.4 percent. Money and prices no longer rise at nearly the same rate, so money now has little to do with inflation."

"Money *does* play the most fundamental role in determining the level of money prices," replied Adam quite fundamentally. "But money has never been the only determinant of prices. And when other variables alter, then the particular relationship of money to prices will be affected."

"I don't like to see a mouse weasel," said Karl cattily, "but just what is the nature of the relationship between money and the price level?"

"Considering money in isolation," patiently exposited Adam, "cannot tell us anything. But considering *money in relation to the output on which it is spent* can tell us much. If money increases much faster than output, we can reasonably expect prices to rise. Money per unit of output did increase in both periods—1966 to 1981 and 1981 to 1986—and prices did rise in both periods."

"So the two periods were nearly identical in these money, output, and price considerations?" asked Karl.

"No, not identical," cautioned Adam. "One conspicuous difference was an abrupt fall in monetary velocity, the average rate at which a dollar is spent. When the increase in money is supplemented by an increase in monetary velocity, prices can rise rapidly, as in the earlier period. When velocity rises little—or actually declines a bit, as in the later period—an increase in the ratio of money to output will have less effect on prices. So," Adam concluded, "the *correlation* between *money per unit of output* and the *price level* is still very large, almost as big as in the period through 1981. But, because of the smaller velocity, the upward *trend* of prices measured against the ratio of money to output has fallen."

(October 1987)

Production Capacity, Money, and Inflation

What do you want to see in the overall performance of the economy? High employment and lots of production?

Well, these days, reports of greater employment and output raise fears for some that further expansion in an economy already quite fully employed will result in substantial inflation and consequently higher interest rates. And the economy supposedly is straining, for its factories and mines supposedly are being used near to capacity.

Inflation fears do have some foundation—but not because we have robust production.

When the community spends more on national output, the market value of the output rises, of course. That money value is determined by both the physical *amount* of the output and *prices* of the various goods. If the amount of output increases at the same rate that spending rises, the price level will be unchanged. Greater output is thus the *enemy*, not the cause, of inflation: for a given amount of spending the greater the output, the lower are prices. If inflation is our fear, we should like to have vigorously expanding production—and the associated fall in unemployment.

But, nervous Nellies cry, we *cannot* have continued vigorous expansion of output, for we already have a high and still increasing rate of manufacturing "capacity utilization." It is true that we live in a world of finite production capacity; and it is true, further, that it is easier to increase the amount of money and thereby the amount of money spending than to increase production of the goods being bought.

Still, the problem of inflation is not that we have limited remaining production capacity. Rather, the problem is that we permit spending on production to outrun the production. Being at a high level of capacity utilization need not result in inflation—if we mind our monetary manners.

Indeed, since World War II, the basic pattern of changes in the capacity utilization rate bears little relation to the path of the inflation rate. From the late 1940s to the mid 1960s, inflation was low, rising but slowly while capacity utilization bounced again and again within the wide range of 74 percent to 91 percent. After hitting its highest peak in 1966, capacity utilization—while continuing to bounce wildly—began a *downward* trend just as the rate of inflation *surged*. Most recently, from 1982 to 1987, utilization of capacity rose again—although still well below levels of many earlier years—while the inflation rate has *fallen*.

Meanwhile, over the forty year period, a 300 percent increase in money has driven up prices some 470 percent.

Producing much of goods—operating at a high level of capacity and low unemployment—is compatible with a stable price level. But producing much of money—increasing money faster than we increase goods—will give us inflation.

(November 1988)

Central Banking

Mr. Magoo and the Making of Economic Policy

Karl, the usually moody mouse, was chipper. "I believe in progress," he chirped. "Every day in every way, the economy grows and improves."

Adam, the mouse who mixes his optimism with realism, was bemused. "To what do you attribute this supposed economic advancement?" he asked.

"To wise government guidance, of course," Karl replied. "How could we not do better? Knowledge accumulates. As time goes on, we not only learn more about technology and physical productivity, we progress also in thought and public policy."

"We do learn some things," agreed Adam. "But the results of growing and increasingly hyperactive government do not uniformly represent progress. And government certainly is becoming more conspicuous. Compare the first half of the period since World War II, 1946–1965, with the second half, 1966–1985. In the early postwar period, the budget was virtually balanced; in the later period, the average annual deficit has been $64 billion. And as a proportion of gross national product, government spending expanded from an average of less than 19 percent to nearly 22 percent."

"It's OK for government to grow bigger," countered Karl, "when it does better."

"Better in what sense?" asked Adam. "By obvious criteria, the economy's performance has been worse in the second half of the postwar period than it was in the first half."

"That can't be true—can it?" Karl said hesitantly. "If government spending and the deficit both have been increasing, that had to stimulate the economy, increasing employment and output."

"Look at the record," replied Adam. "The average *unemployment rate* has been considerably larger in the later period; *real output* has grown considerably more slowly; *inflation* has been vastly greater; and both short-term and long-term *interest rates* have been ridiculously greater. By and large, the government-guided economy from 1966 to 1985—with its highly erratic monetary and fiscal policies and its interventions and regulations—performed miserably relative to the less government-dominated economy of 1946 to 1965."

"So you blame the worsening performance of the economy on worsening public policy?" whimpered a chastened Karl.

"It is hardly a matter of falling I.Q. or polluted hormones," said Adam grimly. "We have afflicted ourselves with the Mr. Magoo Syndrome, as described by Professor Karl Brunner, of the University of Rochester. Largely blind and wholly myopic, we stumble and lurch from one immediate problem to another, always concerned with only the independent short run, trying to appeal to the gallery by being frenetically—even if aimlessly—active, thereby causing concern and confusion among consumers, savers, investors, and managers. Mr. Magoo was an amusing and fetching little cartoon character. But he ought not to be directing our economy."

(June 1986)

The Fed: Denial of Monetary Analysis and Policy

It hurts too much to laugh, but it is not macho to cry. The subject of the whimper could be the Federal Reserve, its misconstrued policy mandate, and its misdirected policy diddling.

Economists outside the organization have extensively noted the failures and futilities of the Fed. Occasionally, complaints and dissents come from some who are, or have been, inside the Fed. The latest inside criticism comes from Laurence K. Roos, former president of the Federal Reserve Bank of St. Louis, writing in the journal of the Cato Institute.

The proper policy province and operational procedures of the Fed are limited but of enormous significance. The central responsibility of the central bank is monetary policy. There is much to be said for generating slow, steady growth of the amount of money. Enormous, erratic swings in the rate of money expansion are a consequence of past failure and a cause of future failure. The Fed cannot determine the money growth rate with perfect precision, but it can do vastly better than it has done. By doing as well as it can do, the Fed can contribute mightily to a long-term monetary stability, and thus predictability, which is conducive to prosperity.

But Mr. Roos found that the Fed persistently eschews its rightful role. It devotes little attention to formulation of proper policy to achieve clearly defined and consistent long-run goals. The decision-makers of the Fed do not *try* to control the money supply, commonly being preoccupied with interest rates, over which they have only limited and roundabout influence. Indeed, they presume that the amount of money *cannot* be controlled. And in analytic know-nothing nonsense, it is doubted in the Fed that it much *matters* if money is controlled.

The attitude with the Fed has been: what will be, will be—and don't blame me. The orientation has been fatalistic and adaptive, with major attention given to covering the flanks of officers through flaunting multiple targets and flashing multiple tools, obfuscating the essential mechanism of market activity and the legitimate processes of market guidance.

While ignoring its legitimate charge of monetary control for the long pull, the Fed is popularly assigned—and does not emphatically reject—diverse obligations, mainly of the short run. Sensible monetary policy can do much for price-level stability and efficient production, but it cannot efficiently specify and peg interest and exchange rates— and it should not decree such market variables, even if it could.

Preoccupied with the very short term—which is precisely the wrong term of emphasis—the Fed has more power than it finds convenient to acknowledge. But it has neither the power nor the wisdom to fine-tune every domestic and international economic variable. The conspicuousness of the Fed is not matched by competence, nor its authority by accountability.

(May 1986)

The Moral of
"The Anguish of Central Banking"

The Federal Reserve—our central bank—is a very important institution. The Fed gathers data, clears checks, and employs some economists. The Fed also largely controls the amount of money. And changes in the money supply have repercussions on the price level, interest rates, national output, and employment.

The Fed does not have a good record in managing money. Commonly, the amount of money goes up much too fast or too slow, and, perhaps worst, it goes up much too erratically. So we have fluctuations in overall economic activity which could be smaller, at an average level of activity which could be higher.

During most of the 1970s, Arthur F. Burns was one of the most distinguished chairmen of the Board of Governors in the history of the Fed. He presided in a period of devastating inflation. In an address not long after leaving the Fed, Dr. Burns described "The Anguish of Central Banking."

"One of the time-honored functions of a central bank," he said, "is to protect the integrity of its nation's currency, both domestically and internationally. In monetary policy central bankers have a potent means for fostering stability of the general price level. By training, if not also by temperament, they are inclined to lay great stress on price stability. . . . And yet, despite their antipathy to inflation and the powerful weapons they could wield against it, central bankers have failed so utterly in this mission in recent years. In this paradox," confesses Dr. Burns, "lies the anguish of central banking."

We are given many supposed reasons for the inflation of the 1970s—deficit financing, dollar devaluation, worldwide boom, crop failures, oil price increases, deceleration of productivity. Money and Federal Reserve management of money also are mentioned. But Congress and the community have gradually diluted the role and usurped the power of the Fed in promoting economic stability. In any case, we are told that the data are too imprecise, the theory is too thin, institutional arrangements are too complex, and social psychology is too perverted to permit clear formulation and effective implementation of decision-rules in monetary management.

Well, if central banking is so difficult and chancy, perhaps the moral to be inferred is that central bankers should try to do strategically more by doing tactically less. Do *not* try to fine-tune prices, interest rates, exchange rates, national income, employment, credit allocation; instead, promote stability with predictability in ground rules and operations, letting the market make its own particular adjustments. The necessity of never-ending adaptation will not be eliminated, and the efficiency of adaptation will not be enhanced by the interventionist hocus-pocus of the central bank.

Members of the community will do their personal productive things best if they have to deal only with changing demands and supplies in the market, unencumbered and undistracted by central bank shenanigans.

(February 1988)

Independence: The Fed, the Government, and the Community

Is the Federal Reserve independent? There is *some* degree of independence. There is also *some* Fed reaction to the White House, the Congress, and the Treasury. How much reaction varies with the significance of the matter, independence being greater on side issues of institutional regulation than on central issues of monetary management, and with the current popularity of the President. Underlining short-term accommodation and adaptation is a possible political business cycle, with monetary policy predictably following the four year presidential election calendar.

Should the Fed be independent? One would expect the central bank to have a considerable voice in economic policy councils—and to have a voice of significance implies substantial room for initiative and weight of authority. Further, to be only a puppet raises the question of who pulls the strings: effective incorporation of the Fed as just an agency controlled by the Treasury or the President or the Congress might simplify, but would not eliminate, internecine competition and conflict within the government.

Still, some simplification some of the time could be welcomed. It can be awkward to have the central bank seriously out of step with the executive or the legislature or the other monetary authorities. Coherency in policy making, with *one* plan of policy supported by *all* members of the government team, assuredly does not guarantee good policy: unanimity in policy formulation and implementation may yield only systematic self-destruction. But things are even less likely to go well if the various molders and executors of policy are lunging in different directions.

Perhaps we come closest to both coherency and efficacy in policy, not by attempted tactics of intimidation by one agency over other agencies, but by minimization of ad hoc, discretionary, seat-of-the-pants, appeal-to-the-gallery shenanigans of government in general. Life is not best lived in a straitjacket, to be sure. A free and robust society is defined largely in such terms as autonomy, imagination, experimentation. But here we speak of the *members* of the community, not of their *government*. The individual members can best do their respective things when living with a government severely constrained, which is confined mainly to delineating and enforcing minimal, general, and stable ground rules for the populace.

Is the Fed independent to an optimal degree? The question can hardly be answered without prior assessment of the larger question of the optimal degree of independence of government itself. Six thousand years of recorded history—decidedly including the twentieth century—make it dismayingly clear to some of us that serving government always contains the potential to grow (and degenerate) into dominating Leviathan. And with domination established, as it has been for most peoples at any time, Leviathon will be curtailed and again controlled only with great effort, much uncertainty, and enormous cost.

(March 1988)

Government and the Coordination of Policies

Inflation: Government, Community, and Love of Poison

"I believe," said mouse Karl quite believably, "that I understand the monetary basis of inflation. I think," he said quite thoughtfully, "that if the amount of *money* increases much faster than the *output* which is bought with money, then the money prices of those goods very likely will be bid up."

"Yes," agreed mouse Adam quite agreeably, "it remains the case that rising money per unit of output is accompanied by a rising price level."

"I can even sort of see," Karl continued while squinting his beady little eyes, "that some people and institutions might gain from inflation redistributing the real wealth of the community. But I have heard that *government* can gain from inflation. I don't want to believe that government people like inflation, for that would be very unstatesman-like."

"You better believe," responded Adam. "Government can gain in *creating* inflation and from the *existence* of inflation. Much of the problem is that people in government are under much pressure to *spend*— partly to provide benefits to constituents directly and partly to help them indirectly through supposedly stimulating the economy. But those in government are loath to tax. So there is a strong tendency toward big budgets, big deficits, and much borrowing."

"And government spending, deficits, and borrowing create inflation!" cried Karl cutely.

"Not inevitably," corrected Adam. "The effects on prices of such over-anxiousness to do good expansively will vary with market circumstances and fiscal techniques. But it *is* realistic to expect rapidly expanding budgets and deficits commonly to be accompanied by rapidly expanding money."

"At least," mused Karl, "bad fiscal policy is partly counter-balanced by the sense of the Federal Reserve. The Fed, as everyone knows, is the heroic fighter of inflation."

"I don't mean to be catty," said mouse Adam, "but the Fed has made its own critical contribution to inflation. It has usually allowed the amount of money to rise much too fast and much too erratically, partly because it has not taken money sufficiently seriously and, in-stead, concentrated on interest rates. And the Treasury can find com-fort in inflation, for rising prices reduce the real value of the govern-ment debt. Meanwhile, government can effectively and surreptitiously, *tax*—obtaining more of the community's wealth and resources—through creating and spending more money and inflating money prices and money incomes without passing an explicit taxation act."

"Gasp," gasped Karl. "The White House, Congress, the Treasury, the Fed—all are involved in choosing those policies and ways of im-plementing policies which conduce inflation. Government likes infla-tion. And," he added soberly, "behind representative government are the people who are represented. Government realistically associates inflation with *power*. The public innocently associates inflation with *prosperity*. So we all tend to love the poison of inflation."

(November 1987)

Deficit Monetization, Inflation, and Interest Rates

Presumably, no one rejoices in the federal budget deficit. The most commonly expressed concern is that large and persistent deficits will contribute to inflation and high interest rates.

If deficits are associated with rising prices and interest rates, it will be mainly through monetary channels. If financing of the deficit results in creation of money, we may have inflation. While the relation between increase in money and increase in prices is imprecise, prices will rise to some extent eventually if the amount of money increases rapidly for a substantial time. And if prices are anticipated to rise appreciably, contractual interest rates will be bloated to offset the reduced purchasing power of the dollars later repaid to lenders.

Do deficits result, then, in increased money growth? Not necessarily. But they may, as deficits are "monetized" by the central bank.

The Treasury finances budget deficits by selling government bonds. The central bank—the Federal Reserve in our country—can buy these government bonds, paying for them with money which is newly created and at the same time providing commercial banks with reserves to create still more money. Not all of the money created through the banking system is inflationary, for, normally, output of the economy also is rising. But if money is persistently created at a faster rate than the goods are produced, we can expect prices to rise. And with inflationary experience, we develop anticipations of further inflation, which makes nominal interest rates higher.

So the budget deficit *can* be monetized, thereby contributing to higher prices and interest rates. But *do* central banks actually monetize the government debt stemming from the deficit, creating money faster than output expands?

International experience has varied considerably since the mid-1970s, when the ratio of government debt to gross national product began to rise in many countries. Economists Aris Protopapadakis and Jeremy Siegel, of the Federal Reserve Bank of Philadelphia, find no systematic relation in ten industrial nations between growth in government debt and growth in the money supply.

In all those countries, debt increased much more rapidly after 1974 than in the dozen preceding years; but in none did money increase its rate of expansion nearly as rapidly as did debt, and in most cases—including the United States—money growth in excess of output growth changed very little in the face of rapidly expanding debt.

Many countries—again including the United States—increased money too quickly (and too erratically) in recent years, with resulting inflation and high interest rates. And money increase can stem in part from monetization of budget deficits. But thus far in our limited experience with huge deficits, massive monetization has not been typical.

(February 1987)

The Compatibility of Sensible Policies

A type whose mouth is the most conspicuous part of his head has been having fun with an alleged inconsistency of two alleged features of the

program of the Reagan administration. The two features are commonly labeled "supply-side economics" and "monetarism."

Each of the analytic approaches and policy strategies—although
not the labels—has a long and splendid history. But now they have
gained conspicuousness in the realm of real-world policy debate. And
some—including some economists of a sort—have chosen to argue
that, whatever the merits of the strategies taken separately, they cannot
be used as policy guides together.

Supply-side economics and monetarism are, indeed, different from
each other: they are different approaches to different problems. But in
this world of general scarcity, we have an abundance of problems.
Policy issues do not obligingly confront us in isolation, one at a time.
And economist David L. Meiselman helps us to understand that supply-side economics and monetarism are useful policy guides simultaneously.

Supply-side economics has to do with productivity—work, savings, investments. It pertains to tax policies impinging on incentives
and efficiency, on capital formation and real wages, on income distribution and the linking of pay with performance and of production
with personal preferences—and thus on economic growth. Its realm is
secular, not cyclical—the realm of planning and acting for ongoing
production and long-range payoff.

Monetarism links the amount of money to total spending and is
pertinent to the long run only indirectly and in shaping general context. A predictable framework of stable prices and low interest rates—
reflecting sensible monetary policy—facilitates business and consumer planning, to be sure. But, more ultimately, real production
stems from use of real resources—labor and its training, capital equipment, technological knowledge, resources, and administrative coordination. Changes in the amount of money largely determine the price
level in the long run, but their effect on output and employment is
largely confined to the short run.

One can envision—even if one would not realistically expect to
see—a vigorously productive economy plagued by high and erratic
inflation. More easily, one can imagine an economy of both low output
and low inflation. But we need not settle for *only* high output *or* steady
prices alone. We are *not* required to buy long-term growth with inflation, or stable prices with stagnation; and we need *not* choose between
growth in productivity and short-term equilibrium. Sensible fiscal

policy and sensible monetary policy are not alternatives: *no* trade-off is required between supply-side economics and monetarism.

But it does require some sense to be sensible, and, over a very long time, we have scorned *both* sensible strategies. Unhappily, we have abundant confirmation that multiple bad policies, too, can be followed at the same time.

(August 1982)

GLOBAL THINKING:
TRADE, FINANCE, DEVELOPMENT

Trade: Purposes, Productivity, Policies, and Politics

Surpluses and Trade

Trade between cities, regions, and nations played an increasingly important role in the late Middle Ages and early modern period. Historians bow to the significance of commerce, describing the goods exchanged, the means of transporting them, and the routes traveled by the traders.

But historians rarely try to explain *why* trade occurs. And when they do, generally they mysteriously allude to exchange of *surpluses*. The vague notion seems to be that a community grinds out more widgets than it can use, so it unloads the excess on foreigners in exchange for gadgets which the foreigners have overproduced.

This explanation is bad economics, and it is, therefore, bad historical interpretation.

Even the great Adam Smith, writing before an analytical explanation of trade was at hand, spoke of the exchange of surpluses. The foreign commerce of a nation, he wrote, "carries out that surplus part of the produce of their land and labor for which there is no demand among them, and brings back in return for it something else for which there is a demand. It gives a value to their superfluities. . . ."

Two generations later, another bright man, John Stuart Mill, complained that Smith's vision of trading partners dumping surpluses on each other is misleading. Exported goods embody valuable resources.

There would be no point in producing those goods if there were no anticipated market for them, and they are to be produced and sold, not for the sheer love of the activity, but in order to buy foreign goods.

The scarce resources used in producing export goods could, as an alternative, be directed to producing things we would like to use domestically. Why not directly produce here, with our own resources, all we consume? Why divert any of our productive power to supplying foreigners in order to provide a market for their output?

It is not a matter of full employment. We can have full employment with or without foreign trade. The point is not simply to make *full* use of our resources, but full and *best* use. Areas and countries, like individuals, differ in their productivities among different goods. Thus, instead of everyone being a jack-of-all-trades, we specialize in accordance with our differing capabilities. And what makes sense in the *domestic* economy—specialized production in anticipation of trade which is then freely carried out in order to obtain the best basket of goods—makes sense also in the *world* market.

So Professor Smith was indeed misleading. The function of international trade is not to enable us to dump unwanted surpluses which we stubbornly continue to spew out. Mr. Mill sees the scene more clearly. Trade enables us, with given productive resources, to obtain more of what we like best. We live on the basis of what we get for our own use: the purpose of trade is not to sell for the sake of selling, not to get rid of surpluses we curiously are obliged to produce.

(August 1986)

Productivity and Competing Internationally

Maybe the very best things in life are free. But most of what we consume and work with must be produced. It must be produced by the sweat of the brow and other resources which are scarce. The more goods we squeeze from those limited resources—the more productive we are—the higher off the hog we eat.

The more we produce, the more we will have—even if we are doomed always to want more than we can produce. It is cause for legitimate concern, therefore, that American productivity—output per labor hour—in recent years has grown very slowly, more slowly than in all other major industrial countries.

While the level and growth of our productivity are critical in determining the level and growth of our standard of living overall, some emphasize a particular consequence of languid productivity. Their specific concern is that we will lose our ability to compete internationally. As our world competitive position ebbs, we are gloomily told that we will eventually be priced out of all foreign markets, for foreigners will outproduce us in everything.

Important as physical productivity is for general well-being, the ability to compete internationally is determined by more than productivity in individual goods.

Potential buyers, in both domestic and foreign markets, look at money prices—assuming that government permits buyers to buy what they please in any market they choose. But the seller of widgets, who has won the money *price* competition in his market, does not necessarily have a physical superiority in producing widgets.

An economy may have a flourishing and balanced foreign trade even though it does not have a physical input-output advantage in any commodity. And a technologically superior country cannot expect to undersell all the rest of the world in everything. Lower Slobbovia is a primitive producer. But its physical inferiority is less in some goods than in others—it is *relatively* productive in certain products even though it is *absolutely* less productive than the United States in every product. And the United States, although it has a larger ratio of output to input than Lower Slobbovia across the board, has a greater degree of superiority in some things than in others.

If trade is not hindered and prices are not pegged, Lower Slobbovia and the United States can engage in mutually beneficial trade, with each country exporting those goods in which it is relatively—whether or not absolutely—more productive. The money prices of goods in the two countries are made comparable through the rate of exchange between the respective countries. Activities of people in the market will generate an exchange rate which will lead to balanced international accounts—*if* Big Brother permits market variables to vary.

None of this denies the importance of productivity. The more efficiently we produce, the more we can produce. And nations which produce much will be wealthier than nations which produce little. But it is true, also, that wealthy nations and poor nations—like wealthy people and poor people within the domestic economy—can trade to mutual benefit.

(May 1981)

Mouse Wisdom: Import Restrictions and Specialization

There are two mice who live in my office, Adam and Karl, whose diverse views on economic theory and policy often give rise to enlightening commentaries. Recently, I overheard them discussing import restrictions on cheese. Karl was muttering angrily.

"Cheese imports from other mouse villages should be restricted," exclaimed Karl. "I just read that more and more of our mice are buying imported cheese rather than cheese made here in our village."

"I can understand that," replied Adam enthusiastically as he licked his fingers. "I just ate several slices of imported cheddar and its quality was superior. Would you like a slice?"

"No!" sniffed Karl. "I prefer to buy cheese made by our own village workers."

"That's your choice," sighed Adam, "but why do you propose to restrict cheese imported from nearby villages?"

"Because the mice in other villages are getting all the jobs producing cheese, while some of our own mice workers are unemployed," said Karl. "Quotas on imported cheese would increase the demand for our own cheese, and that would increase employment of our village workers."

"You mean our village would be more productive because more mice would be busy producing cheese?" asked Adam.

"Exactly," replied Karl, who was beginning to eye Adam's imported cheese.

"If you are correct, then why not limit cheese imports into every household," suggested Adam. "Every time a mouse family buys cheese—even our own village's cheese—it is importing rather than producing the cheese at home. Wouldn't that family be more productive if it were kept busy making its own cheese?"

"That would be silly," responded Karl. "Some mice, including me, don't even know how to make cheese. I would rather buy the cheese and spend my time working at the bread factory."

"Of course it would be silly to produce everything here," Adam agreed. "Compared to other villages, we are better in some lines of production than in others. Imports allow our workers to use their time more efficiently producing the goods and services at which they are most skilled rather than poorly producing everything we consume. We sensibly specialize, concentrating on what we produce relatively best."

"I still think import restrictions on cheese would create more jobs," retorted Karl.

"It is true that more of us would be employed making cheese," explained Adam, "but the cheese would cost more, and it wouldn't taste as good."

"Well, it's not fair that mice in other villages should take jobs away from our own workers," complained Karl. "What will they do? Remain unemployed?"

"They will be employed in the more productive industries of our village, such as baking bread," said Adam. "If we limited the quantity of cheese we buy from other villages, the mice living there would have less money to spend on the bread we export to them. More of our villagers would be making cheese, but fewer would be baking bread. Since we are more productive at baking bread, our village would be worse off, not better off, because of the import restrictions. Are you sure you wouldn't like to try some of my cheese?"

"Well, maybe just a slice," answered Karl. "It does taste good on the splendid bread we make here."

(May 1981)

Silliness and Sense in a Competitive World

Life somehow goes on in this competitive world of scarcity and silliness. But it would go on better if we were not so silly in dealing with scarcity. The scarcity is inevitable; the silliness is largely avoidable.

The essence of market competition is adaptation to perceived and anticipated market circumstances. Investors, managers, and workers have alternatives in determining broadly what they will do and specifically how they will do it and on what terms. They are guided in this adjustment, in this meshing of their activities and resources with the activities and resources of others by market information. Relative prices and their changes—*if* they are permitted to change—lead to calculations of personal gain which induce efficient economic coordination.

This remarkable coordination of acquisitive, largely autonomous people—satisfying as best we can the preferences of the community—goes beyond the *domestic* economy. Increasingly, the United States economy is intertwined with the rest of the world. But the world economy, like the domestic, is efficiently coordinated by market activity on the basis of market calculations—*if* people are permitted to buy and sell and invest as they please in light of freely fluctuating prices.

Not everyone applauds the open market all the time. Perhaps no one clutches freedom to his bosom under all circumstances. As buyers, of course we are delighted to see sellers competing for our favor; but as sellers, we find much merit in being a monopolist.

When competition becomes increasingly effective, sellers can be expected to respond. But there are ways and ways to fight back.

The ways which are conducive to *greater productivity* enhance the well-being of the general community while enabling the producer to prosper. But other strategies of defense try to resolve the difficulties of competition, not by *outcompeting* the competitors, but by *prohibiting* the competition. Instead of *productively* working harder and investing more with better market calculations, we *politically* preclude the community—which includes the sellers themselves—from doing business with the competitors. Instead of sensibly prospering through production, we foolishly prostrate ourselves through protection.

In a miserable world of scarcity, in which we are all consumers, it is the way of silliness to subsidize inefficiency in production and to deny ourselves alternatives in consumption. Because it is, and always will be, a world of scarcity, there is, and always will be, work to be done. We need not use our puny resources badly in order to maintain employment. We do not require tariffs, quotas, and gentlemen's agreements with foreigners in order to have a busy economy.

The real issue is the rationality—the efficiency—of our activity. Will our busyness be silly or sensible as we cope in a competitive world?

(September 1981)

Free Trade is Not a Shoo-In

Our shoe industry is being severely pinched and has holes in its soles. For consumers more and more have been choosing imported over domestic shoes. Imports now account for three-fourths of total sales.

Consumers are telling workers and other resource owners in the United States shoe industry to shift their efforts to other businesses where they would produce goods of greater value. Some years ago, Professor Paul Samuelson, eminent economist of MIT, tried to explain this subtlety on a radio program. He was asked what should be done about the Boston shoe industry, which was losing employment. Professor Samuelson replied that workers should seek more productive jobs in other industries.

The response from listeners was quick—and predictable. The head of the Shoe Workers' Union drew a parallel between Marie Antoinette's supercilious words, "Let them eat cake," and Professor Samuelson's sensible words, "Let them get higher productivity jobs elsewhere." A letter from a shoe worker plaintively objected; "I've lost my job. I didn't have a high school education when I got that job. It's the only industry I've ever worked. I'm fifty-seven. Social Security comes in at sixty-two. Come off it, Professor Samuelson. You know I'm not ever gong to have another job."

So free traders are cast as a callous, heartless bunch, and naive, to boot. How can one be in favor of permitting people to buy and sell as they please when it can bring so much pain? If economists had hearts as well as heads, it is gently suggested, they would see the benefits of protecting domestic producers, such as the shoe industry, from ruinous foreign competition.

But what about the pain caused by the plunder of protectionism? Indeed, by using their heads, economists have demonstrated that the national cost of import quotas far exceeds the benefits received by the protected industry.

In this instance, the U.S. International Trade Commission has estimated that proposed import quotas—which the Commission perversely supports—would cost consumers about $1.3 billion per year in higher shoe prices. For this expenditure, consumers might be saving about 26,000 jobs in the domestic shoe industry. That's $50,000 for each job saved, a job which generates, on average, only $14,000 of wages. We would be better off to pay each of those people $14,000 to do nothing—much less have them move into more valuable work—and spend the remaining $36,000 as we please.

There are too many workers and other resources in our nation's shoe industry. Import quotas would keep them there at the consumers' expense. Quotas freeze resources in disadvantageous uses; they inhibit market adjustment and subsidize inefficiency. Free trade contributes to maximizing our wealth in a poor world. But when good sense is one of our scarce resources, free trade is never a shoo-in.

(July 1985)

Good Economics Over a Crude Barrel

According to one of the myths of economics beloved by some journalists, an increase or decrease in the cost of producing a product will necessarily cause the price of the product to change in the same direction. Consider a major newspaper's editorial about a proposed five-dollar-a-barrel fee on imported crude oil.

The editors champion the import tax as a way to promote energy conservation. By restricting the domestic supply of crude oil, the tax would raise its price in the United States. A higher price of oil would then raise the prices of gasoline and other petroleum products and thereby reduce their consumption. Reduced energy consumption supposedly is desirable, for it would mean less dependence "on unpredictable overseas suppliers and their economically crippling pricing policies."

But the reasoning of the editors has more holes than an oil field. The import fee *would* raise the crude oil price in the United States, but the higher price of crude oil would *not* mean higher prices for petroleum products. For the price of refined products are determined in *world* markets, not in the United States alone. A domestic import fee on crude oil would not alter the *world* price of oil, and it would not change the *world* prices of refined products made from oil.

World prices of refined products are unaffected by the import fee. And United States refiners cannot raise their prices above these levels and continue to sell their products. The dilemma of our refiners is thus similar to that which would result if only a few of the nation's millers had to pay special tax on the wheat they buy. Since most millers would be exempt from the tax, the market price of flour would change little.

The tax would thus fall on the few unlucky millers singled out to pay it, because they would be unable to charge higher prices for flour to offset the tax. Similarly, United States oil refiners would bear the total burden of an import fee. Although they would pay more for crude oil in the United States, domestic refiners could not charge more for their oil products than the prices determined by competitive world markets.

A crude oil tax would affect *costs* of our oil refiners. But the tax would not affect the world-determined *prices* of refiners' outputs. With costs increased and output prices unchanged, *profits* of our refiners would be cut. With smaller profits, domestic refined *output* would fall. But with unchanged oil product prices, domestic *consumption* would be unaffected. And smaller domestic output with unchanged consumption means more *imports* and still greater dependence on those "unpredictable overseas suppliers."

Silly diddling with crude oil taxes in the 1970s confirmed what clear thinking teaches: we cannot insulate ourselves from changes in world oil prices. Until editors understand the international scope of oil markets, they will continue to have sound editorializing over a barrel.

(October 1985)

The Car in Cartel

Government policies are like eating potato chips—easier to start than to stop. Take the so-called voluntary export restraints on automobiles and trucks that the United States government negotiated with Japan in 1981. This agreement was hailed as a major setback for Japanese auto producers, for many Americans believed that fewer sales would reduce the companies' earnings.

But in 1985, when President Reagan announced the intent to end the export restraints, the Japanese government eased, but did not terminate, them. Why would Japan continue a practice that was harmful to its own producers?

The answer is that the export restraints have been a blessing in disguise for Japanese auto firms. Indeed, these restraints on sales have enabled them to raise average prices, eliminate price competition among themselves in the American market, and increase earnings. In short, the agreement promoted a cartel of Japanese auto producers.

The cartel arose to implement the export restraints. The Japanese government issued export quotas to its auto producers. Not only did the government tell each producer the maximum number of vehicles it could sell in the United States, it also policed the agreement in order to assure compliance with the quotas. By acting as enforcer, the Japanese government swept away the obstacles that usually prevent businesses from forming successful cartels.

As the continuing dispute among OPEC nations illustrates, these obstacles appear because producers usually disagree on the cartel's tactics. Not only do they disagree on the price target and on the size of output reduction, but they differ also on how this reduction is to be apportioned among the various producers. Any given producer wants to sell more at the cartel's higher price, so it wants others to bear more of the decrease in output.

Without successful enforcement, the best cartel plans often go awry. But by dictating and enforcing the export restraints, the Japanese government controlled the feuding that commonly fractures cartels. So the export restraints cut the supply of automobiles in the United States, increased their prices, and bloated the earnings of Japanese auto producers. And the effective cartel has encouraged the Japanese to increase their competition in larger, higher-profit automobiles.

The Center for the Study of American Business has documented these results. It describes, for example, how the stock prices of the six major Japanese auto firms jumped immediately after the Japanese government announced the export restraints. The Center also cites evidence estimating that curtailment of exports increased the average price of Japanese cars by well over $1,000 between 1980 and 1984.

No wonder Japan continues its export restraints, despite the fact that our government seeks to end them. Although the restraints have meant concessions, they have been made by American consumers, not by Japanese auto producers.

(October 1986)

Chips and Dip

Techies call them DRAMS: dynamic random-access memory chips. More commonly, they are semiconductors or chips, the electronic brains that power electronic products.

Not long ago, there were more than two dozen American firms selling semiconductors. Now there are two, including Texas Instruments. Many chips are produced also by IBM and AT&T, but each consumes its entire output.

Japan is the other big seller. After building substantial production capacity in the early 1980s, Japanese producers began flooding U.S. markets with chips—a boon to American chip consumers, but a bane to American sellers of semiconductors. And in politics, the interest of sellers typically weighs more heavily than that of consumers. An illustration is the 1986 Semiconductor Trade Agreement imposed by the United States on the Japanese.

The agreement restricted Japanese chip exports to the United States and also set a price floor below which Japanese firms could not sell in our markets. A stated objective was to prevent so-called dumping, in which Japanese producers might sell chips below production costs in order to drive American competitors out of the market, in order then to raise prices of semiconductors.

Ignore the difficulty of accurately defining and measuring the relevant production costs that might define pricing "fairness." Ignore also the analytic and empirical dubiousness of the charge that a sensible seller would choose a policy of "selling below cost." Consider instead the consequences of the 1986 agreement.

One result is a smaller supply and higher price of semiconductors in U.S. markets. Indeed, the agreement effectively cartelized the American chip market for Japanese producers, who before had competed furiously here, as in their own markets. But, thanks to the agreement, Japanese firms were able to cut output, raise prices, and divide up the American market. While the U.S. computer boom fueled chip demand here, the government trade barrier helped push chip prices in American markets to three times their level in Japanese markets.

As prices for semiconductors rose higher here, U.S producers of computers and other electronic products found it harder to compete with the Japanese. Some American firms have rightly condemned the government trade barrier. But others are joining with chip producers in supporting it. In return, they want semiconductor producers to join them in seeking new government restrictions on imports of Japanese electronic goods.

First, we curtail imports of chips; then, in the face of resulting greater production costs, we are to curtail imports of products using chips. So Americans must pay higher prices. In politics, that is chips and dip: some domestic producers remain in the chips—but only by using government to dip into consumers' pockets.

(August 1988)

Purity, Propaganda, and Politics

A syndicated newspaper columnist has castigated U.S. foreign economic policy. Today's policies—in contrast with those of two or three or four decades ago—are not expansive and imaginative. They are not inspired by sensitivity, kindness, and a civilized sense of sharing.

It is true, conceded the journalistic scholar, that the United States economy has been a "locomotive . . . pulling the economies of Europe and Japan." But minding our massive economy well, with happy spill-over effects on the rest of the world, is not enough, he laments. We must emulate "previous periods of American economic strength" in generating "a proliferation of ideas for spreading the wealth and strengthening the global economic system." Shamefully, we do not appropriately proliferate, because today, in contrast to yesterday, we do not have "a generous spirit." Now, "greed sits in the American saddle and economic nationalism holds the whip."

Some of the policies and institutions which stemmed from that past purity of heart—in particular, the International Monetary Fund— were unfortunate. Others—including tariff reductions—deserve applause. But, bad or good, did the ideas of prior generations actually reflect a national self-sacrificing nobility which has been abruptly replaced with greed?

Consider a still earlier era in American tariff history. In the early 1930s, depression plagued the world. Most countries were restricting foreign trade. But Secretary of State Cordell Hull managed to get Congress to pass the Reciprocal Trade Agreements Act, which put the United States in the forefront of efforts to reduce international trade barriers.

Now, what was the case for this liberalized commercial ploy? Did Secretary Hull try to gain support for trade agreements on grounds of generosity? Were we to attempt mutual reduction of trade restrictions as a way of spreading American wealth?

The trade agreements policy—like the later Marshall Plan and other ventures—was sold basically on the proposition that it would help the United States economy. Through the 1930s, Secretary Hull reiterated the rationale of his policy as largely an antidepression strategy; and it would stimulate the economy because it would increase U.S. exports more than imports.

The trade agreements policy may be deemed desirable. The case presented for the policy was analytically unsophisticated but politically predictable. And, analytically and politically, there is nothing sinful or ridiculous in trying to design American policy and use American resources to serve American ends.

National policies are to be criticized, not because they seek to serve national interests, but because they serve national interests badly. Happily, nations—like individuals—commonly can be pleasant neighbors to their mutual benefit. But self-destructive philanthropy is not the essence of appropriate policy.

(January 1985)

International Trade: War and Peace

Does international trade promote peace? Many have hoped so, and some have thought so.

John Stuart Mill, one of the most eminent thinkers of the nineteenth century, found the "intellectual and moral" effects of commerce to be greater than the economic. International contact and communication, between both similar and dissimilar cultures, takes place mainly through trade and is "one of the primary sources of progress." And even the patriot, Mill said, sees in the "wealth and progress [of other nations] a direct source of wealth and progress to his own country. It is commerce which is rapidly rendering war obsolete, by strengthening and multiplying the personal interests which are in natural opposition to . . . [war]."

Mill's remarkable optimism was echoed by Cordell Hull, long a member of Congress and then Secretary of State for President Franklin D. Roosevelt for twelve years. "Economic peace," Hull asserted, "offers the greatest assurance of permanent world peace."

By the same token, Hull went on, "artificial trade barriers inevitably create bitter trade rivalry, vicious trade practices, and economic wars, which in modern times have been the prelude to actual wars. Commercial power or control means political control and often military control as well. It becomes all important," Hull concluded, ". . . to reduce to a minimum those trade discriminations, obstructions, and monopoly combinations, which breed serious antagonisms and strife in the efforts by nations to extend their commercial interests."

Even if one sees war as partially an economic, as well as political, phenomenon, there remains the question of the predominant line of causation. Have conflicting international business interests entangled reluctant governments, or have conflicting governmental interests used reluctant merchants and investors as an excuse and a tool?

A generation ago, the issue was analyzed by Jacob Viner, one of America's splendid economists. In a long list of episodes in the century prior to World War II, in which it has been commonly alleged that greedy, even rapacious, businessmen succeeded in using government military power to protect their investments, Professor Viner found in virtually every case the actual relationship to be the opposite:

> . . . the capitalist, instead of pushing his government into an imperialist enterprise in pursuit of his own financial gain, was pushed, or dragged, or cajoled, or lured into it by his government, in order that, in its relations with the outside world and with its own people, this government might be able to point to an apparently real and legitimate economic stake in the territory involved which required military protection. . . .

It is an enormous exaggeration to hold that trade guarantees peace. But it is a disingenuous distortion to hold that traders generate war.

(March 1987)

Economic Sanctions and Foreign Policy

We sometimes have problems with other nations. We want to be instrumental in changing their conduct. But we want the instrument to be more rapier than club. And, in foreign affairs, what could be more rapier-like than economic pressure?

In modern history, the United States has tried a good many times to twist the economic arms of unfriendly and naughty foreign governments. Usually, the policy has been to stop trade in specific goods;

sometimes, virtually all commerce with the target country as been proscribed. U.S. sanctions were imposed on Japan in the late 1930s and early 1940s; against Cuba since 1960; against Rhodesia beginning in 1965; and, more recently, against Russia, South Africa, Nicaragua, and Libya.

How effective have been such rapier thrusts? Bruce Bartlett, in a Cato Institute essay, finds that trade sanctions generally have been ineffective or perverse in their consequences.

It is not mysterious that sanctions typically have either little effect or an effect opposite to what was desired. Consider some likely conditions for success. For sanctions to work, they had better have modest goals and be directed against a small country; the amount of trade with the country should be large and include commodities which are vital and have poor substitutes; and the sanctions should be imposed by many countries in close cooperation and with strict enforcement. These conditions have never been fully satisfied—and would hardly be sufficient if they were.

Sometimes even in anticipation of sanctions, target countries become more self-sufficient and reduce their dependence on any one supplier. When the United States has curtailed its exports, alternative world suppliers have readily filled the gap: unilateral restrictions have done little more than alter trade patterns. Such disruption as is inflicted on the enemy is felt also by innocent neighbors of the enemy. Meanwhile, the United States, despite its half century espousal of liberalized world trade, is increasingly perceived as an unreliable exporter, and sales are lost, not only in embargoed goods normally sold to the enemy, but also in other goods in other markets. Since there are mutual gains from trade, there will be mutual losses from curtailing trade.

What returns can be balanced against these costs? Historically, the embargo, instead of making the world safer for civilized countries, has consolidated domestic support of the enemy regime, increasing the resolve of the foreign community, intensifying their undesired behavior, and pushing them closer into alliance with our other enemies.

Economic sanctions typically have been mainly gestures of minimal returns and substantial costs. They may have been mainly symbolic even in intent as well as expectation. But we can wonder about the wisdom of a repeated tactic which is seen consistently to yield only short-term exhilaration and long-term negative payoff.

(February 1986)

The Balance of Payments, Exchange Rates, and Adjustment

Mouse Wisdom: Borrowing and Buying

"Internationalwise, we are living in a fool's paradise," eloquently moaned Karl, the fearful and befuddled mouse.

"We are sometimes foolish," replied Adam, the courageous and competent mouse, "but I am counting on this being rather less than paradise."

"It may not be paradise," Karl pouted, "but it could get worse. Look at the balance of international payments. We have a deficit in goods, services, and investment income. That import balance is possible only because we are borrowing from foreigners. If foreigners get tired of lending to us, the imports will not be financed, and the balance of payments won't balance."

"Things can't get *that* bad," laughed Adam. "The balance of payments *always* balances. With double-entry bookkeeping, the accounts *must* balance—it can't be otherwise. If we have net imports of goods, it is financed by net exports of our IOUs. If foreigners sell more stuff to us than they buy, they must lend to us. And if they lend less, they will sell less."

"That's nice," smiled a relieved Karl. "At least I am happy that the accountants and statisticians keep their books in balance. But, at a minimum, isn't it demeaning and embarrassing for the United States to be buying things on credit? In fact, isn't net imports of goods a reflection of economic weakness?"

"Not necessarily," corrected Adam. "Prior to World War I, the United States was a persistent long-term borrower. It made sense for a young, growing economy with great prospects to borrow, and it was an attractive economy in which to invest. And it has been a relatively attractive place of investment in recent years—inflation has been down, output has been rising, rates of return have been substantial, and there are no fears of Big Brother expropriating assets or forbidding their being taken home by foreign investors. So both American and foreign capital has been channeled into this economy because it has been strong, not weak."

"So capital inflow—and the accompanying goods inflow—is evidence of great economic health," concluded Karl.

"Again, not necessarily," Adam cautioned. "It is nice to obtain the fruits of foreign production—that contributes to our standard of living. But the panic borrowing and consumption of a panhandler or a victim of catastrophe is very different from the shrewd borrowing and consumption of a wealthy individual who has his affairs in order and is blessed with encouraging prospects. Do you borrow simply for short-term, hand-to-mouth survival—or for long-term, calculated growth? The United States is not in the position of either Lower Slobbovia or of Europe and Japan immediately after World War II."

"It seems pretty apparent," Karl concluded, "that we are neither hopeless paupers nor devastated victims. We and the rest of the world invest here—and we import—because our economy is stronger and more promising than most."

(May 1985)

Untruths About the Balance of Payments

Most people earn their incomes and spend their money with a degree of attention and shrewdness. But the aggregate commercial and financial transactions of the entire nation in the world economy is outside their range of professional interest. Their knowledge of and impressions about the balance of international payments stem from journalists and politicians.

May the saints preserve us! Note some of the factual error and analytic nonsense spread by innocence and deviousness.

It is not true that the balance of payments is *unbalanced*. The balance of payments is a double-entry accounting record of transactions of United States residents with the rest of the world. Since each transaction is balanced, then over any period the total of transactions necessarily balances.

It is not true that only *merchandise* buying and selling are recorded. Many additional things are included—services, investment income, claims, gold, gifts. Each of these subcategories can be (and almost always is) unbalanced, but all of them added together balance.

It is not true that an ideal trade pattern consists of *balanced exchange* with each trading partner. We naturally have big imbalances with some countries and small ones with others, and some of those imbalances are net imports and others net exports.

It is not true that imports of *goods* is undesirable. Individuals, households, and firms really can gain by buying things. And when some of the things are made abroad, we benefit from use of foreign resources and production.

It is not true that the considerable merchandise import balances of the 1980s stem from a *binge of buying* from abroad. As a proportion of gross national product, imports now are nearly the same as in 1979—but exports have fallen by one-fourth. Our imports have been maintained as our economic health has been maintained; exports have fallen while the rest of the world economy has weakened.

It is not true that our imports are solely for direct consumption. Nearly 40 percent of current imports consist of industrial materials and capital goods—an investment proportion which has steadily grown in the past decade.

It is not true that import of *capital* is undesirable. Borrowing, like spending, can be done well and wisely, making efficient use of borrowed resources.

It is not true that the substantial net capital inflow of the 1980s is simply a large *increase in borrowing* from foreigners. The net inflow reflects also a fall in our lending to foreigners. The world in general, including United States residents, has found this economy to be a relatively attractive place in which to invest.

It is not true that federal *budget deficits* have been largely and increasingly financed by borrowing abroad. The proportion of the federal debt now held by foreigners—a bit over 12 percent—is exactly what it was in the 1970s.

We need not go into a tizzy over our international accounts. If we study and work and save and invest and manage much and well, the balance of payments will take care of itself.

(April 1988)

Mouse Wisdom: Foreign Investment in America

"Foreigners are buying all of America," announced alarmed mouse Karl.

"Are you sure?" queried mouse Adam.

"Look around," snapped Karl. "The Japanese own chunks of many U.S. cities, including most of downtown Honolulu. And they are buying controlling interests in U.S. firms and sometimes starting new businesses here."

"Foreigners *have* made substantial investments in U.S. companies and U.S. real estate," responded Adam, "but overall it has had only a modest impact on our economy. In any case, why should this direct investment in physical assets be bad?"

"We are losing control of our economic destiny," growled Karl. "Americans are becoming dependent on foreign landlords and foreign employers—and vulnerable to their diabolical whims."

"Foreign investors have very little of either power or incentive to harm us," corrected Adam. "Indeed, foreigners are staking their wealth on American workers and customers and their productivity and prosperity. If foreign-owned buildings are not to lose money, they must be rented to American tenants. If foreign-owned firms are to flourish, they must hire American workers and sell to American consumers. This is mutual dependence for mutual benefit."

"I understand the interdependence," said Karl thoughtfully, "but I don't see the mutual benefit."

"Foreign direct investment invigorates our economy with new investment, technology, and management. We obtain more goods and services, more jobs, and more income. And foreign investors obtain a higher return on their investments."

"I admit," admitted Karl, "that these voluntary market transactions benefit both domestic mice and foreign investors. Still, the amount of foreign investment in our nation has been enormous and rapidly growing in recent years. In particular, the Japanese seem to be buying up everything in sight."

"You exaggerate," admonished Adam. "Gerald H. Anderson, of the Federal Reserve Bank of Cleveland, points out that total direct investment by the United States abroad continues to exceed foreign direct investment here. At the end of 1987, the book value of U.S. direct investments abroad was $47 billion greater than that of foreigners here. And in terms of market value, our net position is much larger."

"But hasn't our net position fallen in recent years?" asked Karl.

"Yes," affirmed Adam, "but the decline from more than $130 billion in 1980 to $47 billiion in 1987 has resulted more from diminished U.S. investment abroad in the early 1980s than from increased rate of foreign investment here. Moreover, Europe and Canada, not Japan, have been responsible for most of the increased direct investment in our country. At the end of 1987, Europeans had two-thirds of the $262 billion of foreign direct investment; the Japanese held only 13 percent."

"Boy!" concluded Karl. "Fact can be an effective antidote for fear."

(October 1988)

Wage Rates, Exchange Rates, and Competition

If good sense is common, then much of economic analysis is common sense. But while massive genius is rarely required to use economics fruitfully, sometimes a bit of subtlety is involved, innocuous looking booby traps which can lead the unwary astray.

Consider domestic wage rates in the context of international competition. The head of one of the major U.S. automobile companies has complained—and his complaint has been echoed by some editorial writers and even some economists—that high labor costs are an insurmountable disadvantage. Those costs, it is contended, stem from U.S. wage rates being much higher than Japanese wage rates. United States auto workers receive some nineteen dollars an hour, including fringe benefits, compared to the Japanese eleven dollars—and American productivity is *not* 73 percent higher, offsetting the wage differential. So U.S. costs and prices are higher.

Plausible as that initially appears, it is not quite right. Let's try again.

Japanese auto workers are *not* paid eleven dollars an hour. They are not paid dollars, at all. They are paid yen. The number of yen is *calculated* as the *equivalent* of eleven dollars when converted into dollars by the current *exchange rate* between the yen and the dollar. If the Japanese worker receives twenty-two hundred yen and the yen-price of the dollar is two hundred, then we can say that the wage translates into eleven dollars.

But suppose the exchange rate were only one hundred yen per dollar. Then the wage of twenty-two hundred yen would be the equivalent of twenty-two dollars, more than the United States wage.

Now, in a foreign exchange market where people are free to bid as they please and prices are not governmentally or institutionally pegged, exchange rates will be at market-clearing levels. The rates will rise and fall, as they reflect changes in productivity, prices, and anticipations, but the international accounts will be appropriately balanced. There will be no meaningful balance-of-payments deficits or surpluses when exchange rates are free to adjust to market circumstances.

The international accounts of the entire United States economy will not be in disequilibrium when the foreign exchange market is cleared. But particular U.S. industries can get into competitive trouble when the wages they pay get out of line in comparison with those of other American workers of the same ability. In the United States, but not in Japan, wages of auto workers are much greater than wages of many others equally skilled. That is the problem. American auto worker wages are not too high relative to Japanese auto workers; they are too high relative to wages of other Americans.

Market-determined exchange rates keep the United States economy as a whole in balance with the rest of the world economy. But within the United States economy, some try to grab a bigger slice of the social output than their productivity justifies. And the efficient market is hard on those who try to reap more than they have sown.

(October 1981)

Exchange Rate Tinkering and Diddling

In a world well filled with woe, many are tempted to tinker and diddle with details of institutions and gimmicks of governing rather than face the fundamentals of our failures and options. Commonly, it is easier and more glamorous to prescribe for symptoms than to provide solutions.

Fluctuating foreign exchange rates hurt more than help, we are told, for they increase market uncertainty and thereby promote economic instability. When prices of national currencies are allowed to change, as do other prices, risk is increased and the planning horizon is shortened, which inhibits world commerce and investment and unsettles domestic economies.

True, we have our being in a world of change. Most of the changes cannot be fully foretold. Some of the unanticipated changes are unhappy. And unhappy surprises are not sources of joy and productivity. But fixing selected variables by decree, arbitrarily holding some relationships constant against tides of change, will not yield a placid, predictable world.

There are various ways of holding exchange rates constant for indefinite periods in the face of market pressures which seek other rates. Each way has its problems.

Under the classic gold standard before World War I, domestic variables—product prices, interest rates, output, and employment—had to adjust to requirements of international stability. Would those domestic-adjustment rules of the game be accepted today by sovereign nations which belligerently cherish their autonomy? And would the world be more prosperous if each country did mind its manners by holding its own economy hostage to the dictates of fixed exchange rates?

The gold standard does not eliminate problems of uncertainty and instability, for the world doubtless would—and surely should—remain one of change. Still, the gold standard does embody an adjustment mechanism. If the rules are followed and the manners minded, there is an element of automaticity, a built-in machinery of reconciling the domestic economics with each other so as to maintain those stable exchange rates.

But the coherency of the gold standard mechanism is not to be found in the ad hoc arrangement of exchange-rate price controls of the International Monetary Fund. From the late 1940s to the early 1970s, the IMF tried to attain the exchange rate stability of the gold standard with the domestic autonomy of fluctuating exchange rates. It did not achieve either; it could not achieve both. Instead, it added to the inherent uncertainties of the market the imposed uncertainties of bureaucracies.

Economic certainty, stability, predictability, adaptability—these are attractive goals in adopting policies and procedures and pertinent criteria in assessing economies and their performances. But they will not be attained by exchange rate tinkering and diddling.

(October 1986)

Nostalgia for Silliness

A bank officer has referred to "nostalgia for the Bretton Woods monetary system, with its fixed exchange rates"—a "yearning [based on] rather careless reminiscences." Indeed. The disastrous post-World War II financial arrangement under the International Monetary Fund was characterized not only by governmentally pegged exchange rates, but by lack of an adjustment mechanism.

Adjustment has to do with correcting a disequilibrium, an unsustainable imbalance, in the international accounts. A "market mechanism" of adjustment is a built-in process of automatic correction which leads the system back to equilibrium.

But it became common through the 1960s to speak of balance-of-payments imbalances which are simply a *signal* to monetary authorities and a guide to *discretionary policy*. In this macho environment focused on ad hoc policy, it seemed quaintly academic to think in terms of "disequilibrium" to be cured through reliance on a market mechanism.

And, in fact, there was no adjustment mechanism under the IMF arrangement. Recurrent crisis was inevitable. Strain, panic, improvisation, and occasional disaster were, indeed, the continuing thread in international finance for a quarter of a century.

"Dollar shortage" and then "dollar glut" were ascribed to a series of unfortunate specific events—wars, strikes, recessions and recoveries internationally out of phase, differential interest rates and inflation rates. But doubtless forever more there will be phenomena which quickly upset an equilibrium reached or approached. In a changing world, we do not retain static equilibrium. Genuine adjustment, we must anticipate in realism, will be a never-ending pursuit of a *moving* equilibrium.

But, with reliance on contrived method rather than market mechanism, we did not even try to follow a path of "genuine adjustment." The lamentable history of international financial policy was a succession of frenetic efforts to patch and shore-up a jerry-built substitute for the market.

Through the 1950s and 1960s—until the beginning in 1973 of partially fluctuating rates—after all the overt and camouflaged currency realignments, the acts of discrimination and of protectionism, the attempts at international cooperation, the improvised machinations and controls, the exhortations and admonitions and threats and bargaining, the creation of new financial instruments, after all the conferences and perforated ulcers and public misrepresentations, there continued to abound rumors of still more horrendous things to come.

Obviously, exchange rates had not been set at long-continuing equilibrium levels. Yet, in important circles, the lesson was learned but slowly, if at all, that we need not, in some mysterious fashion, determine the equilibrium exchange rate and then peg it—and repeg it again and again as the equilibrium value changes over time and as the spirit (or whatever) moves us to make the alteration. And in their failure to learn, many profess to feel yearnings of nostalgia for such silliness.

(December 1983)

Economic Development: Aid and Ailments

Economic Growth and Growth Expectations

Discussion of world poverty and international income disparities has been polluted by vastly exaggerated hopes of economic growth. The per capita income gap between the wealthiest one-fourth of the nations and the rest of the world is large and growing larger. It will continue to grow larger as long as the growth rate of the relatively poor countries remains smaller, or no greater, than the growth rate of the relatively wealthy nations.

Even if the poorer nations manage to generate and to maintain indefinitely a higher growth rate, the absolute income gap will grow for a while—probably a long while—and closing the gap would be a matter of many decades, probably even centuries. And yet, the "Alliance for Progress" of twenty years ago, with typical rhetoric, presented the goal of "rapidly bringing about a substantial and steady increase in the average level of income in order to narrow the gap" in living standards.

Consider the consequences of some comparative rates of growth in per capita income. For illustration, take income per person in the United States to be $10,000 and in Alpha to be $1,000. This ratio of 10-to-1 is not extreme with respect to much of the world: per capita income is less than $100 in India, less than $400 in Ghana, and less than $800 in Peru. Suppose that the United States per capita income grows 2 percent annually, as has been the trend since the mid-nineteenth century. How fast would Alpha have to grow just to maintain the initial absolute gap of $9,000?

The answer varies with the specified time period, the required Alphian growth rate being smaller, the longer the time horizon. If the income gap is to be $9,000 after twenty-five years, Alpha must grow at more than 8 percent; if we take a period of 100 years, the required growth rate is still over 4 percent. In general, the Alphas of the world do well to grow at 2 or even 1 percent; they are not going to grow at 4, much less 8, percent for prolonged periods.

Even if Alpha grew at a remarkable rate of over 4 percent while the United States maintained its historic 2 percent, the gap would not be constant through all those years. The gap would grow larger for decades, reaching a maximum of nearly $22,000 after seventy-two years, before falling back to the initial $9,000 at the end of a century.

Of course, if Alpha were perennially to grow at any rate faster than the United States, she would eventually close the gap—and from that time on, Alpha's income would become ever larger than that of the United States. If Alpha were to grow at a reasonable 2 percent and the United States at a depressed 1 percent, it would take 234 years to equalize per capita incomes.

All this hardly seems to form a sound basis for Great Expectations, despite frequent reference to the "revolution of rising expectations." Expectations apparently come easy in some quarters; economic growth itself is hard.

(June 1982)

Food Production and World Hunger

Many go hungry throughout the world while surplus farm goods pile up in our country. Much evidence suggests that government welfare and stabilization programs—both in the United States and abroad—have actually worsened hunger in poorer nations. Policies are to be judged by results, not purported intentions.

The destructive efforts of government food policies can be seen in Africa. During the last ten years, total food production increased almost four times faster in Asia and Latin America than in sub-Sahara Africa, where per capita food production was much less in 1983 than in 1973. Drought, war, political chaos, and population growth have helped to deny gains in Africa's per capita food production, but harmful government policies may have been the main cause.

Economist Robert Dunn, Jr., of George Washington University, finds *heavy taxes on agriculture* common in Africa. Food price controls compel farmers to sell to city consumers at low prices; while most Africans live in rural areas, urban elites—mostly government employees—use state policies to force farmers to subsidize their consumption. Stubborn adherence to overvaluation of domestic currencies in the foreign exchange market has hampered exports and bloated imports, to the detriment of agriculture. Such devastation of incentives to produce food has contributed mightily to the decline in African output during the 1970s.

The price controls that restrict food production in Africa are very different from the controls in our own country. Instead of keeping food prices low to force farmers to subsidize consumers, government controls keep our farm prices artificially high to force consumers to subsidize farmers. Price controls created the huge farm surpluses some want to give away to reduce world hunger—and to reduce the embarrassment of having created those surpluses.

We do donate some of these surpluses through the Food For Peace program, created in 1954. This charity, like Africa's perverse agricultural policies, can undermine food producing incentives and make hunger worse. Writer James Bovard believes Food For Peace may be our most harmful foreign aid program. In the 1950s and 1960s, for example, wheat surpluses sent to India depressed food prices in that country and bankrupted thousands of Indian farmers, thereby reducing output. Guatemala in 1976 and Peru in 1982 insisted that our government send no more food gifts, which were ruining their producers. Our food dumping helps to perpetuate the government programs, property arrangements, and inertia that are hindering and misdirecting production in poor nations.

If we want to help the world's hungry people, we should rethink our policies of food aid. With marketplace incentives and guidance, farmers in developing nations would produce more—and probably enough.

(September 1984)

Foreign Aid: Too Anxious to Do Good

Soliciting, granting, and administering of foreign aid soon became big business after the late 1940s. The good it has done is minimal; the harm it has done is considerable; these results are explicable; and the prospects of similar future results are predictable.

Capital goods—highways, buildings, machinery—can contribute much to productivity and general economic well-being. The worst of circumstances can be alleviated and the best improved by an increase in capital. But capital is not the only, or even the dominant, factor in development; it need not be obtained as aid from abroad; and a badly organized and administered society will not be helped much—indeed, it is likely to be hampered—by massive amounts of capital donated to its government. Such are the sobering conclusions of Peter Bauer, specialist at the London School in economic development.

No analyst should anticipate foreign aid to be necessary, much less sufficient, for development. And no historian can demonstrate that any society has ever developed on the basis of required resources donated from outside. Many societies have developed, but not with outside aid. "Economic achievement depends on personal, cultural, social, and political factors"—the quality of people and their organization—and the barriers to progress will be more probably reinforced than overcome by foreign aid.

In the domestic economy, ideas, prospects, and plans precede massive financing. If the potentiality of attractive investment return is perceived, investment funds will be forthcoming. People are willing to forego current consumption and entrust savings to managers if there appears to be high probability of substantial payoff—and also convincing assurances that the payoff will be collectible by the investors and not expropriated or largely taxed away by Big Brother.

The same is true of the international economy. Economically rational investments are fundable with market investment at market interest rates. Some of the poorer nations are now in debt difficulty, not mainly because of lack of funds for appropriate purposes of development, but because too many resources have been too readily available on terms too tempting. The resources having been acquired without satisfying market requirements, they commonly have been used in wasteful ways—for palaces, airlines, and air forces—which do not help production of the income which could finance their repayment.

As borrowed funds are badly used, gifts are squandered. Foreign aid is given to governments, not to private entrepreneurs—even if the decrees of the state and the mores of the society permit or provide room for private entrepreneurs. And the Big Brothers of the poorer nations have shown little interest in sustainable economic development and the prosperity of the community.

A soft heart—genuine compassion and a desire for improvement of the world—surely is a virtue—if not accompanied by a soft brain. For misguided and maladministered charity can subsidize waste and oppression and entrench the wasters and oppressors. One can be too anxious to do good.

(April 1984)

Foreign Aid, Land Reform, and Socialistic Silliness

The foreign aid program is largely a mess, at best wasting resources and commonly making bad situations worse. It is a mess partly because it is poorly planned, ignoring the massive inherent difficulties in promoting growth in primitive societies through outside resources and directives; and it is a mess partly because the aid program has been disastrously directed, both by those giving the aid and those receiving it.

In 1980, the new government of El Salvador began "land reform" by taking over large farms and converting them into "cooperatives" and also providing credit to peasants for purchase of land fragments. The program of expropriation and "garden-plot statism" was from the outset a political ploy of purported social equity; it could not be an economic strategy of real economic development.

Not only is there the dubious morality, but also the questionable psychology and the ridiculous economics, of taking land from those who have capital and managerial expertise and scattering it among many who are unequipped with tools and techniques to use it well.

Those from whom the land was taken have not been compensated—and most victims of the government banditry have not been enormously wealthy. Those who have lost land have been made unproductive; those who anticipate losing land have no incentive to be productive.

Those for whom the land supposedly was taken have not been given ownership. Along with lacking implements, seed, fertilizer, even sacks in which to transport harvested crops, and experience as independent farmers, they also lack land as their own salable asset. Without ownership rights, they do not have ownership: they are simply impoverished but unmotivated serfs, whether in coercive but uncoordinated state-created coops or in isolated, inefficient plots.

To top it off, centralized government effectively dominates the market. Farmers sell their output to the state at prices dictated by the state. The prices are so low—and the puny payments by government are so long delayed—that the farmers can barely survive and assuredly cannot prosper. The predictable result has been drastically falling output.

This silly socialism has been carried out with not only the awareness of the United States government, but with the active encouragement and considerable financial support of our Agency for International Development.

AID administrators have persistently claimed that "real progress is being made" by the hundreds of thousands of small and previously poor farmers who "now own their own land." In so saying, the administrators are very loose with truth. In actuality, the basically misconceived and abysmally administered experiment with land reform in agricultural El Salvador is a classic illustration of what not to do and how not to do it.

(August 1986)

The Marshall Plan: Then and Now

A glamorous former Secretary of State—not known for his interest or competence in issues of economics—has proposed a massive "Western Hemisphere development program," "the modern philosophical equivalent of the Marshall Plan." He is not the first. Over more than a third of a century, there have been philosophical calls for a Latin American Marshall Plan. The philosophy is historically and analytically dubious.

First, the context of the Marshall Plan for Europe in the late 1940s and early 1950s bears little resemblance to the Latin American circumstance of the mid-1980s. Europe was trying to rebuild after the catastrophe of World War II. The rebuilding job was massive, but the Europeans could draw on traditions, institutions, and expertise developed over the preceding two centuries and more. Regaining strength and stature are different from their initial attainment; returning to a long-established growth path is different from leaving the stultification of perennial non-performance. The Europeans were to begin doing again what they had long done well; the Latin Americans are hoping to start doing belatedly what they have never done well.

Second, even if there could be a modern Latin American counterpart to the European Marshall Plan of a generation ago, would that earlier effort be a good guide, a program to emulate? Economist Tyler Cowen, in a Heritage Foundation publication, finds fundamental deficiencies and defects in the Marshall Plan, and he fears that romantically incorrect assessment of that experience long ago in a different world can mislead us in foreign aid policies today.

Contrary to nearly universally held mythology, Mr. Cowen finds that the Marshall Plan was not a significant factor in European postwar recovery, it did not encourage development of productive enterprise, it did not stimulate and enrich the United States economy, it was not immune to shaping and guiding by private special interests in the United States, and it did not represent or contribute to a policy of free trade.

United States aid through the Marshall Plan was hardly trivial—some thirteen billion dollars, mainly over two years—but it did not bulk large in the economy of any one of the several recipient nations. Not only was European recovery associated with circumstances and developments other than Marshall Aid, but the Marshall Plan administration—favoring centralized controls and directives and subsidizing inefficiencies—diluted and distorted productive incentives.

As a big, dramatic gesture of hope and support for peaceful progress, as a statement of intent to preclude further Russian advance in Western Europe, the Marshall Plan was significant. But it was generally inadequate and commonly misdirected as an economic policy. Rather, it was basically a political strategy in economic clothing—and the quality of the economic clothing was pretty shoddy.

(September 1985)

About the Author

WILLIAM R. ALLEN is professor of Economics at the University of California, Los Angeles, and vice president of the Institute for Contemporary Studies.

After serving as a bombardier of the Army Air Corps, he obtained his A.B. (1948) from Cornell College and his Ph.D. (1953) from Duke University. He instructed at Washington University prior to joining the UCLA faculty in 1952. He has been a visiting professor at Northwestern University, the University of Wisconsin, the University of Michigan, Southern Illinois University, and Texas A&M University, and he has been on the faculty of the Colorado School of Banking. He has been a consultant to the Balance of Payments Division of the Department of Commerce and a director of the Yardney Corporation. He was chairman of the UCLA Department of Economics from 1967 to 1969. A recipient of various scholarship awards as a student, his professional research—largely in International Economics, Monetary Economics, and the History of Economic Theory—has been supported by grants from the Social Science Research Council, the Ford Foundation, the National Science Foundation, and the Earhart Foundation. He has received the UCLA Alumni Association Award for the Art of Teaching, the Western Economic Association Distinguished Teaching Award, and the Freedoms Foundation at Valley Forge Award for Excellence in Private Enterprise Education. He has been vice president and president of the Western Economic Association, vice president of the History of Economics Society, vice president and a member of the Executive Committee of the Southern Economic Association, and a director of the University Professors for Academic Order. He is on the editorial board of the *Social Science Quarterly* and was on the advisory board of the *History of Political Economy*. He has participated extensively in conference, seminar, and lecture programs, and he is a nationally syndicated radio commentator and newspaper columnist. He has authored, co-authored, and edited eight books and contributed widely to professional journals in the United States and elsewhere. In 1974, he was appointed the first president of the International Institute for Economic Research. He is now vice president of the Institute for Contemporary Studies, with which IIER merged in 1986.